Fodor's Family

WASHINGTON D.C. WITH KIDS

1st Edition

Where to Eat and Stay
for All Budgets

Must-See Sights
and Local Secrets

Ratings You Can Trust

WITHDRAWN

Excerpted from *Fodor's Washington, D.C.*

Fodor's Travel Publications New York, Toronto, London, Sydney, Auckland

www.fodors.com

FODOR'S FAMILY WASHINGTON D.C. WITH KIDS

Editors: Paul Eisenberg, Eric B. Wechter

Production Editor: Jennifer DePrima
Writer: Kathryn McKay
Editorial Contributors: Mary Beth Bohman, Coral Davenport, Valerie Hamilton, Beth Kanter, Cathy Sharpe, Elana Schor, Mitchell Tropin
Maps & Illustrations: David Lindroth, Mark Stroud, *cartographers*; Bob Blake and Rebecca Baer, *map editors*; William Wu, *information graphics*
Design: Fabrizio La Rocca, *creative director*; Guido Caroti, *art director*; Ann McBride, *designer*; Melanie Marin, *senior picture editor*
Cover Photo: Jason Horowitz/zefa/Corbis (top), Alfred Wekelo/Shutterstock (bottom)
Production Manager: Angela McLean

COPYRIGHT

Copyright © 2009 by Fodor's Travel, a division of Random House, Inc.

Fodor's is a registered trademark of Random House, Inc.

1st Edition

ISBN 978-1-4000-0888-9

ISSN 1943-0140

SPECIAL SALES

This book is available for special discounts for bulk purchases for sales promotions or premiums. Special editions, including personalized covers, excerpts of existing books, and corporate imprints, can be created in large quantities for special needs. For more information, write to Special Markets/Premium Sales, 1745 Broadway, MD 6-2, New York, New York, NY 10019, or e-mail specialmarkets@randomhouse.com.

AN IMPORTANT TIP & AN INVITATION

Although all prices, opening times, and other details in this book are based on information supplied to us at press time, changes occur all the time in the travel world, and Fodor's cannot accept responsibility for facts that become outdated or for inadvertent errors or omissions. **So always confirm information when it matters,** especially if you're making a detour to visit a specific place. Your experiences—positive and negative—matter to us. If we have missed or misstated something, **please write to us.** We follow up on all suggestions. Contact the Family Washington D.C. with Kids editor at editors@fodors.com or c/o Fodor's at 1745 Broadway, New York, NY 10019.

PRINTED IN THE UNITED STATES OF AMERICA

10 9 8 7 6 5 4 3 2 1

Be a Fodor's Correspondent

Your opinion matters. It matters to us. It matters to your fellow Fodor's travelers, too. And we'd like to hear it. In fact, we *need* to hear it. When you share your experiences and opinions, you become an active member of the Fodor's community. Here's how you can help improve Fodor's for all of us.

Tell us when we're right. We rely on local writers to give you an insider's perspective. But our writers and staff editors also depend on you. Your positive feedback is a vote to renew our recommendations for the next edition.

Tell us when we're wrong. We update most of our guides every year. But things change. If any of our descriptions are inaccurate or inadequate, we'll incorporate your changes in the next edition and will correct factual errors at fodors.com *immediately*.

Tell us what to include. You probably have had fantastic travel experiences that aren't yet in Fodor's. Why not share them with a community of like-minded travelers? Share your discoveries and experiences with everyone directly at fodors. com. Your input may lead us to add a new listing or a higher recommendation.

Give us your opinion instantly at our feedback center at www. fodors.com/feedback. You may also e-mail editors@fodors.com with the subject line "Family Washington D.C. with Kids Editor." Or send your nominations, comments, and complaints by mail to Family Washington D.C. with Kids Editor, Fodor's, 1745 Broadway, New York, NY 10019.

Happy Traveling!

Tim Jarrell, Publisher

CONTENTS

MAPS

ABOUT THIS BOOK

Our Ratings

We wouldn't recommend a place that wasn't worth your time, but sometimes a place is so experiential that superlatives don't do it justice: you just have to be there to know. These sights, properties, and experiences get our highest rating, **Fodor's Choice**, indicated by orange stars throughout this book. Black stars highlight sights and properties we deem **Highly Recommended**, places that our writers, editors, and readers praise again and again for consistency and excellence.

Credit Cards

Want to pay with plastic? **AE, D, DC, MC, V** after restaurant and hotel listings indicate whether American Express, Discover, Diners Club, MasterCard, and Visa are accepted.

Restaurants

Unless we state otherwise, restaurants are open for lunch and dinner daily. We mention dress only when there's a specific requirement and reservations only when they're essential or not accepted—it's always best to book ahead.

Hotels

Unless we tell you otherwise, you can assume that the hotels have private bath, phone, TV, and air-conditioning. We always list facilities but not whether you'll be charged an extra fee to use them, so when pricing accommodations, find out what's included.

Many Listings

★	Fodor's Choice
★	Highly recommended
⊠	Physical address
✦	Directions
⬠	Mailing address
☎	Telephone
🖷	Fax
⊕	On the Web
✉	E-mail
▨	Admission fee
☉	Open/closed times
Ⓜ	Metro stations
▭	Credit cards

Hotels & Restaurants

⬚	Hotel
⇨	Number of rooms
⬧	Facilities
⦿	Meal plans
✕	Restaurant
⬥	Reservations
⤫	Smoking

Outdoors

⛳	Golf
⛺	Camping

Other

⇨	See also
⊠	Branch address
☞	Take note

WHAT'S WHERE

1 The Mall. Stretching from the Capitol to the Washington Monument, the Mall is lined by some of America's finest museums.

2 The Monuments. D.C.'s most famous monuments are concentrated west of the Mall and along the Tidal Basin.

3 The White House Area & Foggy Bottom. The Corcoran, the DAR Museum, and, of course, the most famous home in the United States.

4 Capitol Hill. The Capitol, the Supreme Court, and Library of Congress, as well as the Smithsonian Postal Museum and the best food court for families at Union Station.

5 Downtown. The Federal Triangle and Penn Quarter attract visitors to Ford's Theatre, the International Spy Museum, the National Portrait Gallery, and the American Art Museum.

6 Georgetown. A terrific neighborhood for strolling and shopping. Teens enjoy the street scene; younger children are attracted to the mule-drawn boat rides along the C&O Canal.

7 Dupont Circle. A hub of fashionable restaurants and shops. The Kalorama neighborhood is an enclave of embassies, luxurious homes, and small museums.

8 Adams-Morgan. Ethnically diverse, with offbeat restaurants, shops, and a happening nightlife.

9 Upper Northwest. This mostly residential swath of D.C. holds two must-see attractions: the National Cathedral and the National Zoo.

10 U Street Corridor. Trendy boutiques and hip eateries in the area around 14th and U.

ADAMS-MORGAN

Columbia Rd. NW

Florida Ave. NW

8

18th St. NW

Florida Ave. NW

U St. NW **10** U STREET U St. NW

New Hampshire Ave. NW

16th St. NW

15th St. NW

17th St. NW

S St. NW S St. NW

14th St. NW

Vermont Ave.

Florida Ave.

New Jersey Ave. NW

Dupont Circle

DUPONT CIRCLE

7

P St. NW

Logan Circle

Rhode Island Ave. NW

9th St. NW

7th St. NW

6th St. NW

Connecticut Ave. NW

O St. NW

N St. NW Scott Circle

Thomas Circle

N St. NW N St. NW

19th St. NW

M St. NW

16th St. NW

15th St. NW

M St. NW

Massachusetts Ave. NW

M St. NW

EAST END

K St. NW

Mt. Vernon Square

2nd St. NW

Pennsylvania Ave.

THE WHITE HOUSE AREA

New York Ave. NW

FOGGY BOTTOM

3

5

E St. NW The White House

13th St. NW

14th St. NW

E St.

DOWNTOWN

Virginia Ave. NW

17th St. NW

15th St. NW

The Ellipse

Pennsylvania Ave. NW

D St. NW

Constitution Ave. NW

National Gallery of Art

US Capitol

THE MALL **1** Smithsonian Institution

Washington Monument

Jefferson Dr. SW

Maryland Ave.

2

Kutz Bridge

Independence Ave. SW

National Air and Space Museum

4

THE MONUMENTS

Martin Luther King Jr. Memorial (under construction)

Outlet Bridge

Southwest Fwy.

FDR Memorial

Tidal Basin

Inlet Bridge

Jefferson Memorial

Francis Case Memorial Bridge

Washington Canal

0 500 yards

0 500 meters

TOP EXPERIENCES

Washington, D.C., is filled with kid-friendly attractions. These sights are some of our favorites.

Bureau of Engraving and Printing. Any youngster who gets an allowance will enjoy watching as bills roll off the presses. Despite the lack of free samples, the self-guided, 35-minute bureau tour is one of the city's most popular attractions.

D.C. Duck. What do you get when you cross a tour bus with a boat? Well, you get a bus-boat, of course—a standard 2½-ton GM truck in a water-tight shell with propellers—aka a D.C. Duck! Tour the city by both land and water aboard these unusual amphibious vehicles.

International Spy Museum. This museum elevates the art of espionage beyond typical movie presentations. Even the most cynical preteens and teenagers are enthralled with all the cool gadgetry. Note that this museum is best for older tweens and teens—if you bring along a younger sibling, you could be in for a workout: there aren't many places to sit down, and strollers aren't allowed in the museum.

Jefferson, Lincoln, and FDR Memorials. The key to all three of these memorials is to stop, stand, and read the writing on the walls. There's nothing quite like reading the Gettysburg Address as the massive marble statue of Lincoln broods behind you. Ponder the first lines of the Declaration of Independence at the Jefferson Memorial, and remember the line "The only thing we have to fear is fear itself" as you encounter the stark monuments to poverty and war at the FDR Memorial. Even non-readers can make the connection between Lincoln and his likeness on the penny, appreciate the view from the Jefferson Memorial, or enjoy the tradition of rubbing the ears and nose of Roosevelt's dog, Fala, depicted in a statue with his owner at the memorial.

Mount Vernon. Farm animals, a hands-on discovery center, an interactive museum, movies about the nation's first action hero, and more make George Washington's plantation in Alexandria a place where families can stay all day. And while they're having fun, kids learn about the father of our country.

Museum of Natural History. Say hello to Henry. One of the largest elephants ever found in the world, this stuffed beast has greeted generations of kids in the rotunda of this huge museum dedicated to natural wonders. Take your kid to the O. Orkin Insect Zoo, home to live ants, bees, centipedes, tarantulas, roaches (some as large as mice), and other critters you wouldn't want in your house.

National Air and Space Museum. There's a good reason why this place is the most popular museum in the world: kids love it. The 23 galleries here tell the story of aviation and space from the earliest human attempts at flight. All three gift shops sell freeze-dried astronaut food—not as tasty as what we eat on Earth, but it doesn't melt or drip.

National Museum of American History. Oh say you can see . . . the flag that inspired "The Star Spangled Banner," Oscar the Grouch, the ruby-red slippers from the Wizard of Oz, an impressive collection of trains, and more pieces of Americana can be found here.

National Zoo. Known more for its political animals than its real animals, D.C. nevertheless has one of the world's foremost zoos. From familiar farm favorites to rare and endangered species, more than 5,000 animals live here. If your child is wild about the wild, this is an absolute must—it's huge!

Washington Monument. Kids say it looks like a giant pencil, and from the top some think D.C. looks like Legoland. Older kids like to find the White House and other D.C. landmarks.

White House. Even though it takes significant advance planning to visit, touring the most famous house of the most famous person in the county is worth it for any kid who has studied American history.

IF YOUR KID LIKES

An Early Start. Even if it wasn't your idea to get out of bed, Washington awaits. The grounds of the National Zoo open at 6 AM daily. (Not to fear, so does the Starbucks across the street.) On the Mall, you can imitate the poses on the sculptures starting at 7:30 and then head to the Smithsonian Castle Building at 8:30 to get oriented and use the facilities. While most of the Mall's monuments and memorials are open 24/7, restrooms don't open until 9:30. Other early-morning opportunities: Mount Vernon at 8 April to August and at 9 the rest of the year, the Newseum at 9 AM and National Geographic Explorers Hall, Monday through Saturday at 9. If New York is the city that never sleeps, Washington is the city that never sleeps in.

A View From the Top. Soar up to the top of the Washington Monument for a bird's-eye view of the nation's Capitol. But if you can't get a ticket, head to the Washington National Cathedral's Pilgrim Observation Gallery (Massachusetts and Wisconsin avenues) or the Old Post Office Pavilion (100 Pennsylvania Ave., at 12th St., NW). If exploring one of Washington's highest spots isn't enough, head to the Smithsonian's Air and Space Museum. For a fee, kids can fly an airplane simulator as high as their imagination takes them.

Cold, Hard Cash. The big bucks—some $637 million—roll off the presses every weekday at the Bureau of Engraving and Printing. And everywhere around you the symbols on your dollars and cents loom larger than life. Get a newfound appreciation for the penny's Lincoln Memorial, the nickel's Jefferson Memorial, and the dollar bill's George Washington image as you behold the original painting in the Corcoran Gallery of Art. John Trumbull's painting, *The Declaration of Independence,* pictured on the back of the $2 bill, is on display in the rotunda of the U.S. Capitol.

Lincoln. Learning about Honest Abe is easy in D.C. Read his Gettysburg Address etched on the wall at Lincoln Memorial. See his top hat at the Museum of American History. If you're lucky enough to get White House tickets, try imagining Lincoln's son Tad taking a pair of goats through the East Room. Tour the home of Frederick Douglass, one of Lincoln's advisors and an abolitionist whose oratory skills rivaled Lincoln's. Then visit Ford's Theatre, where our 16th president was shot, and the National Museum of Health of Medicine, where the bullet that killed him is on display.

National Treasures. Imagine wearing a fancy dress at the First Ladies exhibit at the National Museum of American History. Read the Declaration of Independence at the National Archives. Salute at the Tomb of the Unknown Solider at Arlington National Cemetery.

Playing Politics. Learn about how and why the United States started electing presidents at George Washington's Mount Vernon and see where every president since has lived: the White House. Look all the presidents in the eye at the National Portrait Gallery. Arrange to meet one of your legislators at the U.S. Capitol.

Room to Roam. Washington prides itself on its tree-lined streets and parks. Rock Creek Park, twice the size of New York's Central Park, meanders through northwest D.C. from Foggy Bottom past the National Zoo into Montgomery County, Maryland. It's also the only place in the city where you can ride horses, just like presidents Teddy Roosevelt and Ronald Reagan did. The National Arboretum gives growing kids plenty of room to play tag and hide-and-go seek. At Kenilworth Aquatic Gardens, trails meander through ponds with flowers as gorgeous as a Monet painting.

To Laugh. Quack up with your kids on a big, yellow D.C. Duck tour over land and sea. Giggle at the antics of puppets at historic Glen Echo's Puppet Company or slapstick comedians at National Theater on Saturday morning. Join in the fun as your preteens cozy up to the stars at Madame Tussauds.

Wild Things. Live ants, bees, centipedes, tarantulas, and roaches—some as large as mice—live in the O. Orkin Insect Zoo in the National Museum of Natural History, which also houses some of nature's most beautiful insects—butterflies. Sharks and fish swim in rectangular tanks at the National Aquarium. Farm animals, exotic species, and most creatures in between live at the National Zoo, but if your kid wants to see dinosaurs, head to the National Museum of Natural History. At the U.S. Botanic Gardens, walk on pathways marked with footprints from baby and grown-up dinosaurs in the Garden Primeval.

BAD-WEATHER PLANS

Washington, D.C.'s overall climate is generally tolerable year-round. In summer, however, an above-90-degree day with 90% humidity can quickly wither even the hardiest of families. Unremitting April showers can go on for 36 hours, and winter temperatures can fall well below freezing. On such days, when rough weather simply won't pass, you need an accessible, indoor activity that the whole family can enjoy. Here are the top choices to keep everyone entertained and comfortable on a bad-weather day.

The Smithsonian American Art Museum and the National Portrait Gallery. Two museums in one! Both museums share space in the historic old Patent House Building. The National Portrait Gallery is like a "Who's Who?" of Americans, including all U.S. presidents as well as athletes, musicians, and Hollywood types. The American Art features realism and abstraction, sculpture, photography, prints and drawings, contemporary crafts, and folk art that's more accessible to kids than more traditional work. But the best part of the experience might be what you can do in the enclosed courtyard between the two collections: Go barefoot. Lined by ficus and black olive trees, water scrims that look like long, rectangular puddles are perfect places to play. Free public wireless Internet access (Wi-Fi) and a café with casual dining from 11:30 to 6:30 add to the options that pass the time.

National Building Museum. The Big Bad Wolf won't blow this house down! More than 15 million bricks make up this building, but it's the inside that awes budding builders and architects. The site of many inaugural balls is also 15 stories tall and the eight 75-foot Corinthian columns are among the world's largest. With so much space, families don't feel like they're cooped up inside. Treasure hunts for different age kids and lots of drop-in activities like bridge building are free. For five bucks, you can borrow one of three tool kits, geared for kids ages 3 to 7 and 8 to 11. And if your kid catches the do-it-myself bug, the gift shop—known as one of the best museum shops in the city—sells lots of take-home buildings supplies for kids.

Take Your Pick of the Top Three. The Air and Space Museum, the Museum of Natural History, and the Museum of American History—the three most visited museums in Washington are all Smithsonians, on the National Mall, and they're all huge places with exhibits galore, IMAX movies, and food courts, where you can spend the day and still not see everything.

FOR FREE

It would almost be easier to list what's not free in D.C. All the Smithsonian museums and national memorials are free, as are many other museums—too many, in fact, to list here. Many of the top attractions are also free, like Ford's Theatre and Dumbarton Oaks. Summertime is heaven for budget travelers when free outdoor concerts and festivals occur every week.

Free Attractions
Arlington National Cemetery

Bureau of Engraving and Printing

Dumbarton Oaks (free from November 1 to March 14)

Ford's Theatre

Kenilworth Aquatic Gardens

Kennedy Center tours

National Arboretum

National Archives

National Building Museum

National Gallery of Art

National Geographic Museum at Explorer's Hall

National Museum of Medicine and Health

National Shrine of the Immaculate Conception

Old Post Office Pavilion

Old Stone House

Rock Creek Park (See the stars in a planetarium show)

Roosevelt Island

Supreme Court of the United States

U.S. Botanic Garden

U.S. Capitol

Washington National Cathedral

White House

Free Performances
The Kennedy Center hosts performances every day at 6 PM on the Millennium Stage. Also, every September the Prelude Festival kicks off the Kennedy Center's fall performance schedule with many free events. Choral and church groups perform at the National Cathedral, often at no charge.

Performances of military music take place around the city. From June through August, the U.S. Navy Band, U.S. Air Force Band, U.S. Marine Band, and U.S. Army Band take turns playing concerts on the grounds of the U.S. Capitol weekdays at 8 PM. You can also see the U.S. Marine Band every Friday night from May through August during the Evening Parade at the Marine Barracks.

D.C. is a city of festivals, many of which are free to the public (food and souvenirs cost extra). Check the National Mall lawn

FOR FREE

and Pennsylvania Avenue for music and dance performances, concerts, talks, cooking demonstrations, parades, and more. For a complete list of annual events, visit Destination D.C. at ⊕*www.washington.org.*

Birds aren't the only ones singing at the zoo on Thursday nights in the summer. At 6:30 from late June through early August, Sunset Serenades concerts range from rock and blues to folk and jazz.

TICKETPlace sells half-price tickets to D.C.'s theater and music events. If you're visiting in late October, reserve your seats early for D.C.'s Free Night of Theater.

Almost every day of the year, the Politics and Prose independent bookstore on Connecticut Avenue invites fiction and nonfiction authors to the store for book readings, talks, and Q&A sessions. Often, they're children's book authors.

WHEN TO GO

D.C. has two delightful seasons, spring and autumn, although families tend to visit in spring and summer during school breaks. In spring the city's ornamental fruit trees are budding, and its many gardens are in bloom. By autumn most of the summer crowds have left, and you can enjoy many of the sights in peace. Summers can be uncomfortably hot and humid, but late summer can be the most economical time to see Washington, as many hotels reduce their rates and free festivals flourish all over town. Winter weather is cold but mild by northern East Coast standards, and a handful of modest to heavy snowstorms each year bring this Southern city to a standstill.

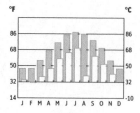

Exploring Washington, D.C.

WORD OF MOUTH

". . . we took our kids for the first time when they were 6 and 8 and they loved it—the monuments, Mount Vernon, the White House, in fact, there was very little they didn't like. Our favorite museum is the American History museum—just seeing the original "star spangled banner" (in the repair room) was a highlight of the trip."

—sf7307

Updated
by Kathryn
McKay

WHAT CHILD WOULDN'T BE EXCITED to touch a moon rock, see Dorothy's slipper, or cruise along the C&O Canal in a boat pulled by mules? Washington may seem like a place for grown-ups and school trips, but the city of the White House and the Supreme Court is also home to the International Spy Museum, the National Museum of Natural History, and National Zoo. History that may seem dry and dusty in the classroom comes alive for children as they visit landmarks they've seen on TV and the Web, stand where Martin Luther King Jr. delivered his "I have a dream" speech, and watch thousands of dollars roll off the presses at the Bureau of Engraving and Printing. A big plus in Washington is that most attractions are free.

Washington is a city of vistas—pleasant views that shift and change from block to block, a marriage of geometry and art. Unlike other large cities, it isn't dominated by skyscrapers, largely because, in 1899, Congress passed a height-restrictions act to prevent federal monuments from being overshadowed by commercial construction. The result: the world's first planned capital is also one of its most beautiful. And although the federal government dominates many of the city's activities and buildings, there are always places where you can leave politics behind.

The possibilities for together time are limitless in D.C. From exploring the Smithsonian's treasures to trying new ethnic cuisines to learning about the Constitution by reading the original, you'd need to try really hard to run out of things to do with your kids here. D.C. is an extremely compact city, so you're never too far from your next attraction—or, if you stay in the District, your hotel room for that mid-afternoon nap.

HOW D.C. CAME TO BE

The city that invented American politicking, back scratching, and delicate diplomatic maneuvering is itself the result of a compromise. Tired of its nomadic existence after having set up shop in eight locations, Congress voted in 1785 to establish a permanent federal city. Northern lawmakers wanted the capital on the Delaware River, in the North; Southerners wanted it on the Potomac, in the South. A deal was struck when Virginia's Thomas Jefferson agreed to support the proposal that the federal government assume the war debts of the colonies if New York's Alexander Hamilton and other Northern legislators would agree to locate the capital on the banks of the Potomac.

George Washington himself selected the site of the capital, a diamond-shape, 100-square-mi plot that encompassed the confluence of the Potomac and Anacostia rivers, not far from his estate at Mount Vernon. To give the young city a head start, Washington included the already thriving tobacco ports of Alexandria, Virginia, and Georgetown, Maryland, in the District of Columbia. In 1791 Pierre-Charles L'Enfant, a French engineer who had fought in the Revolution, created the classic plan for the city.

It took the Civil War—and every war thereafter—to energize the city, by attracting thousands of new residents and spurring building booms that extended the capital in all directions. Streets were paved in the 1870s, and the first streetcars ran in the 1880s. Memorials to famous Americans such as Lincoln and Jefferson were built in the first decades of the 20th century, along with the massive Federal Triangle, a monument to thousands of less-famous government workers.

EXPLORING WASHINGTON, D.C.

GETTING YOUR BEARINGS

Four Quadrants: The address system in D.C. takes some getting used to. The city is divided into the four quadrants of a compass (NW, NE, SE, SW), with the U.S. Capitol at the center. Because the Capitol doesn't sit in the exact center of the city (the Washington Monument does), Northwest is the largest quadrant. Northwest also has most of the important landmarks, although Northeast and Southwest have their fair share. The boundaries are North Capitol Street, East Capitol Street, South Capitol Street, and the National Mall. That's where street addresses start and climb as you move up the numbers and alphabet. Fortunately for kids, the city is full of statues of animals, many of which are best viewed from a vehicle. From the pair of lions (one sleeping, one roaring) at each end of the Taft Bridge on Connecticut Avenue to the traditional generals on horseback, there seem to be enough creatures to fill Noah's ark.

Numbered Streets & Lettered Streets: Within each quadrant, numbered streets run north to south, and lettered streets run east to west (the letter J was omitted to avoid confusion with the letter I). The streets form a fairly simple grid—for instance, 900 G Street NW is the intersection of 9th and G streets in the northwest quadrant of the city. Likewise, if you count the letters of the alphabet, skipping

J, you can get a good sense of the location of an address on a numbered street. For instance, 1600 16th Street NW is close to Q Street, Q being the 16th letter of the alphabet if you skip J.

Avenues on the Diagonal: As if all this weren't confusing enough, Major Pierre L'Enfant, the Frenchman who originally designed the city, threw in diagonal avenues recalling those of Paris. Most of D.C.'s avenues are named after U.S. states. You can find addresses on avenues the same way you find those on numbered streets, so 1200 Connecticut Avenue NW is close to M Street, because M is the 12th letter of the alphabet when you skip J.

When you arrive at a sight, be prepared to walk through metal detectors and open your bag for security personnel. Some places such as the National Gallery of Art, may require that you check your bag. Visit the information desk for maps and brochures, and inquire about children's programs. Also, show kids how to recognize staff or security people and designate a time and place—some visible landmark—to meet in case you become separated.

THE MALL

GETTING ORIENTED

This expanse of green, which stretches due west from the Capitol to the Washington Monument, is lined on the north and south by some of America's finest museums, almost all of which are free. Lindbergh's Spirit of St. Louis, the Hope Diamond, the flag that inspired "The Star Spangled Banner," a tyrannosaurus rex, and myriad other modern and classical artifacts await you. Of course, the 300-foot-wide Mall is more than just a front yard for museums: it's a picnicking park and a running path, an outdoor stage for festivals and fireworks, and America's town green. During your visit here you might see residents playing soccer, protestors wielding signs and banners, or children cavorting on the restored 1947 carousel. First one on gets to ride the dragon.

PLANNING YOUR TIME

Don't try to see all the Mall's attractions in a day. Few people have the stamina for more than a half day of museum or gallery going at a time; children definitely don't. To avoid mental and physical exhaustion, try to devote at least two days to the Mall. ■TIP➔ **The Mall stretches more than two miles. Comfortable shoes are necessary as are stroll-**

TOP 5 MALL EXPERIENCES

1

■ **Bureau of Engraving and Printing**. Show me the money! It's here—some $637 million printed daily—and it's all for show as you watch the money roll off the presses.

■ **National Air and Space Museum**. There's a good reason why this is the most popular museum in the world: Kids love it!

■ **National Museum of American History**. The incredible diversity of artifacts from Lincoln's top hat to Kermit the frog are again on dis-

play after major architectural renovations.

■ **National Museum of Natural History**. From tiny little insects to the tremendous dinosaurs, the natural wonders here amuse young and old.

■ **Washington Monument**. Some kids say it looks like a giant pencil. Visible from nearly everywhere in the city, it's a landmark for tourists and lost motorists and a beacon for anyone who yearns to shoot to the top and see Washington appear as small as a village made from Legos.

ers for young children. Do the north side one day and the south the next. Or split your sightseeing on the Mall into a walking day, when you take in the scenic views and enjoy the architecture of each museum and a museum day, when you go back to spend time with the exhibits that catch your interest. Afterward, plan something relaxing that doesn't require more walking—picnicking or getting a snack in one of the many museum cafeterias probably makes more sense than, say, shopping.

WHAT TO SEE

Bureau of Engraving and Printing. Paper money has been printed here since 1914, when the bureau relocated from the redbrick-towered Auditors Building at the corner of 14th Street and Independence Avenue. In addition to the paper currency in the United States, military certificates and presidential invitations are printed here, too. You can only enter the bureau on the tours, which last about 35 minutes. From March through August, same-day timed-entry tour passes are issued starting at 8 AM at the Raoul Wallenberg Place SW ticket booth. For the rest of the year, tickets aren't used. On beautiful spring and summer days, waits to get in can be up to two hours, and if a tour bus arrives as you do, you may be in line longer. September through February is considered an off-peak time, so tickets aren't required and

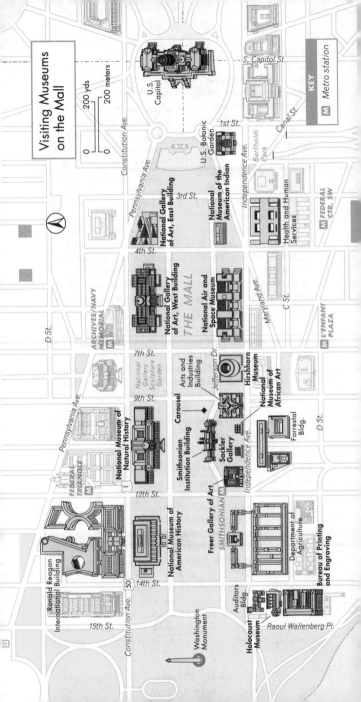

Visiting Museums on the Mall

0 — 200 yds
0 — 200 meters

KEY

M Metro station

U.S. Capitol

S. Capitol St.

Canal St.

Constitution Ave.

Pennsylvania Ave.

U.S. Botanic Garden

1st St.

Bartholdi Park

National Gallery of Art, East Building

3rd St.

National Museum of the American Indian

Independence Ave.

Health and Human Services

M FEDERAL CTR. SW

4th St.

National Gallery of Art, West Building

National Air and Space Museum

THE MALL

Maryland Ave.

C St.

M L'ENFANT PLAZA

ARCHIVES/NAVY MEMORIAL M

D St.

7th St.

National Gallery Sculpture Garden

Arts and Industries Building

Jefferson Dr.

Hirshhorn Museum

National Museum of African Art

Forrestal Bldg.

D St.

9th St.

Carousel

Smithsonian Institution Building

Sackler Gallery

Pennsylvania Ave.

National Museum of Natural History

FEDERAL TRIANGLE M

12th St.

Freer Gallery of Art

Independence Ave.

M SMITHSONIAN

National Museum of American History

Ronald Reagan International Building

15th St.

14th St.

Constitution Ave.

50

Department of Agriculture

Bureau of Printing and Engraving

Auditors Bldg.

Holocaust Museum

Raoul Wallenberg Pl.

Washington Monument

waits likely will not be long. While waiting you could examine the money in your wallet and amuse the kids with fun facts. For example: If you spent $1 every second, it would take 317 years to spend $10 billion; a mile high stack of currency would contain more than 14½ million notes or dollars. It may sound crazy to adults, but kids like to buy shredded bags of money in the gift shop. ⊠ *14th and C Sts. SW, The Mall* ☎ *202/874–8888, 877/874–4114 tour information* ⊕ *www.moneyfactory.gov* ✇ *Free* ☉ *Sept.– Apr., weekdays 9–10:45 and 12:30–2; May–Aug., weekdays 9–10:45, 12:30–2, and 5–7* Ⓜ *Smithsonian.* 5+up

Franklin Delano Roosevelt Memorial. Unveiled in 1997, this 7½-acre memorial to the 32nd president includes waterfalls and reflection pools, four outdoor gallery rooms—one for each of Roosevelt's presidential terms—and 10 bronze sculptures. The granite megaliths connecting the galleries are engraved with some of Roosevelt's famous statements, including, "The only thing we have to fear is fear itself."

The statue of a wheelchair-bound Roosevelt near the entrance of the memorial was added in 2001. Originally, the memorial showed little evidence of Roosevelt's polio, which he contracted at age 39. He used a wheelchair for the last 24 years of his life but kept his disability largely hidden from public view. The statue was added after years of debate about whether to portray Roosevelt realistically, or to honor his desire not to display his disability.

A bronze statue of First Lady Eleanor Roosevelt stands in front of the United Nations symbol in the fourth room. She was a vocal spokesperson for human rights and one of the most influential women of her time.

You're encouraged to touch the handprints along the columns in the second room, which represent the working hands of the American people. With older kids, take your time walking through the four "rooms." With wee ones, head straight to the third room. Though your youngsters can't sit on Roosevelt's lap, they can pet Fala, his Scottish terrier. The tips of Fala's ears are shiny from all the attention. For all families, this memorial presents one of the best places for photographs. Have your family take a place in the bread line. For merchandise featuring the presidential pouch, check out the bookstore. ⊠ *West side of Tidal Basin, Washington, DC, The Mall* ☎ *202/426–6841* ⊕ *www.nps.gov/fdrm* ✇ *Free* ☉ *Open 24 hrs; staffed daily 8 AM–midnight* Ⓜ *Smithsonian.* All ages

★ **Freer Gallery of Art and the Arthur M. Sackler Gallery.** Together these galleries comprise the National Museums of Asian Art and are connected by an underground exhibition space. When Charles Freer endowed the gallery that bears his name, he insisted on a few conditions: objects in the collection could not be lent out, nor could objects from outside the collections be put on display. Because of the restrictions, it was necessary to build a second, complementary museum to house the Asian art collection of Arthur M. Sackler, a wealthy medical researcher and publisher who began collecting Asian art as a student in the 1940s. Sackler allowed Smithsonian curators to select 1,000 items from his ample collection and pledged $4 million toward the construction of the museum. The collection includes works from China, Southeast Asia, Korea, Tibet, and Japan. Objects in the permanent collection include Chinese ritual bronzes, jade ornaments from the third millennium BC, Persian manuscripts, and Indian paintings in gold, silver, lapis lazuli, and malachite. The lower level connects to the Freer Gallery of Art.

Free highlight tours meet at 12:15 every day, except Wednesday and federal holidays, at the information desks. Ask about the free ImaginAsia program. Armed with guidebooks and pencils, families take self-guided tours, searching for artwork and filling out pages in an activity booklet. Afterward, they meet in an education room in the Sackler Gallery to create take-home crafts. Recent activities included printing on T-shirts, making stick puppets, and creating scrapbook pages. ImaginAsia is a drop-in program; reservations are needed only for groups of eight or more. Kids must be accompanied by an adult. The museum recommends ImaginAsia for kids eight and up. ImaginAsia takes place most days throughout the summer and on weekends during the school year. ⊠ *12th St. and Jefferson Dr. SW, The Mall* ☎ *202/633-1000* ⊕ *www.asia.si.edu* ⊠ *Free* ⊘ *Daily 10–5:30* Ⓜ *Smithsonian.* 7+up

Hirshhorn Museum and Sculpture Garden. Sculpture on the National Mall is mostly marble columns and dead presidents, but in 2003 the Hirshhorn made a bold addition: a 32-foot-tall yellow cartoon brushstroke sculpture by pop-art iconographer Roy Lichtenstein. It became a beloved local landmark and an apt symbol of the Hirshhorn itself. Conceived as the nation's museum of modern and contemporary art, the Hirshhorn is home to more than 11,000 works by masters like Pablo Picasso, Joan Miró, Piet Mondrian, Willem de Kooning, and Andy Warhol.

Visiting Memorials
on the Mall

These are displayed in a 1974 round, poured-concrete building. Designed by Gordon Bunshaft, it was dubbed the "Doughnut on the Mall" when it was built, but today it's seen as a fitting home for contemporary art. Most of the collection was bequeathed by the museum's founder, Joseph H. Hirshhorn, a Latvian immigrant who made his fortune in uranium mines.

The internationally renowned sculpture collection inside has masterpieces by Henry Moore, Alberto Giacometti, and Constantin Brancusi. Outside, sculptures dot a grass-and-granite garden, which, in addition to the Lichtenstein, boasts Henri Matisse's *Backs I-IV* and Auguste Rodin's *Burghers of Calais*. Don't miss the giant Alexander Calder mobiles. The collection is constantly updated with the best of contemporary art, which often includes fun interactive installations, such as Danish artist Olafur Eliasson's *Round Rainbow*, a room in which a rotating prism transforms a beam of light into undulating colors bathing visitors' faces.

Exhibitions change regularly, so there's no guarantee that a particular piece from the permanent collection will be on view when you visit. If you're looking for a specific work or artist, browse the museum Web site's "Collection Search" feature, which will tell you whether a work is on display or archived. The coolest art for kids is outside in the Sculpture Garden. Looking through Dan Graham's "For Gordon Bunshaft" with two-way mirrors gives a fun-house effect. "Man Passing Through Door" by Jean Ipoustegy may remind "muggles" of when Harry Potter boarded the train to Hogwarts. Take a peak at the star inside Kenneth Snelson's tall sculpture "Needle Tower." Inside the museum, the Alexander Calder mobiles on the third floor are favorites with kids. Family programs are limited, but occasionally artists will lead workshops for older children and teens. ⊠*Independence Ave. and 7th St. SW, The Mall* ☎*202/633–1000* ⊕*www.hirshhorn.si.edu* ▤*Free* ⊘*Museum daily 10–5:30, sculpture garden 7:30–dusk* Ⓜ *Smithsonian or L'Enfant Plaza (Maryland Ave. exit).* 5+up

Lincoln Memorial. Many consider the Lincoln Memorial the most inspiring monument in Washington, but that hasn't always been the case: early detractors thought it inappropriate that a president known for his humility should be honored with what amounts to a grandiose Greek temple. The memorial was intended to be a symbol of national unity, but over time it has come to represent social justice and civil rights. In its shadow, Americans marched for integrated schools in 1958, rallied for an end to the Vietnam War in 1967, and laid wreathes in a ceremony honoring the Iranian hostages in 1979. It may be best known, though, as the site of Martin Luther King Jr.'s "I Have a Dream" speech. Even the littlest kids are familiar with the president on the penny and the five-dollar bill. Children eager to show off their counting skills can count the columns, representing the 36 states in the country at the time of Lincoln's death. Challenge kids 10 and up to practice their oratorical skill by reciting two of Lincoln's speeches—the Second Inaugural Address and the Gettysburg Address—which are carved on the north and south walls. Kids can even find the exact spot where Martin Luther King Jr. gave his "I Have a Dream" speech. ⊠ *West end of Mall* ☎ *202/426–6895* ⊕ *www.nps. gov/linc* 🎫 *Free* ⊙ *Open 24 hrs; staffed daily 8 AM–midnight* Ⓜ *Foggy Bottom.* All ages

National Air and Space Museum. This is the world's most visited museum, attracting 9 million people annually to the world's largest collection of historic aircraft and spacecraft. Its 23 galleries tell the story of aviation from the earliest human attempts at flight to supersonic jets and spacecraft. For more giant jets and spaceships, visit the **National Air and Space Museum Steven F. Udvar-Hazy Center,** at Washington Dulles International Airport in northern Virginia. A shuttle bus runs from the museum entrance on the Mall to the outdoor center, where you can see a Concorde, the space shuttle *Enterprise,* and the *Enola Gay* (which in 1945 dropped on Japan the first atomic devices to be used in war). "Fun for all ages" isn't a cliché at this museum. On Saturday at 11 and 1, Flight of Fancy features a professional storyteller for toddlers. An activity board at the gallery entrance lists times for paper airplane contests and demonstrations by museum Explainers, high school and college students who encourage kids to participate. At the Explore the Universe exhibit, kids seven and up may enjoy how past stargazers mapped the heavens and what mysteries about our universe still remain. Don't let long lines deter you from seeing a show in the five-story IMAX Theater. Films like To Fly!, a family favorite, make you feel positively airborne. Strollers aren't allowed at the movies, but then kids under four may find the noise and larger-than-life images frightening anyway. The flight simulators, two- and four-person capsules that spin and whirl you through a simulated air fight, are often the highlight of kids' entire

Washington, D.C., visit. Before you leave, go to Milestones of Flight to touch the moon rock, one of only three on earth you can feel. ⊠*Independence Ave. and 6th St. SW, The Mall* ☏*202/357–1729, 202/357–1686 movie information, 202/357–1729 TDD* ⊕*www.nasm.si.edu* ☑*Free, IMAX $8.50, children 2–12 $7, planetarium $8.50, children 2–12 $7* ⊙*Daily 10–5:30 Smithsonian.* All ages

National Gallery of Art, East Building. The East Building opened in 1978 in response to the changing needs of the National Gallery, especially its growing collection of modern art. Masterpieces from every famous name in 20th-century art—Pablo Picasso, Jackson Pollock, Piet Mondrian, Roy Lichtenstein, Joan Miró, Georgia O'Keeffe, and dozens of others—fill the galleries. Many children find the colorful, modern art here a bit more accessible than the more traditional works in the West Building. Even kids too young to have tried making their own mobiles with coat angers or wire can appreciate Alexander Calder's 76-foot long mobile in the atrium. The free Film Program for Children and Teens features recent flicks and classic foreign and domestic films aired in the 500-seat auditorium. Art workshops for kids are held in both buildings. Find out about family programs through the information desk, the Web site, or by calling. Free weekend (and some weekday) workshops include tours and activities. ⊠*Constitution Ave. between 3rd and 4th Sts. NW, The Mall* ☏*202/737–4215, 202/789–3030 family programs, 202/842–6176 TDD* ⊕*www.nga.gov* ☑*Free* ⊙*Mon.–Sat. 10–5, Sun. 11–6* Ⓜ*Archives/Navy Memorial.* 5+up

National Gallery of Art, West Building. The two buildings of the National Gallery hold one of the world's foremost collections of paintings, sculptures, and graphics, from the 13th to the 21st centuries. If you want to view the museum's holdings in (more or less) chronological order, it's best to start your exploration in the West Building. The only painting by Leonardo da Vinci on display in the Western Hemisphere, *Ginevra de'Benci,* is the centerpiece of the collection's comprehensive survey of Italian Renaissance paintings and sculpture. The gallery of gorgeous French Impressionist masterworks by superstars such as Claude Monet, Auguste Renoir, and Edgar Degas, is unmissable. Computers in the Information Room allow you to preview works before you go to the galleries. Adventures in Art family audio tours, which explore Dutch and Flemish paintings (*$3 per tour, $2 for extra headphones*), recommended for ages 7 to 12, are available in the rotunda. Find out about family programs through the information desk, the Web site, or by calling. Free weekend (and some weekday) workshops include tours and activities. But the best part of a visit, particularly for those under five, might be the outdoor sculpture garden, adjacent to the West building. The massive *Spider* by Louise Bourgeois and the rabbit *Thinker on a Rock* by Barry Flanagan may remind kids of nursery rhymes, but the only sculpture kids can touch is Scott Burton's *Six-Part Seating*, with its polished granite chairs. In the center of all the sculpture, a fountain spews until winter when the pool becomes an ice rink. The Pavilion Café sells sandwiches, salads, and fruit. ⊠*The Mall*☎*202/737–4215, 202/789–3030 family programs, 202/842–6176 TDD* ⊕*www.nga.gov* ⊠*Free* ⊙*Mon.–Sat. 10–5, Sun. 11–6* Ⓜ*Archives/Navy Memorial.* 3+up

National Museum of African Art. This unique underground building houses galleries, a library, photographic archives, and educational facilities. Its rotating exhibits present African visual arts, including sculpture, textiles, photography, archaeology, and modern art. Long-term installations explore the sculpture of sub-Saharan Africa, the art of Benin, the pottery of Central Africa, the archaeology of the ancient Nubian city of Kerma, and the artistry of everyday objects. The museum's educational programs include films with contemporary perspectives on African life, storytelling programs, festivals, and hands-on workshops for families, all of which bring Africa's oral traditions, literature, and art to life. Workshops and demonstrations by African and African-American artists offer a chance to meet and talk to practicing artists. Kids enjoy the displays of masks, beaded art, and many objects that incorporate animals. About once a month at free or low-cost Afri-Kid programs, kids may hear stories, tour the gallery hunting for certain objects, and/or make music. Designed for children ages 5 to 11, these drop-in programs are usually held once a month on Saturday throughout the school year and on at least one weekend and one weekday each month in summer. Inquire at the front desk about an activity brochure connected with a current exhibit. Occasionally the museum has activities for teenagers such as photographing art with their cell phones and e-mailing the images to a designated Web site. ⊠*950 Independence Ave. SW, The Mall* ☎*202/633–1000, 202/357–1729 TDD* ⊕*www.nmafa.si.edu* ⊠*Free* ⊙*Daily 10–5:30* Ⓜ*Smithsonian.* 5+up

WHERE CAN I FIND . . . ON THE NATIONAL MALL?

Quick Meals

Smithsonian Castle	1000 Jefferson St. SW	Basic sandwiches and salads; faster in and out than other museums on the mall.
On the Fly	Front of Hirshhorn and American History museums	Look for lime green and white carts. BBQ, tacos, and veggie options, too.

Ice Cream/Gelato

Espresso and Gelato Bar at National Gallery of Art	6th and Constitution Ave. NW	Some people bypass the art for the gelato, 19 flavors.

Good Coffee

Espresso and Gelato Bar at National Gallery of Art	6th and Constitution Ave., NW	Look for seasonal flavors, iced and over ice cream, too.

Grocery Stores

Farmers' Market	12th and Independence Ave. NW	Friday 10–2, June–October, fruits, veggies, home-baked breads, and treats.

Fun Stores

Museum of Natural History shops	Constitution Ave. and 10th St. NW	Lots of animal action—stuffed and plastic animals, yard-long gummy snakes, and more.
Museum of American History	14th St. and Constitution Ave. NW	Americana toys and games, presidential memorabilia.

Playgrounds

National Mall	From the Capitol to the Washington Monument	Bring your Frisbee, softball and mitt, or soccer ball.
Carousel	Outside of Castle	$2.50 a ticket. Only one dragon ride in this ring of horses.

Public Bathrooms

Sackler/Freer Gallery	1050 Independence Ave.	Clean, not crowded, and super close to Smithsonian Metro.
National Gallery of Art West Building	East End Ave. and 77th St.	Less crowded than the most popular Smithsonian museums.

National Museum of American History. The 3 million artifacts in the country's largest history museum explore America's cultural, political, technical, and scientific past, with holdings as diverse and iconic as the desk on which Thomas Jefferson wrote the Declaration of Independence, the top hat Abraham Lincoln was wearing the night he was assassinated, and Judy Garland's ruby slippers from *The Wizard of Oz.* The original Star-Spangled Banner: the 15-stripe and 15-star American flag that flew over Fort McHenry during the British bombardment of Baltimore Harbor in 1814, and inspired Francis Scott Key to write the national anthem, is the centerpiece of the museum's vast collections. Head to the first floor if your kids are into transportation. Farm machines, antique automobiles, a 1939 school bus painted "double deep" orange, and an early steam locomotive await. Nearby, SparkLab! has enough interactives to keep kids busy for about an hour. A corner of the lab is set up with building blocks and more for the under-five set, where adults must accompany children. On the second floor, you'll find the flag that inspired "The Star-Spangled Banner," the first ladies' inaugural gowns, and presidential possessions, including George Washington's sword, Abraham Lincoln's top hat, and the portable wooden desk (some call it an early laptop) that Thomas Jefferson designed and used to draft the Declaration of Independence. The third floor houses some of the most famous kid-pleasing treasures, including the shoes from Oz, Oscar the Grouch from *Sesame Street,* and Dumbo the flying elephant from Disneyland. ⊠*Constitution Ave. and 14th St. NW, The Mall*☎*202/633–1000, 202/357–1729 TDD* ⊕*www.american history.si.edu* ✆*Free* ⊙*Daily 10–5:30; call for hrs of Hands on History and Hands on Science rooms* Ⓜ*Smithsonian or Federal Triangle.* All ages

National Museum of the American Indian. The Smithsonian's newest museum opened in 2004 and is the first national museum devoted entirely to Native American artifacts, presented from a Native American perspective. The exterior, clad in limestone from Minnesota, evokes natural rock formations shaped by wind and water. Inside, four floors of galleries cover 10,000 years of history of the native tribes of the Western Hemisphere, with exhibitions of wood and stone carvings, headdresses, beadwork, textiles, paintings, baskets, pottery, and nearly a million other crafts and works of art from the Americas. Part of the lure of this building is the architecture, which may be lost on kids. Request a copy of the family activity guide, which includes photos that can be used as a pictorial treasure hunt. Unless you're purchasing a souvenir, skip the second floor. Move on to the top floors where exhibits often focus on one item, such as gold, guns, swords, and arrow points, allowing kids to make comparisons and look for the largest, the most ornate. Under some display cases are drawers, which kids can pull out. In Our Universes, kids can beat drums, poke their hands through holes, and look through a sculpture of a raven. Who We Are, a 13-minute presentation on the fourth floor is a great introduction to contemporary native life, but preschoolers and children who cover their ears during thunderstorms might not appreciate the loud noises. To give kids a taste of Indian food, dine at the museum's Mitsitam Native Foods Café, known as one of best museum restaurants in D.C. ⊠*4th St. and Independence Ave. SW* ☎*202/633–1000* ⊕*www.americanindian.si.edu* ☜*Free* ☉*Daily 10–5:30* Ⓜ*L'Enfant Plaza.* 5+up

National Museum of Natural History. This is one of the great natural history museums in the world. The giant dinosaur fossils, glittering gems, creepy-crawly insects, and other natural delights—124 million specimens in all—attract nearly 6 million visitors annually. Some kids refer to this museum as the one with the elephant. "Henry," one of the world's largest elephants on display, has greeted generations of visitors in the rotunda. In the popular Dinosaur Hall, fossilized skeletons range from a 90-foot-long diplodocus to a tiny *Thesalorsaurs neglectus* (so named because it sat for years in a museum drawer before being assembled). Across the rotunda is the Hall of Mammals with 274 creatures, including lions and tigers and bears, plus more exotic mammals. Older children may enjoy the Janet Annenberg Hooker Hall of Geology, Gems & Minerals, which takes rock collecting to new heights and includes a neat exhibit on volcanoes and earthquakes. The O. Orkin Insect Zoo is home to live ants, bees, centipedes, tarantulas, and roaches—some as large as mice. Toddlers like crawling around the model of an African termite mound. Tarantula feedings usually take place at 10:30, 11:30, and 1:30 Tuesday through Friday and 11:30, 12:30, and 1:30 on weekends. In the Butterfly Pavilion (*Adults $6, children $5, free with timed entry passes on Tues.*), winged insects fly overhead. The Discovery Room (*Tues.–Sun. 10:30–3:30*) features hands-on activities for children ages 5–11. ⊠*Constitution Ave. and 10th St. NW, The Mall* ☎*202/633–1000, 202/357–1729 TDD* ⊕*www.*

mnh.si.edu ⊠*Free, IMAX $8.50, $7 ages 2–12* ⊙*Museum daily 10–5:30; Discovery Room Tues.–Fri. noon–2:30, weekends 10:30–3:30; free passes for Discovery Room distributed during regular museum hrs near Discovery Room door* Ⓜ*Smithsonian or Federal Triangle.* All ages

Smithsonian Institution Building. The first Smithsonian museum constructed, this red sandstone, Norman-style building is better known as the Castle. It was designed by James Renwick, the architect of St. Patrick's Cathedral in New York City. Although British scientist and founder James Smithson had never visited America, his will stipulated that should his nephew, Henry James Hungerford, die without an heir, Smithson's entire fortune would go to the United States, "to found at Washington, under the name of the Smithsonian Institution, an establishment for the increase and diffusion of knowledge." The museums on the Mall are the Smithsonian's most visible example of this ideal, but the organization also sponsors traveling exhibitions and maintains research posts in outside-the-Beltway locales such as the Chesapeake Bay and the tropics of Panama.

The Smithsonian Institution was finally established on August 10, 1846. The Castle building was completed in 1855 and originally housed all the Smithsonian's operations, including the science and art collections, research laboratories, and living quarters for the institution's secretary and his family. The statue in front of the Castle's entrance is not of Smithson but of Joseph Henry, the scientist who served as the institution's first secretary. Smithson's body was brought to America in 1904 and is entombed in a small room to the left of the Castle's Mall entrance.

▮TIP→ **Today the Castle houses the Smithsonian Information Center, which can help you get your bearings and decide which attractions to visit.** An 18-minute video gives an overview of the Smithsonian museums and the National Zoo, and monitors display information on the day's events. Interactive touch-screens provide more detailed information on the museums as well as other attractions in the capital. The center opens at 8:30 AM, an hour before the other museums, so you can plan your day without wasting sightseeing time. It also has a good café, offering one of the better options for lunch on the Mall, and a gift shop. The touch-screen monitors are at heights for both children and adults. Interactive videos provide more detailed information on the museums as well as other attractions in the city. Although they weren't designed for children, an electronic map and a braille map of the city draw kids nonetheless. And, of course, there's the historic carousel just behind the building. ✉*1000 Jefferson Dr. SW, The Mall* ☎*202/633–1000, 202/357–1729 TDD* ⊕*www.si.edu* ✆*Free* ⏱*Daily 8:30–5:30* Ⓜ*Smithsonian.* All ages

Thomas Jefferson Memorial. In the 1930s, Congress decided that Thomas Jefferson deserved a monument positioned as prominently as those honoring Washington and Lincoln. Workers scooped and moved tons of the river bottom to create dry land for the spot directly south of the White House where the monument was built. Jefferson had always admired the Pantheon in Rome, so the Jefferson Memorial's architect, John Russell Pope, drew on it for inspiration. His finished work was dedicated on the bicentennial of Jefferson's birth, April 13, 1943. The memorial's bronze statue of Jefferson, standing on a 6-foot granite pedestal, looms larger than life. You can get a taste of Jefferson's keen intellect from his writings about freedom and government inscribed on the marble walls surrounding his statue. Children and adults may be surprised that Jefferson didn't list being president as one of his greatest accomplishments. He wanted to be remembered as the "Author of the Declaration of American Independence, of the Statute of Virginia for religious freedom, and Father of the University of Virginia." To learn more about Jefferson, kids can talk to National Park Service rangers at the memorial and visit an exhibit called Light and Liberty on the lower level, which provides a time line of world history during his lifetime and a 10-minute video. ✉*Tidal Basin, south bank* ☎*202/426–6821* ⊕*www.nps.gov/thje* ✆*Free* ⏱*Daily 8 AM–midnight* Ⓜ*Smithsonian.* 5+up

United States Holocaust Memorial Museum. Museums usually celebrate the best that humanity can achieve, but this museum instead documents the worst. This museum's permanent exhibition tells the stories of the millions of Jews, Gypsies, Jehovah's Witnesses, homosexuals, political prisoners, the mentally ill, and others killed by the Nazis between 1933 and 1945. The exhibitions are detailed and graphic; the experiences memorable and powerful. Timed-entry passes (distributed on a first-come, first-served basis at the 14th Street entrance starting at 10 AM or available in advance through tickets.com) are necessary for the permanent exhibition. Allow extra time to enter the building in spring and summer, when long lines can form.

Like the history it covers, the Holocaust Museum can be profoundly moving and emotionally complex, so parents need to first decide whether their children can appreciate it. The recommended ages published by the museum are guidelines only. During the tourist season (March–August), the museum is often crowded, making it difficult to obtain tickets. The average visit is long, often two to three hours, and exhibits involve lots of reading. All that said, a trip here will be memorable for a preteen or teenager. You don't need a pass for Remember the Children: Daniel's Story, an interactive exhibit that tells the history of the Holocaust through the perspective of a young boy growing up in Nazi Germany. Children know from the beginning that Daniel survives to tell his story. ⊠*100 Raoul Wallenberg Pl. SW, enter from Raoul Wallenberg Pl. or 14th St. SW, The Mall* ☎*202/488–0400, 800/400–9373, tickets.com* ⊕*www.ushmm.org* ☜*Free* ☉*Daily 10–5:30* Ⓜ*Smithsonian. Remember the Children* 7+up, *Museum* 12+up

Vietnam Veterans Memorial. "The Wall," as it's commonly called, is one of the most visited sites in Washington. The names of more than 58,000 Americans who died in the Vietnam War are etched in its black granite panels, creating a somber, dignified, and powerful memorial. The memorial was conceived by Jan Scruggs, a former infantry corporal who served in Vietnam, and designed by Maya Lin, a 21-year-old architecture student at Yale. The Wall was unveiled in 1982. The statues near the wall came about in response to controversies surrounding the memorial. In 1984, Frederick Hart's statue of three soldiers and a flagpole was erected to the south of the wall, with the goal of winning over veterans who considered the memorial a "black gash of shame." A memorial plaque was added in 2004 at the statue of three servicemen to honor veterans who died after the war as a direct result of injuries suffered in Vietnam but who fall outside Department of Defense guidelines for remembrance at the wall. The Vietnam Women's Memorial was dedicated on Veterans Day 1993. Glenna Goodacre's bronze sculpture depicts two women caring for a wounded soldier while a third woman kneels nearby; eight trees around the plaza commemorate the eight women in the military who died in Vietnam. Sometimes kids think all the soldiers listed on the Wall are buried at the monument. They aren't, of course, but the memorial may have some kids asking serious questions about war and death. You can look up names in books posted at the entrance and exits of the memorial or ask rangers or volunteers wearing yellow caps for help. They also carry graphite pencils and paper to make rubbings of names. Kids may enjoy decoding symbols on the wall. Every name is preceded (on the West Wall) or followed (on the East Wall) by a symbol designating status. "A diamond indicates "killed, body recovered." A small percentage of names have plus signs, indicating "killed, body not recovered." ⊠*Constitution Gardens, 23rd St. and Constitution Ave. NW* ☎*202/634–1568* ⊕*www. nps.gov/vive* ☑*Free* ⊙*24 hrs; staffed daily 8 AM–midnight* Ⓜ*Foggy Bottom.* 7+up

Washington Monument. At the western end of the Mall, the 555-foot, 5-inch Washington Monument punctuates the capital like a huge exclamation point. Inside, an elevator takes you to the top for a bird's-eye view of the city. The monument was part of Pierre L'Enfant's plan for Washington, but his intended location proved to be marshy, so it was moved 100 yards southeast to firmer ground. (A stone marker now indicates L'Enfant's original site.) Construction began in 1848 and continued, with interruptions, until 1884. The design called for an obelisk rising from a circular colonnaded building, which was to be adorned with statues of national heroes, including Washington riding in a chariot. When the Army Corps of Engineers took over construction in 1876, the building around the obelisk was abandoned. Upon its completion, the monument was the world's tallest structure. It's still the tallest in Washington. An elevator whizzes to the top of the monument in 70 seconds—a trip that in 1888 took 12 minutes via steam-powered elevator. From the viewing stations at the top you can take in most of the District of Columbia, as well as parts of Maryland and Virginia. There's a story behind the change in color of the stone about a third of the way up the monument. In 1854, six years into construction, members of the anti-Catholic Know-Nothing party stole and smashed a block of marble donated by Pope Pius IX. This action, combined with funding shortages and the onset of the Civil War, brought construction to a halt. After the war, building finally resumed, and though the new marble came from the same Maryland quarry as the old, it was taken from a different stratum with a slightly different shade. Arrive at the monument at the appointed time. Although lines tend to be long, particularly during the tourist season and on good-weather weekends, they move quickly. If children are restless, have them count the flags surrounding the monument. (There are 50: one for each state, though none for the District of Columbia.) Two of the four viewing stations are equipped with a step so younger or shorter children can see out the windows. Older children may enjoy finding Washington's landmarks. (A street map, available in the gift shop, is helpful for this.) ✉*Constitution Ave. and 15th St. NW* ☎*202/426–6841, 877/444–6777 for advance tickets* ⊕*www.nps.gov/wamo, www.recreation.gov for advance tickets* 💵*Free; $2 service fee per advance ticket* ⊙*Daily 9–5* Ⓜ*Smithsonian.* 5+up

THE WHITE HOUSE AREA & FOGGY BOTTOM

Tops on many first-timer's D.C list is a visit to the White House. The home of every U.S. president but George Washington, the 132-room mansion is as impressive in real life as it is on television.

In a city full of famous places, none is more familiar than the White House. But the neighborhood holds other attractions such as the Corcoran Gallery of Art and the Kennedy Center for the Performing Arts that often host fun programs for families.

Many visitors take a tour of the White House, then head straight to the Tidal Basin and the monuments where kids don't have to worry about keeping off the furniture.

GETTING HERE

The White House can be reached by the Red Line's Farragut North stop or the Blue and Orange lines' McPherson Square and Farragut West stops. Foggy Bottom has its own Metro stop, also on the Blue and Orange lines. A free shuttle runs from the station to the Kennedy Center. Many of the other attractions are a considerable distance from the nearest subway stop. If you don't relish long walks or time is limited, check the map to see if you need to make alternate travel arrangements to visit specific sights.

PLANNING YOUR TIME

Touring the area around the White House could easily take a day or even two, depending on how long you visit each of the museums along the way. To see Foggy Bottom's more westerly sights will add still more time.

If you enjoy history, you may be most interested in the Decatur House, DAR Museum, and State Department. If

TOP WHITE HOUSE AREA EXPERIENCES

■ **DAR Museum.** Kids five to seven discover what life was like 150 years ago as part of the Colonial Adventure program.

■ **White House.** America's most famous house is still open to the public—a thrill, even if you're only allowed into 8 of the 132 rooms.

■ **White House Visitor Center.** If you didn't plan your visit months in advance with a group of 10, you can still get a look at White House life. Here the videos and photos capture first families. Unlike the actual White House, kids can roam around here, sit on the furniture, use the restroom, and drink from the water fountains.

it's art you crave, devote the hours to the Corcoran and Renwick galleries instead. Save the Kennedy Center and Watergate for the evening, when you can catch a performance or enjoy dinner in the area.

WHAT TO SEE

Corcoran Gallery of Art. The Corcoran is Washington's largest nonfederal art museum, as well as its first art museum. Founded "for the purpose of encouraging American Genius," the Corcoran's extensive collection of 16,000 works of 18th- through 21st-century American art represents most significant American artists, as well as a fine collection of European art. At the heart of the Corcoran's collections are masterworks by the great early American artists: John Copley, Gilbert Stuart, Rembrandt Peale, Mary Cassatt, and John Singer Sargent. Family workshops on Sunday mornings are a tradition for many local families. Registration is required, but it's best to call at least four weeks ahead of time. During the Corcoran's Family Days usually held two weekends a year, the museum becomes a funfest for kids. To celebrate presidential birthdays, for example, a February program may involve looking for portraits of presidents. During DIY, or Do-It-Yourself, weekends, you can follow a list of suggested activities in a guide and follow up with hands-on activity. All exhibits have exploration galleries with interactive activities such as a photo booth that projects images on a wall. ⊠*500 17th St. NW, White House area*☎*202/639–1700* ⊕*www.corcoran. org* ⊠*$14* ⊙*Sun., Mon., and Wed. 10–6, Thurs. 10–9, Fri. and Sat. 10–5* Ⓜ*Farragut W or Farragut N.* 5+up

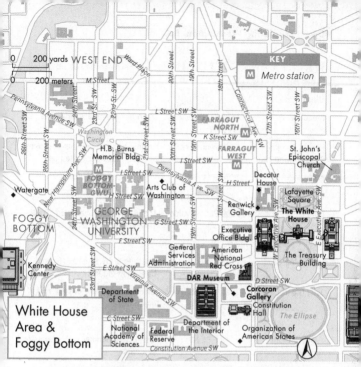

DAR Museum. The headquarters of the Daughters of the American Revolution, the beaux arts Memorial Continental Hall was the site of the DAR's annual congress until the larger Constitution Hall was built around the corner. An entrance on D Street leads to the museum. Its 30,000-item collection includes fine examples of colonial and Federal furniture, textiles, quilts, silver, china, porcelain, stoneware, earthenware, and glass. Thirty-one period rooms are decorated in styles representative of various U.S. states, ranging from an 1850 California adobe parlor to a New Hampshire attic filled with 18th- and 19th-century toys. Two galleries—one of them permanent—hold decorative arts. Docent tours are available weekdays 10 to 2:30 and Saturday 9 to 5. In the "Touch of Independence" education center for children, families can explore early American life through period games and costumes. During the "Colonial Adventure" tours, held the first and third Sunday of the month at 1:30 and 3 from September through May, costumed docents use the objects on display to teach children ages five to seven about day-to-day life in colonial America. Reservations are required two weeks in advance. Two weeks' advance registration is required for the Colonial

WHERE CAN I FIND . . . IN THE WHITE HOUSE AREA & FOGGY BOTTOM?

Quick Meals

Breadline	1751 Pennsylvania Ave. NW	Fresh-baked bread, sandwiches.
Ronald Reagan Building food court	1300 Pennsylvania Ave. NW	Cajun, sushi, and deli; lots of choices and 980 chairs to choose from
Ecco	1706 G St. NW	Over-the-counter Italian

Ice Cream

Cone-E Island	2000 Pennsylvania Ave. NW	The usual flavors plus Muddy Sneakers and Moose Tracks ice cream

Good Coffee

M.E. Swing Co.	17th and G Sts. NW	Roasting in DC since 1916, traditional and organic coffees.
Java Green Café	1020 19th St. NW	Organic coffee and organic milk, green menu.

Grocery Stores

Foggy Bottom Grocery	2140 F St. NW	Small store popular with university students
Watergate Safeway	2550 Virginia Ave. NW	Small store carries the basics, no bakery

Fun Stores

Gift shop at Corcoran Gallery of Art	500 17th St. NW	Art kits and Corcoran ornaments are an annual favorite
DAR Museum Shop	1776 D St. NW	Cute shop with colonial crafts and toys

Playgrounds

Pershing Park	14th St. and Pennsylvania Ave. NW	Limited parking, ice skating in winter, more of a green space than a playground
The Ellipse	17th St and Constitution Ave. NW	Play on land that was once the president's backyard, great green space, national Christmas tree lighting in December

Public Bathrooms

White House Visitor Center	1450 Pennsylvania Ave. NW	Need to go through security first
Renwick Gallery	1661 Pennsylvania Ave. NW	Check out the "game fish" sculpture while you're here

Adventure program, where boys wear vests and three-corner caps and girls don long white aprons, because proper Colonial ladies never showed their ankles. Docents, who are all DAR members and who also wear Colonial garb, lead the children on one tour while the parents and any other siblings tour the museum separately. For regular docent-led tours, let the guide know if children have any particular interests. For example, kids with an ear for music might enjoy seeing the antique instruments in the Rhode Island room. Other rooms of special interest include the Oklahoma room, set up like a Colonial kitchen (try to find the toaster), and the Georgia Room, which depicts a tavern where citizens gathered for the state's first reading of the Declaration of Independence. The Wisconsin Room depicts a one-room house like those that serve as a reminder that the majority of people in our nation's early history were not to the manor born. ✉ *1776 D St. NW, White House area* ☎ *202/879–3241* ⊕ *www.dar.org* ✈ *Free* ☉ *Weekdays 9:30–4, Sat. 9–5* Ⓜ *Farragut W.* 5+up

The White House. America's most famous house is open to visitors, but getting in requires planning. You'll need to contact your representative or senator—arrangements are made through their offices. To visit in spring or summer, you should make your request about six months in advance. For a January visit, a month might suffice. Non-U.S. citizens make arrangements through their embassy. You also need a group of 10 or more in order to visit. Don't have 10? The office of your representative or senator may be able to place you with another group. Before your visit, you'll be asked for the names, birthdates, and Social Security numbers of everyone in your group, and you'll be told where to meet and what you can bring. On the morning of your tour, call the White House Visitors Office information line, 202/456–7041. Tours are subject to last-minute cancellation. Arrive 15 minutes early. Your group will be asked to line up in alphabetical order. Everyone 15 years or older must present photo ID. Going through security will probably take as long as the tour itself: 20 to 25 minutes. Tours go through the East Room (where Teddy Roosevelt allowed his children to ride a pony and where one of Abraham Lincoln's sons caused a stir by sending a goat through a reception), the Green Room, the Blue Room, and the State Dining Room (where Bill Clinton's daughter Chelsea hosted pizza parties). For some kids, the actual tour might be a bit boring since there aren't any interactive things to do, but there's an undeniable thrill of being inside America's most historic house. Many children hope to see the president or at least a presidential pet. The chances of glimpsing either are nil, but youngsters can e-mail the president at president@whitehouse.gov or send a formal letter to the White House. The president and first lady even have their own zip code: 20500. ✉*1600 Pennsylvania Ave. NW* ☎*202/208–1631, 202/456–7041 24-hr info line* ⊕*www.whitehouse.gov* ✆*Free; reservations required* ⊗*Tours Tues.–Sat. 7:30–12:30* Ⓜ*Federal Triangle, Metro Center, or McPherson Sq.* 5+up

CAPITOL HILL

Kids who love American history will find lots of opportunities for extra credit on Capitol Hill. Not only can you tour these hallowed halls on the Capitol, you can also sit in on a Supreme Court hearing and marvel at the Library of Congress's Great Hall.

Even kids too young to have heard about history can enjoy smelling the roses and more at the Botanic Garden.

GETTING HERE

From the Red Line's Union Station stop, you can easily walk to most destinations on Capitol Hill. From the Blue and Orange Line, the Capitol South stop is close to the Capitol and Library of Congress, and the Eastern Market stop leads to the market and the Marine Corps Barracks. The Numbers 30, 32, 34, 35, and 36 buses run from Friendship Heights through Georgetown and Downtown to Independence Avenue, the Capitol, and Eastern Market. Street parking is available.

PLANNING YOUR TIME

Touring Capitol Hill could take about four hours, allowing for about an hour each at the Capitol, the Botanic Garden, and the Postal Museum. If you want to see Congress in action, contact your legislator in advance, and bear in mind that the House and Senate are usually not in session during August. Supreme Court cases are usually heard October through April, Monday through Wednesday, two weeks out of each month.

TOP 5 CAPITOL HILL EXPERIENCES

1

■ **The Capitol:** See democracy in action. Watch congressmen and women debate, insult, and wrangle their way through the job of making laws in the Capitol's House and Senate chambers.

■ **DC Ducks:** During the 1½-hour ride in an amphibious vehicle over land and water, a wise-quacking captain mixes historical anecdotes with trivia.

■ **Eastern Market:** The main building of one of D.C.'s most beloved weekend destinations

was destroyed by a fire in 2007, but while rebuilding is under way you can still listen to live music, sample fresh produce, and purchase locally made crafts.

■ **National Postal Museum:** It gets a stamp of approval from kids and parents for its doable size and displays.

■ **United States Botanic Garden:** Wrinkle your nose at the corpse flower, explore the jungle, gawk at the orchids, or stroll the paths of the new National Garden.

WHAT TO SEE

The Capitol. Beneath its magnificent dome, the day-to-day business of American democracy takes place: senators and representatives debate, coax, and cajole, and ultimately determine the law of the land. For many visitors, the Capitol is the most exhilarating experience Washington has to offer. It wins them over with a three-pronged approach: It's the city's most impressive work of architecture. It has on display documents, art, and artifacts from 400 years of American history. Its legislative chambers are open to the public. You can actually see your lawmakers at work, shaping the history of tomorrow. To see the Capitol you're required to go on a 30- to 40-minute tour conducted by the Capitol Guide Service. The first stop is the Rotunda, followed by the National Statuary Hall, the Hall of Columns, the old Supreme Court Chamber, the crypt (where there are exhibits on the history of the Capitol), and the gift shop. Note that you don't see the Senate or House chambers on the tour—you'll need to contact your senator or representative in advance to arrange to see congress in session. Kids can find Pocahontas in three places in the Rotunda. (Hint: she doesn't resemble Disney's cartoon.) Kids who follow elections may be interested in meeting their representative or senator, but even if Congress isn't in session, kids can look for their state's statues. (Every state has two.) They range from Colorado's (and Apollo 13's)

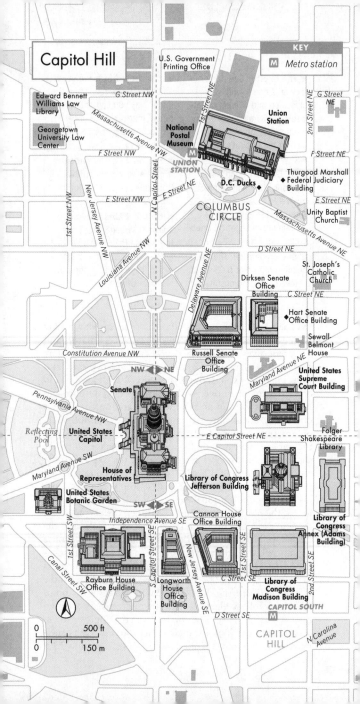

Capitol Hill

KEY

Ⓜ Metro station

U.S. Government Printing Office

Edward Bennett Williams Law Library

Georgetown University Law Center

G Street NW

Massachusetts Avenue NW

1st Street NE

2nd Street NE

G Street NE

Union Station

National Postal Museum

Ⓜ UNION STATION

F Street NW

F Street NE

New Jersey Avenue NW

N Capitol Street

E Street NE

E Street NW

D.C. Ducks

Thurgood Marshall Federal Judiciary Building

E Street NE

Unity Baptist Church

COLUMBUS CIRCLE

1st Street NW

Louisiana Avenue NW

D Street NE

Massachusetts Avenue NE

St. Joseph's Catholic Church

Delaware Avenue NE

Dirksen Senate Office Building

C Street NE

Hart Senate Office Building

Sewall-Belmont House

Russell Senate Office Building

Constitution Avenue NW

NW ◄ ► NE

Pennsylvania Avenue NW

Senate

Maryland Avenue NE

United States Supreme Court Building

Reflecting Pool

United States Capitol

Maryland Avenue SW

E Capitol Street NE

Folger Shakespeare Library

House of Representatives

Library of Congress Jefferson Building

SW ◄ ► SE

United States Botanic Garden

Independence Avenue SE

Cannon House Office Building

Library of Congress Annex (Adams Building)

1st Street SE

New Jersey Avenue SE

C Street SE

Canal Street SW

1st Street SW

Rayburn House Office Building

S Capitol Street SE

Longworth House Office Building

2nd Street SE

Library of Congress Madison Building

CAPITOL SOUTH Ⓜ

D Street SE

CAPITOL HILL

N. Carolina Avenue

0 ___ 500 ft

0 ___ 150 m

Jack Swigert to Utah's Philo Farnsworth, the father of TV. Hawaii's Kamehameha I in Statuary Hall is one of the heaviest in the collection. ⊠*East end of Mall* ☎*202/224–4048, 202/225–6827 recorded updates, 202/224–4049 TDD* ⊕*www.aoc.gov, www.senate.gov, www.house.gov* ⊠*Free* Ⓜ*Capitol S or Union Station.* 7+up

D.C. Ducks. Tour the city by land and water without leaving your seats aboard these amphibious vehicles: standard 2½-ton GM trucks in watertight shells with propellers and seats for 28 intrepid passengers. During the 1½-hour ride, a wise-quacking captain entertains with anecdotes and historical trivia. The captain may even quiz kids about sights along the way. Answer correctly and *ding*—the bell rings! Often children are invited to take the captain's seat and steer the duck. Midway through the ride, captains pass out "quackers," bright yellow blowers that look like cartoon beaks and sound like ducks. ⊠*Union Station main entrance, Massachusetts Ave., NE, near N. Capitol St.* ☎*202/966–3825 recorded updates, 202/224–4049 TDD* ⊕*www.aoc.gov, www.senate.gov, www.house.gov* ⊠*$32* $16 children 4–12 Ⓜ *Union Station.* 5+up

Library of Congress. The largest library in the world has more than 134 million items on approximately 530 mi of bookshelves. Only 32 million of its holdings are books—the library also has 2.8 million recordings, 12 million photographs, 5.3 million maps, and 59 million manuscripts. Also here is the Congressional Research Service, which, as the name implies, works on special projects for senators and representatives.

The Jefferson Building opens into the Great Hall, richly adorned with mosaics, paintings, and curving marble stairways. The grand, octagonal Main Reading Room, its central desk surrounded by mahogany readers' tables under a 160-foot-high domed ceiling, inspires researchers and readers alike. Computer terminals have replaced card catalogs, but books are still retrieved and dispersed the same way: readers (18 years or older) hand request slips to librarians and wait patiently for their materials to be delivered. Researchers aren't allowed in the stacks, and only members of Congress and other special borrowers can check books out. Items from the library's collection—which includes one of only three perfect Gutenberg Bibles in the world—are on display in the Jefferson Building's second-floor Southwest Gallery and Pavilion. Information about current and upcoming exhibitions, which can include oral-history projects, presidential papers, photographs, and the like, is available by phone or Web. ■TIP→ **To even begin to come to grips with the scope and grandeur of the library, taking one of the free hourly tours is highly recommended.** Well-informed docents are fonts of fascinating information about the library's history and holdings; they can decode the dozens of quirky allegorical sculptures and paintings throughout the building, and can bring you into spaces—such as the glassed-in observation deck over the Main Reading Room—that are closed to solo visitors. While the grandeur of this glorious building might even make a kindergartner look up in awe, there isn't enough to keep most children busy for more than a minute or two. For parents who want to see the Library and have children in tow, encourage the kids to look for animals in the artwork and show them the computer images of the Grand Hall that let you zoom in on selected artwork. ⊠ *Jefferson Bldg., 1st St. and Independence Ave. SE, Capitol Hill* ☎ *202/707–4604, 202/707–5000, or 202/707–6400* ⊕ *www. loc.gov* 🎫 *Free* ☉ *Mon.–Sat. 10–5:30; reading room hrs may extend later. Free tours Mon.–Sat. at 10:30, 11:30, 1:30, and 2:30, and weekdays at 3:30* Ⓜ *Capitol S.* 12+up

DID YOU KNOW? Men and women aren't the only ones who have delivered mail. Camels, birds, reindeer, and dogs have helped, too. Although Owney the Dog never carried any, he was still the mascot of the railway service in the late 19th century. Thanks to taxidermy, you can actually see Owney at the National Postal Museum.

The Supreme Court. The court convenes on the first Monday in October and hears cases until April. There are usually two arguments a day at 10 and 11 in the morning, Monday through Wednesday, in two-week intervals. On mornings when court is in session, two lines form for people wanting to attend. The "three-to-five-minute" line shuttles you through, giving you a quick impression of the court at work. The full-session line gets you in for the whole show. If you want to see a full session, it's best to be in line by at least 8:30. The *Washington Post* carries a daily listing of what cases the court will hear. In May and June the court takes to the bench Monday morning at 10 to release orders and opinions. Sessions usually last 15 to 30 minutes and are open to the public. When court isn't in session, you can hear lectures about the court, typically given every hour on the half hour from 9:30 to 3:30. Teenagers who follow political and national news may be fascinated with the rituals of the court, so arrive early to see the Justices make their grand entrance. ⊠*1 1st St. NE, Capitol Hill* ☎*202/479–3000* ⊕*www.supremecourtus.gov* ⊠*Free* ⊙*Weekdays 9–4:30; court in session Oct.–June* Ⓜ*Union Station or Capitol S.* 12+up

United States Botanic Garden. Established by Congress in 1820, this is the oldest botanic garden in North America. The recently renovated glass building, a Victorian design, sits at the foot of Capitol Hill, in the shadow of the Capitol building. It offers an escape from the stone and marble federal office buildings that surround it; inside are exotic rain-forest species, desert flora, and trees from all parts of the world. A special treat is the extensive collection of rare and unusual orchids. Walkways suspended 24 feet above the ground provide a fascinating view of the plants. A relatively new addition is the National Garden, which emphasizes educational exhibits. The two-year-old garden features the Rose Garden, Butterfly Garden, Lawn Terrace, First Ladies' Water Garden, and Regional Garden. Allow about an hour to see what's in bloom. To really dig in, head to the Children's Garden (open spring and summer) where children can try out gardening tools, meander through a tunnel made of bamboo and hang out in a thatched-roof cottage the size of a playhouse. Pushing a hand pump sends a fish spouting water into a fountain. Indoors, children need to be encouraged to use indoor voices and not touch unless the staff invites them to, but there's enough to see to engage even the littlest children. See plants that prehistoric creatures might have munched in the Garden Primeval, which even has footprints from baby and grown-up dinosaurs. Kids can see how bananas grow upside down from 20-foot stalks. Older kids might want to check out the therapeutic uses of the Medicinal Plants garden. Encourage them to read the signs and they can look for the devil's shoestring, the sticky monkey flower, the bearded orchid and more flowers with funny names. ⊠*1st St. and Maryland Ave. SW, Capitol Hill* ☎*202/225–8333* ⊕*www.usbg.gov* ⊠*Free* ⊙*Daily 10–5* Ⓜ*Federal Center SW.* All ages

WHERE CAN I FIND . . . CAPITOL HILL?

Quick Meals

Union Station food court	50 Massachusetts Ave. NE	Deli, sushi, grill, wraps, etc.
Tunnicliffs	222 7th St. SE	Peanut-butter-and-jelly pizza anyone?
The Market Lunch	306 7th St. SE	Famous for blueberry pancakes

Ice Cream

Ben & Jerry's	50 Massachusetts Ave. NE 327 7th St. SE	Kids cones, too!
Haagen-Dazs	50 Massachusetts Ave. NE 703 7th St. SE	Two locations

Good Coffee

Bread & Chocolate	666 Pennsylvania Ave. SE	Lavazza coffee beans, hot chocolate, too
Ebenezer's Coffeehouse	201 F St. NE	Fair trade coffee; all proceeds benefit the National Community Church's outreach projects

Grocery Stores

Capitol Hill Supermarket	241 Mass. Ave. NE	Family-run and friendly service; fresh fruits, veggies, meats, and cheeses; no paper goods

Fun Stores

Fairy Godmother	319 7th St. SE	Children's books and traditional toys
Destination DC	50 Massachusetts Ave. NE	Political souvenirs galore—serious and irreverent, too

Playgrounds

Stanton Park	C St, between 4th and 6th Sts. NE	Small climbing wall, slides, seesaw, picnic table
Lincoln Park	East Capitol and 11th St. NE	A favorite for families and dog walkers, impressive statue of Mary McLeod Bethune with two children, small playground

Public Bathrooms

Union Station	50 Massachusetts Ave.	Convenient but crowded

DOWNTOWN

GETTING ORIENTED

In Downtown—the area within the diamond formed by Massachusetts, Louisiana, Pennsylvania, and New York avenues—are Chinatown, Ford's Theatre, and several museums. The National Portrait Gallery is like a who's who of famous people, and the Smithsonian American Art Museum proves that art is made of much more than paint and canvas.

Within Federal Triangle, a few blocks away and bordered by Pennsylvania and Constitution avenues and 15th Street NW, you can find the National Archives, which houses the original Declaration of Independence, the Constitution, and the Bill of Rights. The National Building Museum has the largest columns in the world as well as displays devoted to architecture. Other nearby museums include the National Museum of Women in the Arts, the National Portrait Gallery, and the Smithsonian American Art Museum. The Old Post Office Pavilion is also here, as is the International Spy Museum.

The downtown area can be divided into several sections, each with its own personality. The Federal Triangle is the wedge-shape area south of Pennsylvania Avenue, north of Constitution Avenue, and east of 15th Street. It's the neighborhood's serious side, with its imposing gray buildings and all-business milieu. The Penn Quarter makes up the area directly to the north of Pennsylvania Avenue. This is Downtown's party side, where restaurants and bars mix with popular museums. Chinatown gives the neighborhood an international flair, and Judiciary Square, immediately to the east, is like a stern older uncle frowning about the goings-on.

GETTING HERE

Take the Metro to Federal Triangle or Archives-Navy Memorial to visit the government buildings along Pennsylvania Avenue. The Gallery Place–Chinatown stop gives direct access to the Verizon Center, Chinatown, and the American Art and Spy museums. Judiciary Square has its own stop, and Metro Center is the best choice for the National Theater. Bus routes crisscross the area as well. Street parking is available; it's easier to find on nights and weekends, away from the main Chinatown and Verizon Center area. Several parking garages in the neighborhood offer convenience, at a price.

PLANNING YOUR TIME

Downtown is densely packed with major attractions—far too many to see in one day. You'll need at least an hour inside each attraction, so pick the two that appeal most and stroll past the rest. Art loving kids might focus on the National Portrait Gallery and Smithsonian American Art Museum. Future historians might limit themselves to touring the National Archives. Families with preteens or teens may prefer the International Spy Museum and the Newseum, while families with toddlers will appreciate the cozy National Aquarium with aisles wide enough for double strollers.

SAFETY

Downtown's blocks of government and office buildings become something of a ghost town when the working day is done. You may prefer not to walk alone in this area after dark. The recently revitalized Penn Quarter still carries some vestiges of its grittier past, so stick to the main commercial areas at night.

WHAT TO SEE

Ford's Theatre. In 1859, Baltimore theater impresario John T. Ford leased the First Baptist Church building that stood on this site and turned it into a successful music hall. The building burned down late in 1863, but Ford built a new structure on the same spot. The events that occurred less than two years later would shock the nation. On the night of April 14, 1865, during a performance of *Our American Cousin,* John Wilkes Booth entered the state box and shot Abraham Lincoln in the back of the head. The stricken president was carried across the street to the house of tailor William Petersen. Charles Augustus Leale, a 23-year-old surgeon, was the first man to attend to the president. To let Lincoln know that someone was nearby, Leale held his hand throughout the night. Lincoln died the next morning. In 2007 the Ford's Theater Society launched a two-year, $50-million campaign to transform the theater and its basement museum of Lincoln artifacts into a block-long, Lincoln-centered cultural campus commemorating the president. Scheduled to open in early 2009, it will include a renovated Ford's Theatre, which will run a full schedule of plays; a new Lincoln museum; the historically restored home of William Peterson; and a new Center for Education and Leadership focused on Lincoln's life and presidency. Except in the busy spring and summer months, allow about a half hour to take a self-guided tour of the museum and theater and to cross the street to Peterson House to see the

TOP 5 DOWNTOWN EXPERIENCES

■ **International Spy Museum.** Junior James Bonds and young Nancy Drews dive into the art of espionage.

■ **The National Archives.** Gawk at the Declaration of Independence, Constitution, and Bill of Rights; suddenly school history isn't so abstract.

■ **National Building Museum** takes building blocks to new heights as kids can strap on a tool belt and design their own cities.

■ **National Portrait Gallery and Smithsonian American Art Museum.** These sister museums have something for everyone from presidential portraits to art made from aluminum foil, bottle caps, and even television sets.

■ **Newseum.** Kids experience the stories behind the headlines and can even broadcast the news in front of the camera.

bedroom where Lincoln died. During peak tourist times, allow about an hour. Ask about a Junior Ranger handout, aimed at kids 6 to 12, which includes a scavenger hunt that sends young detectives scouting for a replica of the booth where Lincoln was shot, the Derringer pistol that Booth used, and the suit that Lincoln wore that night. Families fascinated by Lincoln may also want to see the actual bullet that killed him at the National Museum of Health and Medicine. ✉ *511 10th St. NW, East End* ☎ *202/426–6924* ⊕ *www.fords.org* ✆ *Free* ⊙ *Daily 9–5; theater closed to visitors during rehearsals and matinees, generally Thurs. and weekends; Lincoln museum in basement remains open at these times* Ⓜ *Metro Center or Gallery Pl.* 7+up

★ Fodor'sChoice **International Spy Museum.** Cryptologists, masters of disguise, and former CIA, FBI, and KGB operatives are among the advisers of this museum, which displays the world's largest collection of spy artifacts. These artifacts range from the coded letters of Revolutionary War überspy Benedict Arnold, to the KGB's lipstick pistol, to high-tech 21st-century espionage toys, showcased with theatrical panache in a five-building complex (one, the Warder-Atlas Building, held Washington's Communist party in the 1940s). Fittingly, the museum is a block away from FBI headquarters. The high-tech feel of this metallic and wood museum is particularly cool to preteens and teenagers. Younger children might get bored, and seating is limited and strollers aren't allowed in the museum. Despite all the cool gadgetry that makes some kids want to speed too quickly in hot pursuit

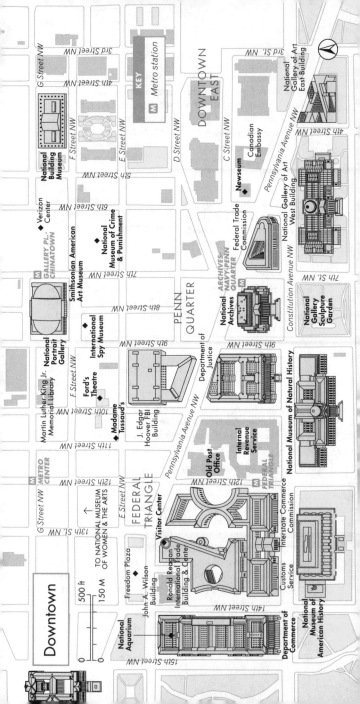

1

of adventure, take your time at the replica of James Bond's Aston Martin sports car. Just like in the films, gadgets galore pop out. Kids can crawl through the museum's ductwork to peek through the vents. Also watch how people transform themselves into spies on videos and find the larger-than-life-size flies that transmit information to undisclosed locations. For kids 12 and up who want to put their sleuthing skills to work, they can crack a safe, conduct a polygraph of a suspect, and more through Operation Spy (an additional $7), a one-hour program to give participants a chance to act like intelligence officers. Operation Spy runs about every 10 to 15 minutes. ⊠*800 F St. NW, East End* ☎*202/393-7798* ⊕*www.spymuseum.org* ⊠*$18, $15 children 5–11, under 5 free* ☉*Apr.–Oct., daily 9–8; Nov.–Mar., daily 10–6; hrs subject to change; check Web site before visiting* Ⓜ*Gallery Pl./Chinatown.* 5+up

Madame Tussauds. The D.C. branch of this famous London-based waxworks franchise opened in late 2007, with a focus on local history: you can see (and pose for pictures with) uncanny likenesses of the founding fathers and political heavyweights like Bill and Hilary Clinton, and even sit in an Oval Office painstakingly re-created in wax. If you want a taste of the celebrity, you can enter a nightclub room populated with waxen recreations of Julia Roberts, J.Lo, and Brad Pitt, among many others. Beyond the photo ops with a virtual who's who of movies, music, sports, and, of course, politics, kids can putt with Tiger Woods and sit at a desk like the one in the Oval Office. In Behind the Scenes, see how the wax figures are made and compare their hands, feet, and even eyes to lifelike replicas of famous folk. You can make wax molds of your own hands for $10 or $12. At the exit of the museum, Katie Couric invites all visitors for a mock-interview about their experience. Save 15% off the admission by flashing your American Automobile Association (AAA) card. *1025 F St. NW, East End* ☎ *202/942–7300* ⊕*www. madametussaudsdc.com* ⊠*$18, $12 children 4–12* ☉ *Daily 10–6.* Ⓜ*Metro Center and Gallery Pl./Chinatown.* 9+up

National Aquarium. Established in 1873, this is the country's oldest public aquarium, with more than 1,200 fish and other creatures—such as eels, sharks, and alligators—representing 270 species of fresh- and saltwater life. Seekers of a transcendent aquarium experience will probably be happier visiting the Baltimore National Aquarium, which is routinely ranked among the nation's best. But the easy-to-view tanks, accessible touching pool (with crabs and sea urchins), low admission fee, and lack of crowds make this a good outing with children. There are also animal keeper talks and feedings every day at 2. Preteens and teens expecting state-of-the-art displays might be disappointed. But parents of youngsters who want to find Nemo appreciate the aisles wide enough for double strollers. The aquarium generally isn't crowded, and you can circle through it in about 20 minutes. Special events are held a few times a year. On Shark Day (usually in July or August), kids can watch a shark dissection and dig for shark teeth. ⊠*14th St. and Constitution Ave. NW, East End* ☎*202/482–2825* ⊕*www.nationalaquarium.com* ⊠*$7 $3 ages 2–10* ☉*Daily 9–5, last admission at 4:30; sharks fed Mon., Wed., and Sat. at 2; piranhas fed Tues., Thurs., and Sun. at 2; alligators fed Fri. at 2* Ⓜ*Federal Triangle.* All ages

National Archives. The National Archives are at once monument, museum, and the nation's memory. Headquartered in a grand marble edifice on Constitution Avenue, the National Archives and Records Administration is charged with preserving and archiving the most historically important U.S. government records. Its 8 billion paper records and 4 billion electronic records date back to 1775. The star attractions, which draw millions of reverential viewers every year, are the Declaration of Independence, Constitution, and Bill of Rights. These are housed in the Archives' cathedral-like rotunda, each on a marble platform, encased in bulletproof glass, and floating in pressurized helium, which protects the irreplaceable documents. The movie National Treasure, starring Nicholas Cage, has given the reverential documents housed here additional mystique for kids. Cage's character steals the Declaration of Independence to discover a hidden treasure map on the backside. No such map on the Declaration, but there is an upside-down note on the bottom front that reads ORIGINAL DECLARATION OF INDEPENDENCE, dated 4th July 1776. Other objects in the archive's vast collection that may interest school-age kids and teens are immigration records, treaties, recordings of Teddy Roosevelt's voice, and satellite maps. Kids can make their own Great Seal, guess the use of a patent, and create their own documentary film. Unless you're visiting on a blustery day in February, be prepared for 30-minute lines ⊠*Constitution Ave. between 7th and 9th Sts. NW, The Mall*☎*202/501–5000, 202/501–5205 tours* ⊕*www.nara.gov* ⊠*Free* ☉*Apr.–Labor Day, daily 10–9; Labor Day–Mar., daily 10–5:30; tours weekdays at 10:15 and 1:15* Ⓜ*Archives/Navy Memorial.* 7+up

WHERE CAN I FIND . . . DOWNTOWN?

Quick Meals

Austin Grill	750 E St. NW	Tex-Mex in a wind-powered restaurant
Farragut smartkafe	1101 Connecticut Ave. NW	Wraps, hummus, energy drinks—lots of organic offerings
California Tortilla	728 7th St. NW	Colorful décor, kids' menu with four choices; sign up for e-mail and get a free taco

Ice Cream

Maggie Moo's	11th and E Sts. NW	Cotton candy ice cream, anyone? National franchise with a silly mascot
Giffords	E & 10th Sts. NW	Ice cream in D.C. area since 1938, roasted coconut on a cone plus the unusual suspects

Good Coffee

Big Bear Cafe	1700 1st St. NW	No decaf here—single bean and blends from Counter Culture
Swing Coffee Shop	1702 G St. NW	Brewin' since 1916, 30 choices plus hot cocoa and ice cream

Grocery Stores

Safeway	5th and K Sts. NW	Huge produce aisle
CVS	435 8th St. NW	Yogurt, milk, bread, and staples (no fresh fruit)
Farmers' Market	North end of 8th St. between D and E Sts. NW	Thurs. afternoons Apr.–Dec.; fresh fruits and veggies, cookies, and breads

Fun Stores

International Spy Museum Store	800 F St. NW	Disguises and gadgets galore
Cowgirl Creamery	919 F St. NW	Hundreds of cheeses from the U.S. and Europe

Public Bathrooms

Macy's Department Store	1201 G St. NW	Easy in and out, no key needed
National Portrait Gallery	8th and F Sts. NW	You may need to check your bag in a locker. Bring a quarter. It will be returned.

National Building Museum. Devoted to architecture, design, landscaping, and urban planning, the National Building Museum is the nation's premier cultural organization devoted to the built environment. The open interior of the mammoth redbrick edifice is one of the city's great spaces and has been the site of many presidential inaugural balls. The eight central Corinthian columns are among the largest in the world, rising to a height of 75 feet. Although they resemble Siena marble, each is made of 70,000 bricks that have been covered with plaster and painted. For years, the annual *Christmas in Washington* TV special has been filmed in this breathtaking hall.

The permanent exhibit "Washington: Symbol and City" tells the story of the birth and evolution of the backwater that eventually became the nation's capital (beginning by debunking the myth that Washington was built on a swamp!). You can touch the perfectly scaled, intricately detailed models of the White House, the Capitol, the Washington Monument, and the Lincoln and Jefferson memorials, and look at original drawings, building plans, maps, videos, and photographs that trace the city's architectural history.

Among the most popular permanent exhibits is the Building Zone, where kids ages two to six can get a hands-on introduction to building by constructing a tower, exploring a kid-size playhouse, or playing with bulldozers and construction trucks.

There's also a constant series of temporary exhibits: recent ones have covered environmentally sustainable architecture, Shakespeare's Globe Theatre, and the influential work of modernist designer Marcel Breuer.

Before entering the building, walk down its F Street side. The terra-cotta frieze by Caspar Buberl between the first and second floors depicts soldiers marching and sailing in an endless procession around the building. Architect Meigs lost his eldest son in the Civil War, and, though the frieze depicts Union troops, he intended it as a memorial to all who were killed in the bloody war. Tours are offered at 12:30 Monday through Wednesday; 11:30, 12:30, and 1:30 Thursday through Saturday; and 12:30 and 1:30 on Sunday. Family programs are available at 2:30 on weekends. Stop at the Information Desk to learn about drop-in activities, most of which are free, such as interactive readings on Tuesday and bridge-building demonstrations on weekends. You can also pick up free Treasure Hunt (kids 6 to 11) and Adventures in Architecture (for preteens) booklets for $5. Or borrow one of three tool kits, geared for kids 3 to 7, 7 to 10 and 8 to 11. Kits may include craft projects, hammers and nails, and other building materials. At the Washington: Symbol and City exhibit, children can handle plastic models of the Capitol, White House, Washington Monument, and Lincoln Memorial. In the Building Zone, developed for two to six year olds, children don hard hats and goggles and strap on a tool belt to look like Bob the Builder. The gift shop here is known as one of the best museum shops in the city. ⊠*401 F St. NW, between 4th and 5th Sts., East End* ☎*202/272–2448* ⊕*www.nbm.org* ⊠*Suggested donation $5* ⊙*Mon.–Sat. 10–5, Sun. 11–5* Ⓜ*Judiciary Sq.* 5+up

National Museum of Crime and Punishment. Explore the history of crime and punishment in America, from pirates and Wild West outlaws to white-collar criminals and computer hackers. The museum was created in partnership with "America's Most Wanted" host John Walsh and includes a studio where the show is filmed and a behind-the-scenes look at the program. Exhibits range from a medieval torture chamber to the actual getaway car used by John Dillinger. There are plenty of opportunities for interactive displays: you can put your hands in pillory stocks, take a lie-detector test, and experience a simulated crime-scene investigation. The museum recommends purchasing advance tickets on the Web site: tickets are hourly with a specific date and time. This museum isn't for everyone. The typical visit is lengthy, about two hours, and there aren't many places to sit. Pace yourself. There's a rifle shooting range with a Wild West backdrop for $2 and computer questions on crime throughout the museum. Some of the best interactives, which are at the end of the tour and are free, include joining a lineup, getting in front of a camera with a John Walsh voice-over declaring you as America's Most Wanted, riding a police motorcycle, joining a simulated high speed police chase, and going inside a prison cell. ⊠*575 7th St. NW, East End* ☎*202/393–1099 TDD* ⊕*www.crimemuseum.org* ⊠*$17.95, $14.95 kids 5–11* ⊙*Sept.–Feb., daily 10–6; Mar.–Aug., daily 9–7* Ⓜ*Gallery Pl./Chinatown.* 8+up

National Museum of Women in the Arts. Works by female artists from the Renaissance to the present are showcased at this museum. The beautifully restored 1907 Renaissance

Revival building was designed by Waddy B. Wood; it was once a Masonic temple, for men only. In addition to displaying traveling shows, the museum has a permanent collection that includes paintings, drawings, sculpture, prints, and photographs by Georgia O'Keeffe, Mary Cassatt, Élisabeth Vigée-Lebrun, Frida Kahlo, and Camille Claudel. Free family programs for children and role-model workshops for teens are held about once a month. Reservations are required for most programs. Once a year, the museum is transformed for children as they dance, hear stories, and make crafts at the annual Family Festival. Usually celebrating another culture, the event is generally held in spring, but the date varies. By October, the museum staff usually knows the date. If you're not attending a children's program, stop by the Education Gallery to learn more about special exhibits and get an Artventure, brochure, designed for kids ages 6 to 10, which suggests ways to look at art through the elements of line, shape, color, and texture. From early June through mid-September, local school kids have their art on display. ⊠*1250 New York Ave. NW, East End* ☎*202/783–5000* ⊕*www.nmwa.org* 🎫*$10* ⊙*Mon.–Sat. 10–5, Sun. noon–5* Ⓜ*Metro Center.* 6+up

National Portrait Gallery. Devoted to the intersection of art, biography, and history, this collection houses nearly 20,000 images of men and women who have shaped U.S. history. There are prints, paintings, photos, and multimedia sculptures of subjects from George Washington to Madonna. This museum shares the landmark Old Patent Office Building with the Smithsonian American Art Museum. The building itself is a highlight: Built between 1836 and 1863, this gracious marble edifice is considered one of the country's finest examples of Greek Revival architecture.

The gallery has the only complete collection of presidential portraits outside the White House, starting with Gilbert Stuart's iconic "Lansdowne" portrait of George Washington, and bushy-browed, cigarillo-smoking humorist Samuel Clemens, aka Mark Twain.

From a moving bronze sculpture of Martin Luther King Jr. to Andy Warhol's Marilyn Monroe prints, to Madonna's 1985 *Time* magazine cover, the third-floor gallery of 20th-century Americans offers a vibrant and colorful tour of the Americans who shaped the country and culture of today. The Portrait Gallery and American Art Museum are two different entities set up in the same building to complement

1

one another. For example, on the first floor, the Portrait Gallery takes up the building's west wing, and the American Art Museum is in the east—but they reverse on the second floor. Exhibits are set up so that the art you see in transition will complement the portraits, setting up a rich dialogue between the two.

At the Portrait Connection computer kiosks you can search a database of the gallery's collections. Look up the portrait's subject and the database can tell you where in the gallery it is and show you an image, even if it's not currently on exhibit. There are free docent-led walk-in tours most days at 11:45, 1, and 2:15. Check the Web site to confirm times. At the Lunder Conservation Center on the third and fourth floors, you can watch conservators preserving and restoring works from both the Portrait Gallery and American Art Museum. From presidents to sports heroes to military figures, kids will find familiar faces to point at. Remarkably, the presidential portraits are a favorite. ⊠*8th and F Sts. NW, East End* ☎*202/633–1000* ⊕*www.npg.si.edu* ⊠*Free* ⊙*Daily 11:30–7* Ⓜ*Gallery Pl./Chinatown.* 7+up

Newseum. The brand-new Newseum opened to great fanfare in 2008, in a landmark $450 million glass-and-silver structure on Pennsylvania Avenue, set smack between the White House and the Capitol: a fitting location for a museum devoted to the First Amendment and the essential role of a free press in maintaining democracy. The museum has a serious purpose, but the space and exhibits are high-tech, interactive, multimedia, and sometimes shamelessly fun. Visitors enter into a 90-foot-high media-saturated atrium, overlooked by a giant breaking news screen and a news helicopter suspended overhead. From there, 14 galleries display 500 years of the history of news, including exhibits on the First Amendment, global news, the rise of multimedia, and the way radio, television, and especially the Internet have transformed how we find out about the world. Live news programs—from presidential debates to town hall meetings—are regularly filmed in the museum's central live news studio, and audiences are often welcome to watch.

The largest piece of the Berlin wall outside Germany, including a guard tower, is permanently installed in an exhibit explaining how a free press was a key contributor to the fall of the Wall. Five state-of-the art theaters, including an eye-popping 4-D theater and another with a 90-foot-long screen, show features, news, sports, and documentaries throughout the day. In the interactive games gallery, you can create your own standup newscast, be a photographer in an action news event, and win or lose at making ethics decisions on deadline.

ABC's *This Week* with George Stephanopoulos is filmed live here every Sunday morning; museum visitors are welcome to watch. Celebrity chef Wolfgang Puck designed the menu for the food court, as well as for the well-reviewed restaurant the Source, adjoining the museum.

The best way to tour the museum is by viewing the orientation films on the ground floor, then taking the elevator up to the top floor and working your way down.

Tickets for the Newseum are date-specific and subject to availability; purchasing them in advance on the Web site is recommended. The top-floor terrace offers one of the best public views of the Capitol, and looks directly down onto Pennsylvania Avenue.

Most exhibits have a cool component that will impress kids. For example, in the Great Books section, even kids who could care less about Thomas Paine's Common Sense will enjoy flipping through a digital version on an electronic monitor. The interactive newsroom on level two is the best bet for kids: the Be a Reporter gets kids interviewing subjects (even animals) to find the who, what, where, when and how for a story about animals escaping from the circus. Parents, be mindful that because news can concern war and death, a few exhibits, such as the one on 9/11 and some photos in the Pulitzer Gallery, may be intense for young children. For $5 your child or entire family can appear on camera, reading news in front of backdrops, including the White House, a weather map or the Newseum and then download the broadcast for 30 days. Prices in the quality food court are surprisingly reasonable. ✉*555 Pennsylvania Ave. NW, East End* ☎*888/639–7386* ⊕*www.newseum. org* ✎*$20, $13 ages 7 to 12, under 6, free* ☉*Daily 9–5* Ⓜ*Archives/Navy Memorial.* 7+up

QUICK BITES. **Cheap eats abound in Chinatown. Watch the chef stretching noodles by the window before you head into Chinatown Express (✉*746 6th St. NW, 20001* ☎*202/638–0424*). At Marvelous Market (✉*730 7th St. NW, 20001* ☎*202/628–0824*) you can get fresh sandwiches, soups, chips, and other bakery fare, including the best brownies in Washington.**

Old Post Office Pavilion. Insiders know that if you want a bird's-eye view of D.C. and you don't have tickets to the Washington Monument, you can ride up the elevators to an observation deck in the Tower 270 feet above street level. National Park Service rangers take people up every five minutes. On the way down, you can see the Bells of Congress, a gift from England to the United States in celebration of our bicentennial, but the best reason to visit goes beyond the bells. The second-highest view in the city is spectacular. Keep in mind, the deck is outdoors so the National Park Service rangers will stop tours in bad weather. A food court with choices ranging from pizza to Chinese gives families choices for lunch and dinner. ⊠ *1100 Pennsylvania Ave. NW, Downtown* ☎ *202/606-8691* ⊕ *www.oldpostofficedc. com/clock_tower.html* ☐ *Free*Free ⊗ *1stt weekend June– Labor Day, weekdays 9–7:45, weekends 10–5:45; Labor Day–Memorial Day, weekdays 9–4:45, weekends 10–5:45* Ⓜ *Metro Center.* 5+up

Smithsonian American Art Museum. Home to the United States' first federal art collection, the Smithsonian American Art Museum is considered the world's biggest and most diverse collection of American art. Its more than 41,000 holdings span three centuries, from colonial portraits to 21st-century abstractionists. Among the thousands of American artists represented are John Singleton Copley, Winslow Homer, Mary Cassatt, Georgia O'Keeffe, Edward Hopper, David Hockney, and Robert Rauschenberg. This museum is in the Old Patent Office Building along with the National Portrait Gallery.

At any given time, more than 3,000 of the museum's holdings are in storage, but you can view them all at Luce Foundation Center's glassed-in archives on the third and fourth floors. At computer kiosks set among the archives, you can look up any work and find out exactly where it is in the exhibits or archives. The third floor Upper West Side café offers a good rest stop, with drinks, snacks, and a view into the Luce Foundation Center's glassed-in archives. There are free docent-led tours every day at noon and 2. The museum regularly holds lectures, films, and evenings of live jazz among the exhibits. Check the Web site for what's on during your visit. Ask children what they would do with hundreds of rolls of aluminum foil. For more than 12 years using salvaged objects and reams of silver and gold foil, James Hampton, a janitor, built Throne of the Third Heaven of the Nations Millennium General Assembly. An unknown artist created Bottlecaps Giraffe in the late 1960s. Nam June Paik turned 343 televisions into Electronic Superhighway: Continental U.S., Alaska, Hawaii. You can pick up a scavenger hunt sheet for the Luce Foundation Center at the Center's information desk on the mezzanine. Playing on the museum's acronym for itself, SAAM I AM free art programs for kids occur once a month, usually on the second Saturday. Previous activities include chalk drawing on the sidewalk, making baseball cards, and painting on canvas. Running isn't allowed in the museum's courtyard. ⊠*8th and G Sts. NW, East End* ☎*202/633–1000* ⊕*www.oldpostofficedc. com/clock_tower.html* ⊠*Free* ☉*Daily 11:30–7* Ⓜ *Gallery Pl./Chinatown.* 5+up

GEORGETOWN

GETTING ORIENTED

Georgetown can be thought of in four sections: the shopping and nightlife area, the university, the historical residential neighborhoods, and the waterfront. The most popular area is the first, located mainly on M Street and Wisconsin Avenue. Georgetown's students claim the university as their turf; the streets of town houses belong to well-to-do homeowners, museumgoers, and strollers. The C&O Canal is a sylvan spot for a bike ride, morning jog, or pleasant paddle, while the riverfront restaurants at Washington Harbour let visitors enjoy sedentary water views as well.

The hub of Georgetown is the intersection of M Street and Wisconsin Avenue. By day, the lengths of these thoroughfares are crowded with shoppers. The area is known for its high-end clothing boutiques, antiques stores, and fancy furniture shops, now squeezing cheek-to-jowl with chain stores such as J. Crew and Banana Republic or cheap-and-chic H&M and Zara.

GETTING HERE

There's no Metro stop in Georgetown, so you have to take a bus or taxi or walk to this part of Washington. It's about a 15-minute walk from Dupont Circle or the Foggy Bottom Metro station. Perhaps the best transportation deal in Georgetown is the Circulator. For a buck you can ride from Union Station along Massachusetts Avenue and K Street to the heart of Georgetown. Or try the Georgetown Metro Connection. These little blue buses have two routes, one along Wisconsin Avenue and K Street to the Foggy Bottom

Metro, and the second along M Street to the Dupont Circle and Rosslyn Metros.

Other options include the G2 Georgetown University Bus, which goes west from Dupont Circle along P Street, and the 34 and 36 Friendship Heights buses, which go south down Wisconsin Avenue and west down Pennsylvania Avenue toward Georgetown.

PLANNING YOUR TIME

Adults can easily spend a pleasant day in Georgetown, partly because some sights (Tudor Place, Dumbarton Oaks, Oak Hill Cemetery, and Dumbarton House) are somewhat removed from the others, and partly because the street scene, with its shops and people-watching, invites you to linger. Teens who like to shop also enjoy the street scene, with its stores and people-watching, invites you to linger. For kids the best way to experience Georgetown is by a mule-drawn boat along the C&O Canal. Georgetown is almost always crowded. It's not very car-friendly either, especially at night; driving and parking are usually difficult. The wise take the Metro to Foggy Bottom or Dupont Circle and then walk 15 minutes from there, or take a bus or taxi.

WHAT TO SEE

C&O Canal. This waterway kept Georgetown open to shipping after its harbor had filled with silt. George Washington was one of the first to advance the idea of a canal linking the Potomac with the Ohio River across the Appalachians. Work started on the Chesapeake & Ohio Canal in 1828, and when it opened in 1850 its 74 locks linked Georgetown with Cumberland, Maryland, 184.5 mi to the northwest (still short of its intended destination). Lumber, coal, iron, wheat, and flour moved up and down the canal, but it was never as successful as its planners had hoped it would be. Many of the bridges spanning the canal in Georgetown were too low to allow anything other than fully loaded barges to pass underneath, and competition from the Baltimore & Ohio Railroad eventually spelled an end to profitability. Today the canal is part of the National Park System; walkers follow the towpath once used by mules while canoeists paddle the canal's calm waters.

You can glide into history aboard a mule-drawn **canal boat ride.** The National Park service provides the hour-long rides from about mid-April through late October; they are available across the canal, next to the Foundry Building. The schedule varies by season, with limited rides in the spring

TOP GEORGETOWN EXPERIENCES

■ **C&O Canal:** Walk or bike along the path here, which offers bucolic scenery from Georgetown all the way to Maryland.

■ **Dumbarton Oaks:** Stroll through the 10 acres of for-

mal gardens—Washington's loveliest oasis.

■ **Canal Boat Rides:** Let Molly and Ada pull you along on a mule-drawn barge along the C&O.

and fall. In summer the boats run at least twice a day from Wednesday through Sunday. Call the visitor center for the exact schedule on the day of your visit. Canal boat rides also depart from the Great Falls Tavern visitor center in Maryland. Most children are fascinated by the canal boats' engines: four mules named Ada, Molly, Lil, and Nell take turns pulling the barge along the towpath. Amid tales of canal life, the guides dressed in costumes from the 1870s may treat you to some music and a few jokes. Sometimes they'll even put a kid "in charge" of the boat. ⊠*George-town Canal Visitor Center, 1057 Thomas Jefferson St. NW, Georgetown* ☎*202/653–5190* ⊕*www.nps.gov/choh* ⊗*$5 4 and up; 3 and under free; Apr.–Oct., Wed.–Sun. 9–4:30; Nov.–Mar., weekends 10–4, staffing permitting.* 3+up

NEED A BREAK? Next to Dumbarton Oaks, **Montrose Park** has green fields, a boxwood maze, and a creek with crayfish in the mud. To pick up a "crawdad" or "craymom" without getting pinched, use thumb on forefinger on the crustacean's midsection. *Upper Northwest* ⊕*nmhm.washingtondc.museum* ⊠*Free.* All ages

Old Stone House. What was early American life like? Here's the capital's oldest window into the past. Work on this fieldstone house, thought to be Washington's oldest surviving building, was begun in 1764 by a cabinetmaker named Christopher Layman. Now a museum, it was used as both a residence and a place of business by a succession of occupants. Five of the house's rooms are furnished with the simple, sturdy artifacts—plain tables, spinning wheels, and so forth—of 18th-century middle-class life. The National Park Service maintains the house and its lovely gardens, which are planted with fruit trees and perennials. The best part for kids is the yard in back, perfect for playing tag or letting off steam. ⊠*3051 M St. NW, Georgetown* ☎*202/426–6851* ⊕*www. nps.gov/olst/* ⊠*Free* ⊗*Wed.–Sun. 10–5.* 5+up

WHERE CAN I FIND . . . IN GEORGETOWN?

Quick Meals

Booeymonger	3265 Prospect St. NW	Sandwiches made to order with "jazz it up" extras
Johnny Rockets	3131 M St. NW	Burgers, fries, and shakes in a '50s-style setting
The Shops at Georgetown's Food Court	3222 M St. NW	Lots of quick choices— Italian, Chinese, and hot pretzels

Ice Cream

Thomas Sweet	3214 P St. NW	Ice cream, fudge, and munchies
DolceZZa	1560 Wisconsin Ave. NW	Argentinean gelato made with local, fresh fruit

Good Coffee

Bean Counter	1665 Wisconsin Ave. NW	Columbian house brew, neighborhood favorite
Patisserie Poupon	1645 Wisconsin Ave.	Coffee and croissants in a French café atmosphere

Grocery Stores

Dean & Deluca	3276 M St. NW	Gourmet groceries and meals to-go, plus cool retro candies and licorice poodles
Safeway	1855 Wisconsin Ave. NW	Known as the "singles Safeway," but there's an aisle with baby stuff

Fun Stores

Commander Salamander	1420 Wisconsin Ave. NW	Funk and punk clothes and accessories for teens
Piccolo Piggies	1533 Wisconsin Ave. NW	Educational toys and classic kids clothes

Playgrounds

Volta Park	Volta Place at 33rd St.	Public pool, softball diamond, monkey bars and sandbox; crowded on gorgeous days
Montrose Park	R St., east of Dumbarton Oaks	Box maze and creek, plus swings, etc., and tennis courts

Public Bathrooms

Shops at Georgetown	3222 M St. NW	Conveniently located at the entrance
Barnes & Noble	3040 M St. NW	Rest rooms are in the back of the second and third floors

QUICK BITES. Top off your outing with ice cream topped with gummy bears, M&Ms, and sprinkles from **Thomas Sweet Ice Cream and Chocolate Shop** (⊠ *3215 P St. NW, 20007* ☎ *202/337–0616*). Self-service, pizza, and more than 25 kinds of bread make **Marvelous Market** (⊠ *3217 P St. NW 20007* ☎ *202/333–2591*) appealing for families.

UPPER NORTHWEST

GETTING ORIENTED

The upper northwest corner of D.C. is predominantly residential and in many places practically suburban. However, there are several good reasons to visit the leafy streets, including the National Zoo and National Cathedral. You'll have to travel some distance to see multiple attractions in one day, but many sights are accessible on foot.

This area, to the north of Georgetown and stretching up to the Maryland border, is best known for Washington National Cathedral, an eye-catching Gothic-style building completed in 1990 after more than 80 years of construction. About a mile north, just past the Tenleytown/American University Metro stop and at the highest point in the city, is Fort Reno, the site of the only Civil War battle within Washington proper.

GETTING HERE

Connecticut Avenue attractions, such as the Zoo, are accessible from the Red Line Metro stops between Woodley Park/Zoo and Van Ness. If you're going to the zoo, keep in mind that the Cleveland Park Metro stop is a better choice than Woodley Park/Zoo, with an uphill walk to the zoo but a downhill walk when you leave. The Friendship Heights Bus travels north from Georgetown along Wisconsin Avenue and takes you to the National Cathedral.

PLANNING YOUR TIME

The amount of time you spend at the Zoo is up to you; animal enthusiasts could easily spend a full day here. You may want to plan your trip around daily programs, such as the elephant-training session or the eagle feeding. For other itineraries, be sure to leave room in your schedule for travel between sights and, if you have a car, for parking. To maximize your time, call ahead to inquire whether on-site parking is available and when the next tour will begin.

1

WORD OF MOUTH. "About the Zoo. The Conn. Ave entrance (closest to the Metro) is up a considerable hill from the Rock Creek Park entrance (where there's parking. If you don't know this, you can set yourself up for an arduous uphill walk at the end of a longish (hot) afternoon." —Cassandra

WHAT TO SEE

National Zoo. In a town known more for political animals than real animals, Washington nevertheless possesses one of the world's foremost zoos. The pandas Tian Tian and Mei Xiang came from China in 2000, and will stay here until 2010. In 2005 their cub, Tai Shan, was born, the first giant panda cub to survive from birth at the National Zoo and only the third to survive in the United States. The pandas are stars, and their many fans cluster around their bamboo-filled compound.

Carved out of Rock Creek Park, the zoo is a series of rolling, wooded hills that complement the many innovative compounds showing animals in their native settings. Step inside the Great Flight Cage to observe the free flight of many species of birds; this walk-in aviary is open from May to October (the birds are moved indoors during the colder months). Between 10 and 2 each day you can catch the orangutan population traveling on the O Line, a series of cables and towers near the Great Ape House that allows the primates to swing hand over hand about 35 feet over your head. The most ambitious addition to the zoo is Amazonia, an amazingly authentic reproduction of a South American rain-forest ecosystem. You feel as if you are deep inside a steamy jungle, with monkeys leaping overhead and noisy birds flying from branch to branch. Part of the Smithsonian Institution, the National Zoo is one of the foremost zoos in the world. Created by an Act of Congress in 1889, the 163-acre park was designed by landscape architect Frederick Law Olmsted, who also designed the U.S. Capitol grounds. Before the zoo opened in 1890, live animals used as taxidermists' models were kept on the Mall. Start with the must-see creatures on your child's list. On busy days, there may be waits for the popular animal houses, such as the Giant Panda house, Reptile Discovery Center, or Amazonia's tropical rain forest. In summer, early morning is often the best time to catch animals alert; in cooler months, they're more active at midday. Toddlers climb on, stack and move mushrooms, olives, and other pizza toppings in the playground's pizza garden. In summer, they can water the real pizza garden's herbs, tomatoes, and veggies and then see traditional barn animals at the Kids' Farm. Sometimes the zookeepers even let children help groom the goats and miniature donkeys. At the prairie dog playground, children crawl through tubes that resemble prairie dogs' underground tunnels and pop up above ground to scan for cutouts of predators like hawks and ferrets. Kids with MP3 players can go to the zoo's Web site and download an audio tour to use on the Asia Trail. The seals and sea lions put on shows every day at 11:30 in Beaver Valley. Rental strollers are available. Be sure to watch your children carefully; the biggest safety problem here is not animals but children wandering off. ✉ *3001 Connecticut Ave. NW, Woodley Park* ☎ *202/673–4800 or 202/673–4717* ⊕ *www.si.edu/natzoo* ✉ *Free, parking $16* ⊙ *May–mid-Sept., daily 6 AM–8 PM; mid-Sept.–Apr., daily 6–6. Zoo buildings open at 10 and close before zoo closes* Ⓜ *Cleveland Park or Woodley Park/Zoo.* All ages

Washington National Cathedral. Construction of Washington National Cathedral—the sixth-largest cathedral in the world—started in 1907; it was finished and consecrated in 1990. Like its 14th-century Gothic counterparts, the stunning National Cathedral (officially the Cathedral Church of St. Peter and St. Paul) has a nave, flying buttresses, transepts, and vaults that were built stone by stone. State funerals for presidents Eisenhower, Reagan, and Ford were held here, and the tomb of Woodrow Wilson, the only president buried in Washington, is on the nave's south side. ■ TIP→ **The expansive view of the city from the Pilgrim Gallery is exceptional.** The cathedral is Episcopalian, but it's the site of frequent ecumenical and interfaith services.

On the grounds of the cathedral is the compact, English-style **Bishop's Garden.** Boxwoods, ivy, tea roses, yew trees, and an assortment of arches, bas-reliefs, and stonework from European ruins provide a counterpoint to the cathedral's towers. Although budget cuts have affected children's activities, there's still plenty for families to see. You can pick up a printed family guide at the information table at the west end of the cathedral. A stained-glass window with an encapsulated moon rock celebrates the *Apollo 11* space flight, and the flags of all 50 states can be found here. Challenge your child to find statues of Washington and Lincoln. Kids like counting the pennies in the floor of Lincoln Bay, and some visitors even leave food for the poor at his feet. A charming children's chapel tantalizes the imagination with depictions of real and imaginary animals. Kneelers depict the story of Noah's ark. Outside, binoculars are helpful to play an "I spy" game with the cathedral's gargoyles and grotesques. At the east side of St. Peter's tower, is a stone grotesque of Darth Vader, designed by a 13-year-old boy. ✉ *Wisconsin and Massachusetts Aves. NW, Upper Northwest* ☎ *202/537-6200, 202/537-6207 tour information* ⊕ *www.cathedral.org/cathedral* ✉ *Suggested tour donation $3* ⊙ *Weekdays 10–5, Sat. 10–4, Sun. 8–6:30 (8–2:45 for worship only). Tours Mon.–Sat. 10–4, every 30 min. Gardens open dawn–dusk* Ⓜ *Cleveland Park or Tenleytown. Take any 30 bus series.* 5+up

NEED A BREAK? **Friendship Park.** Locals call this neighborhood hangout "Turtle Park" after the turtle statues near the sandboxes. The park is a combination playground with slides and swings and in the summer a spray ground, with water for the under-six set. Basketball and tennis courts and baseball fields can keep older kids busy. ✉ *45th St. and Van Ness Ave. NW, Upper Northwest* ✉ *Free.* All ages

WHERE CAN I FIND . . . UPPER NORTHWEST?

Quick Meals

Lebanese Taverna	2640 Connecticut Ave. NW	Sit-down restaurant near the zoo and Metro; pita pizzas and burgers and fries served with humus
Chipotle	2600 Connecticut Ave. NW	Burritos, tacos, fajitas; order online or in person
Booeymonger	5252 Wisconsin Ave. NW	Creative hot-and-cold sandwiches since 1976

Ice Cream

Baskin Robbins	2604 Connecticut Ave. NW	Classic cones; most flavors are kosher

Good Coffee

Modern Times Coffeehouse at Politics and Prose	5015 Connecticut Ave. NW	French and Mexican roasted coffees, steamed milk, and coco for kids

Grocery Stores

Rodman's Discount Foods and Pharmacy	5101 Wisconsin Ave. NW	Gourmet and basic foods both plus Webkinz
Magruders	3527 Connecticut Ave. NW	Locally owned, lots of fresh produce and cheeses, good prices

Fun Stores

World Market	5335 Wisconsin Ave. NW	Cool housewares plus kids craft kits and novelty candy
Politics and Prose bookstore	5015 Connecticut Ave. NW	Extensive kids section, excellent staff and story times
Child's Play	5536 Connecticut Ave. NW	Superb service, good selection of toys and books

Playgrounds

Friendship Park aka Turtle Park	45th and Van Ness Sts. NW	Huge sandbox, spray area, ball fields
Palisades Park Recreation Center	Off Sherrier Pl., near Edmunds Pl.	Tall tube slides, climbing wall, monkey bars, sandbox; soccer fields nearby

Public Bathrooms

Borders	5333 Wisconsin Ave. NW	Books, too!

Where to Eat

WORD OF MOUTH

"For a fun lunch while checking out the museums on the mall, go to the cafeteria at the American Indian Museum. Enjoy!"

–DoctorCarrie

"For an interesting lunch, do the Native American food cafeteria [at] the Natl. Museum of the American Indian. . . . The kids will like the fry bread (or a buffalo burger) and you can experiment with regional native dishes—better than the traditional fast food at many museums."

–Beachies7500

Updated
by Kathryn
McKay

AS HOST TO VISITORS AND transplants from around the world, Washington benefits from the constant infusion of different cultures. Despite D.C.'s lack of true ethnic neighborhoods and the kinds of restaurant districts found in many other cities, you *can* find almost any cuisine here, from Burmese to Ethiopian. Just follow your nose.

Although most neighborhoods lack a unified culinary flavor, make no mistake: D.C. is a city of distinctive neighborhoods, each with its own style. Adams-Morgan, for example, is known for its small family-run eateries. You'll find Ethiopian restaurants next to Italian trattorias and Asian bistros. These small ethnic spots open and close frequently; it's worth taking a stroll down the street to see what's new.

Downtown you can find many of the city's blue-chip law firms and deluxe, expense-account restaurants, as well as stylish lounges, microbrew pubs, and upscale eateries that have sprung up to serve the crowds that attend games at the Verizon Center.

Wherever you venture forth in the city, there are a few trends worth noting: Spanish tapas eateries and other restaurants serving small tasting portions are bigger than ever. You'll find this style of eating pervasive, whether you're at a modern Greek, Asian, or American restaurant. High-end restaurants in town also have begun to add bar menus with smaller plates that are much less expensive than their entrées but created with the same finesse.

Though Italian, French, and New American spots continue to open at a ferocious pace, Washingtonians are always hungry to try something new, whether it's Chinese smoked lobster, fiery Indian curry, or crunchily addictive Vietnamese spring rolls.

Many of Washington's parks and monument grounds don't allow any food, so parents will need to plan ahead. Downtown is full of predictable fare that many families rely on such as Subway sandwich shops. The small tasting portions and tapas that are popular now are ideal for children with small appetites and for parents encouraging kids to just "try a bite."

When Washingtonians go out for a nice meal at a trendy downtown restaurant, they usually leave the kids at home. That doesn't mean you need to check your children at the door, just that you shouldn't be surprised if you're

TOP 5 RESTAURANT EXPERIENCES

■ **Ben's Chili Bowl.** Since 1958, one of D.C.'s most famous dining destinations has specialized in down-home food: hot dogs. Even adults are surprised that one of D.C.'s most popular dining destinations is famous for hot dogs!

■ **Mitsitam Native Foods Café.** The Museum of the American Indian appeals to all the senses with its restaurant. Translated as "Let's Eat," the Fry Bread is like a cross between a doughnut and a croissant.

■ **Union Station Food Court.** A lifesaver for kids with competing tastes.

■ **Old Glory Barb-B-Que.** In between the mini corn muffins and lollipops, it's okay to lick your fingers at this down-home restaurant with six sauces on each table.

■ **Cactus Cantina.** Tex-Mex foods aren't the only delights here. Check out the display of Stetson hats, a bow-and-arrow set and cowboy boots, plus watch the warm tortillas rolling down a conveyor belt.

one of the few obvious parents in attendance, especially in such neighborhoods as Adams-Morgan and the U Street Corridor, where the restaurants cater to a young, single crowd.

HOURS, PRICES & DRESS

Washington has less of an around-the-clock mentality than other big cities, with many big-name restaurants shutting down between lunch and dinner and closing their kitchens by 11 PM. Weekend evenings spent downtown can also be a hassle for those seeking quick bites, since many popular chain eateries cater to office workers and shut down after 6 PM. Families looking for late lunches should head north from the Mall to find kitchens that stay open between meals.

Some pricier restaurants require jackets, and some insist on ties. In reviews, we mention dress only when men are required to wear a jacket or a jacket and tie. But even when there's no formal dress code, we recommend wearing jackets and ties in $$$ and $$$$ restaurants. If you have doubts, call the restaurant and ask.

If you're watching your budget, be sure to ask the price of daily specials recited by the waiter or captain. The charge for specials at some restaurants is noticeably out of line with the other prices on the menu. Beware of the $10 bottle of water; ask for tap water instead. And always review your bill.

If you eat early or late you may be able to take advantage of a prix-fixe deal not offered at peak hours. Most upscale restaurants offer great lunch deals with special menus at cut-rate prices designed to give customers a true taste of the place.

Credit cards are widely accepted, but many restaurants (particularly smaller ones downtown) accept only cash. If you plan to use a credit card, it's a good idea to double-check its acceptability when making reservations or before sitting down to eat.

Some restaurants are marked with a price range ($$–$$$, for example). This indicates one of two things: either the average cost straddles two categories, or if you order strategically, you can get out for less than most diners spend.

WHAT IT COSTS AT DINNER				
¢	$	$$	$$$	$$$$
under $10	$10–$17	$18–$25	$26–$35	over $35

Price per person for an average main course or equivalent combination of smaller dishes. Note: if a restaurant offers only prix-fixe (set-price) meals, it has been given the price category that reflects the full prix-fixe price.

CAPITOL HILL

Capitol Hill has a number of bars that cater to congressional types who need to fortify themselves with food and drink after a day spent running the country. Dining options are augmented by Union Station's huge food court and restaurants including America!, which focuses on different U.S. regional cooking styles each week.

¢ ✕ **Jimmy T's Place.** *American.* This D.C. institution is tucked into the first floor of an old row house only five blocks from the Capitol. Sassy waiters, talkative regulars, and this small diner's two boisterous owners, who run the grill, pack the place daily. Soak in the local culture or read the paper as you enjoy favorites such as grits, bacon, omelets, or the homey eggs Benedict, made with a toasted English muffin, a huge piece of ham, and lots of hollandaise sauce. **Family Matters:** The anything-goes atmosphere makes it a great

2

place for kids. Breakfast is served all day. Try to get a seat near the windows to people-watch. ⊠*501 E. Capitol St. SE, Capitol Hill* ☎*202/546–3646* ▤*No credit cards* ⊘*Closed Mon. and Tues. No dinner* Ⓜ*Eastern Market.*

¢–$ ✕**The Market Lunch.** *American.* A walk around the Capitol, a stroll through Eastern Market, and then a hefty pile of blueberry pancakes from Market Lunch make for a perfect Saturday morning or afternoon on the Hill. The casual counter service and informal seating make it ideal for kids. Locals wait in long lines to dine on ham, eggs, grits, or pancakes in the morning or crab cakes, fried shrimp, or fish for lunch—and owner Tom Glasgow earned that loyalty by setting up a temporary location after historic Eastern Market was decimated by a fire spring 2007. But don't be mistaken: eating here has never been a leisurely experience. On Saturday you must be in line by noon. **Family Matters:** Patience pays off for families who can wait up to 30 minutes on Saturday mornings. Sit at the long counter or grab a table outside. Service on Sunday doesn't start until 11 ⊠*Tent hall across the street from Eastern Market, 306 7th St. SE, Capitol Hill* ☎*202/547-8444* ▤*No credit cards* ⊘*Closed Mon. No dinner* Ⓜ*Eastern Market.*

$ ✕**Mitsitam Native Foods Café.** *Native American.* Mitsitam (mit-se-TOM) translates into "Let's Eat" from the Native Piscataway and Delaware language. Don't be tempted to get the classic kids' meals. Not only will a burger or chicken fingers with fries and soda set you back $7.25, you'll miss out on authentic dishes. From familiar fare, such as tacos and corn on the cob, to the more exotic such as quahog clam chowder and Peruvian potato causa, the range of food reflecting the American Indian is vast. **Family Matters:** Trail mix, pumpkin cookies, and popcorn are all here, but if you only go for one sweet, order the fry bread, topped off with cinnamon, honey, and powdered sugar. Try to get a seat near the window where it looks as if the water outside disappears under your feet. ⊠*4th St and Independence Ave. SW, Capitol Hill* ☎*202/633–7039* ▤*AE, DC, MC, V* Ⓜ*Capitol South.*

DOWNTOWN

Downtown covers everything between Georgetown and Capitol Hill. The "new downtown," centered at Connecticut Avenue and K Street, has many of the city's blue-chip law firms and deluxe eateries—places that feed expense-account diners and provide the most elegance, most atten-

Where to Eat
in Washington, D.C.

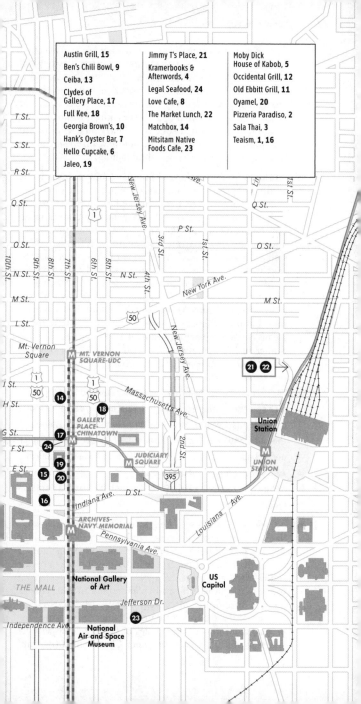

Austin Grill, **15**

Ben's Chili Bowl, **9**

Ceiba, **13**

Clydes of
Gallery Place, **17**

Full Kee, **18**

Georgia Brown's, **10**

Hank's Oyster Bar, **7**

Hello Cupcake, **6**

Jaleo, **19**

Jimmy T's Place, **21**

Kramerbooks &
Afterwords, **4**

Legal Seafood, **24**

Love Cafe, **8**

The Market Lunch, **22**

Matchbox, **14**

Mitsitam Native
Foods Cafe, **23**

Moby Dick
House of Kabob, **5**

Occidental Grill, **12**

Old Ebbitt Grill, **11**

Oyamel, **20**

Pizzeria Paradiso, **2**

Sala Thai, **3**

Teaism, **1, 16**

tive service, and often the best food—but you can also find some of the same chain restaurants that families rely on. But "old downtown," farther east, is where the action is these days. Restaurants of all stripes (usually casual and moderately priced) have sprung up to serve the crowds that attend games at the MCI Center. The entire downtown area, however, has been in a state of culinary flux, with famed restaurants closing their doors and new ones—including some upscale, trendy spots—blossoming.

$$-$$$ ✕ **Ceiba.** *Latin.* At this very popular Latin restaurant the adults will probably want to start with a mojito or a pisco sour cocktail, then taste the smoked-swordfish carpaccio or Jamaican crab fritters. This is a menu meant for grazing, but the main courses, like rib eye with chimichurri sauce and *feijoada* made from pork shanks, still satisfy. Also stellar are desserts such as Mexican vanilla-bean cheesecake with guava jelly, and cinnamon-dusted churros to dip in Mexican hot chocolate. Island-theme murals, angular cream banquettes, an open kitchen, and vaulted ceilings set the scene. **Family Matters:** Families looking to expand their Latin-food horizons beyond Taco Bell should by all means check this place out. Sit by the open kitchen to watch dinner in the making. ✉ *701 14th St. NW, Downtown* ☎ *202/393–3983* ▭ *AE, D, DC, MC, V* ⊗ *Closed Sun. No lunch Sat.* Ⓜ *Metro Center.*

WORD OF MOUTH. "... Just walk a few blocks toward 7th St NW and pick something (there are some chains, like Clyde's or Chipotle or California Tortilla), but I'd go for non-chains, like Jaleo's or the old standby of Old Ebbitt (over by 14th St), or McCormick and Schmick if you like seafood. I also love Rosa Mexicana and Zola's or Zaytinya's, but they are a little more expensive and may not be great with the kids. Up by Dupont, try Pizzeria Paradiso (yum!)." —kaudry

$$-$$$ ✕ **Clydes of Georgetown.** *American.* Clydes has been serving up dependable burgers, chili, and crab cakes since 1963. The children's menu for 10 and under includes a bigger than average burger for kids, grilled chicken breast sandwiches, and more, all served with fruit or ice cream for dessert followed by a toy plane, train, or car made in Sweden specifically for Clydes. **Family Matters:** Ask to be seated in the patio dining room where planes are suspended from the ceiling. Clydes of Gallery Place with its sports theme and Clydes of Chevy Chase with a toy train

that circles above the main dining room are also good options for families. They have the same basic menu and give out the same toys. ☒*707 7th St, NW, Downtown* ☎*202/349–3700* Ⓜ*Gallery Pl./Chinatown* ☒*3236 M St. NW, Georgetown* ☎*202/333–9180 5441* ☒ *Wisconsin Ave, Chevy Chase, MD* ☎*301/951–9600* ▬*AE, D, DC, MC, V* Ⓜ*Friendship Heights.*

$–$$ ✕**Georgia Brown's.** *Southern.* An elegant New South eatery and a favorite hangout of local politicians, Georgia Brown's serves shrimp Carolina-style (head intact, with steaming grits on the side); thick, rich crab soup; and such specials as grilled salmon and slow-cooked green beans with bacon. Fried green tomatoes are filled with herb cream cheese, and a pecan pie is made with bourbon and imported Belgian dark chocolate. ▬TIP➔**The Sunday jazz brunch adds live music and a decadent chocolate fondue fountain to the mix.** The airy, curving dining room has white honeycomb windows and unusual ceiling ornaments of bronze ribbons. **Family Matters:** No children's menu but fried chicken and macaroni and cheese, along with crayons for coloring on tables covered by white butcher paper, might keep kids satisfied. ☒*950 15th St. NW, Downtown* ☎*202/393–4499* ▬*AE, D, DC, MC, V* ⌦*Reservations essential* ☉*No lunch Sat.* Ⓜ*McPherson Square.*

$$ ✕**Jaleo.** *Spanish.* You are encouraged to make a meal of the long list of tapas at this lively Spanish bistro, although entrées such as paella are just as tasty. Tapas highlights include the *gambas al ajillo* (sautéed garlic shrimp), fried potatoes with spicy tomato sauce, and the grilled chorizo. Adventurers are encouraged to sample the octopus with paprika, and sweet tooths should save room for the crisp apple charlotte and the chocolate hazelnut torte. **Family Matters:** A children's menu isn't needed as the choices are vast and tapas are a perfect size for getting kids to taste something new. Lively enough so kids don't need their indoor voices. Reservations recommended for lunch and before 6:30. ☒*480 7th St. NW, Downtown* ☎*202/628–7949* ▬*AE, D, DC, MC, V* Ⓜ*Gallery Pl./Chinatown.*

$–$$ ✕**Matchbox.** *American.* The miniburgers, served on toasted brioche buns with a huge mound of fried onion strings, get the most press, but the main clue to what to order at this convivial triple-decker bar-restaurant is the glowing wood-burning pizza oven. The personal pizzas are New York–style, with a thin, crisp crust. You probably won't mistake them for the very best of New York, but the pizza margherita is good nevertheless. Homey plates such as grilled filet mignon with horseradish potatoes and spicy pecan-crusted chicken add substance to the menu. There's a great lineup of draft beers and oddball martinis. **Family Matters:** Dine before 6:30 to beat the crowds at this hot spot where the burgers are only a wee bit bigger than matchbox cars and the pizzas are just as popular. ⊠ *713 H St. NW, Downtown* ☎ *202/289–4441* ⊙ *Closed Sun.* Ⓜ *Gallery Pl./Chinatown.*

$$–$$$ ✕ **Occidental Grill.** *American.* One of the most venerable restaurants in the city covers its walls with photos of politicians and other notables who have come here for the food and the attentive service. The standbys are best—chopped salad, grilled tuna or swordfish, lamb shank, veal meat loaf. More than half of the menu is seafood. **Family Matters:** Parents who don't want to skip the legendary Washington restaurant that dates back to 1906 can rest assured that there are high chairs and a menu with the usual kids' offerings. ⊠ *Willard InterContinental, 1475 Pennsylvania Ave. NW, Downtown* ☎ *202/783–1475* ☖ *Reservations essential* ⊟ *AE, DC, MC, V* Ⓜ *Metro Center.*

$$ ✕ **Old Ebbitt Grill.** *American.* People flock here to drink at the several bars, which seem to go on for miles, and to enjoy well-prepared buffalo wings, hamburgers, and Reuben sandwiches. The Old Ebbitt also has Washington's most popular raw bar, which serves farm-raised oysters. Pasta is homemade, and daily fresh fish or steak specials are served until 1 AM. Despite the crowds, the restaurant never feels cramped, thanks to its well-spaced, comfortable booths. ■ TIP→ **Service can be slow at lunch; if you're in a hurry, try the café-style Ebbitt Express next door.** **Family Matters:** Staff may be willing to set up some extra tables in the atrium room when it's crowded. The children's menu includes a seasonal fruit plate in addition to the predictable grilled cheese, hot dogs, and pizza. ⊠ *675 15th St. NW, Downtown* ☎ *202/347–4800* ⊟ *AE, D, DC, MC, V* Ⓜ *Metro Center.*

¢ ✕ **Teaism.** *Japanese.* This informal teahouse stocks more than 50 teas (black, white, and green) imported from India, Japan, and Africa, but it also serves healthful and delicious Japanese, Indian, and Thai food, as well as tea-friendly sweets like ginger scones, plum muffins, and salty oat cookies. You can mix small dishes—tandoori kebabs, tea-cured salmon, Indian flat breads—to create meals or snacks. There's also a juicy ostrich burger or *ochazuke,* green tea poured over seasoned rice. The smaller Connecticut Avenue branch (enter around the corner, on H Street; closed on weekends) is tucked neatly on a corner adjacent to Lafayette

Park and the White House, a casual reprieve from neighboring high-price restaurants. It's a perfect spot to grab lunch after touring the nation's power center. Breakfast is served daily. **Family Matters:** Even kids like eating out of little black paper boxes. Bento chicken with chicken, rice, sweet potatoes, and cucumber is a healthier, albeit more expansive option, to the typical chicken fingers on kids' menus. There's no hot chocolate but a nice selection of uncaffeinated teas. The oat cookies may not be for everyone—they're a bit dry. ⊠*400 8th St. NW, Downtown* ☎*202/638–7740* ⊟*D, MC, V* Ⓜ *Archives/Navy Memorial* ⊠*800 Connecticut Ave. NW, Downtown* ☎*202/835–2233* Ⓜ*Farragut West* ⊠*2009 R St. NW, Dupont Circle* ☎*202/667–3827* ⊟*D, MC, V* Ⓜ*Dupont Circle.*

CHINATOWN

Chinatown, centered on G and H streets NW between 6th and 8th, is the city's one officially recognized ethnic enclave, Here Burmese, Thai, and other Asian cuisines add variety to the many traditional Chinese restaurants. The latter entice you with huge, brightly lighted signs and offer such staples as beef with broccoli or spicy kung pao chicken with roasted peanuts.

¢ ✕**Austin Grill.** *Mexican.* With stars on the ceiling and Texas license plates and flags on the walls, the decor is a bit more Texas than Mexico in this popular Tex-Mex restaurant, which can get crowded when there's an event at the Verizon Center. **Family Matters:**The menu reflects the expected tacos, quesadillas, and enchiladas, but kids can get burgers, hot dogs, and peanut butter and jelly. The buzz is loud enough to drown out all but the loudest cries or whines. Up to two kids eat free for every paying adult on Tuesday. ⊠*750 E St. NW, Penn Quarter* ☎*202/393–3776* ⊟*AE, DC, MC, V* Ⓜ*Gallery Place, Chinatown and/or Archive.*

WORD OF MOUTH. **"A kid-friendly place to eat one block from the Portrait Gallery/Museum of Am. Art in Penn Quarter is Austin Grill. It's Tex/Mex food, casual atmosphere." —tahl**

$ ✕**Full Kee.** *Chinese.* Many locals swear by this standout from the slew of mediocre local Chinese joints. Addictively salty shrimp or scallops in garlic sauce cry out for a doggie bag to enjoy again later, as do the wide assortment of Cantonese-style roasted meats. ▰TIP➔ **Order from the house specialties, not the tourist menu; the meal-size soups garnished** with roast meats are the best in Chinatown. Tried-and-true dishes include the steamed dumplings, crispy duck, eggplant with garlic sauce, and sautéed leek flower. **Family Matters:** If kids don't get queasy walking by the roasted ducks in the window, they'll find a menu with oodles of noodles to slurp up. ✉ *509 H St. NW* ☎ *202/371–2233* ▭ *No credit cards* Ⓜ *Gallery Pl./Chinatown.*

$$$ ✕ **Legal Sea Foods.** *Seafood.* The popular Boston-based sea-food chain recently expanded its seating capacity to 200 to meet demand. Two dozen varieties of seafood are available daily. Although best known for oysters and lobsters, its their New England clam chowder that's been served at every presidential inauguration since 1981. **Family Matters:** Legal Sea Foods is recognized as one of the top kid-friendly restaurants of its kind. All kids' meals are served with fresh fruit, and chefs skip the salt on kids' fries. Gluten-free meals are available, and the waitstaff routinely asks about food allergies, but more exciting to kids might be the behemoth lobsters that the chef will bring out upon request when they're available. ✉ *704 7th St. NW Chinatown* ☎ *202/347–0007.*

¢–$ ✕ **Oyamel.** *Mexican.* The specialty at this Mexican stunner is antojitos, literally translated as "little dishes from the street." But the high ceilings, gracious service, and gorgeous Frida Kahlo–inspired decor are anything but street, and even the smallest of dishes is bigger than life when doused with chocolatey mole poblano sauce or piquant lime-cilantro dressing. Standouts include house-made margaritas topped with a clever salt foam, the Veracruz red snapper in a hearty olive-tomato confit, and grasshopper tacos. Yes, those are bugs basted in tequila and pepper sauce—and they're delightful. **Family Matters:** Silver butterflies suspended from the ceiling delight all ages. Kids can get their daily vitamin C from an ever-changing variety of juices such as papaya, pineapple, and watermelon. A tiny taco or quesadilla may satisfy young ones, but parents of big eaters beware: the tab can add up quickly. ✉ *401 7th St. NW, Penn Quarter* ☎ *202/628–1005* ▭ *AE, D, MC, V* Ⓜ *Archives/Navy Memorial.*

GEORGETOWN

At its beginnings in the mid-1700s, Georgetown was a Maryland tobacco port. Today, the neighborhood is D.C.'s premiere shopping district, as well as a tourist and architectural attraction, with its grand row houses, narrow

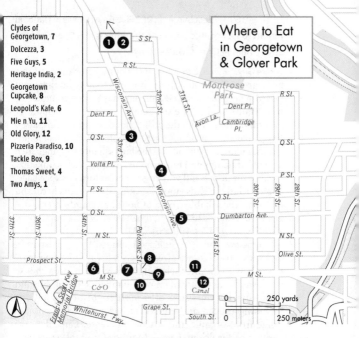

**Where to Eat
in Georgetown
& Glover Park**

cobblestone streets, and European architectural accents. The neighborhood's restaurants range from upscale Italian to down-home barbecue. Still, since its incorporation into D.C. in 1790, Georgetown has retained much of its distinct charm and flair. Georgetown's main thoroughfares, M Street NW and Wisconsin Avenue NW, are always bustling with university students, professionals, and tourists. On a given day, you may encounter political activists on the sidewalks, wedding parties posing for photos, and gossiping teens laden with shopping bags.

$ × **DolceZZa.** *Café.* The handmade gelato and sorbet at this all-white storefront are divine, especially during the heat of summer. The flavors, such as Coconut con Dulce de Leche, are endlessly inventive. Strawberry-, peach-, apple-, and clementine-flavored sorbets are available seasonally. Espresso and churros will warm winter afternoons. **Family Matters:** Kid's-size cones are available, but sprinkles or other toppings that might detract from the flavors are not. ⊠*1560 Wisconsin Ave. NW, Georgetown* ☎*202/333–4646.*

WORD OF MOUTH. "Best burger in DC? Five Guys. One is in National Airport (US Air shuttle terminal), the other is at H Street and 9th Street, right in Chinatown." —mcnyc

¢ ✕ **Five Guys.** *American.* One of the quirky traditions of this homegrown fast-food burger house is to note on the menu board where the potatoes for that day's fries come from, be it Maine, Idaho, or elsewhere. The place gets just about everything right: from the grilled hot dogs and hand-patted burger patties—most folks get a double—to the fresh hand-cut fries with the skin on and the high-quality toppings such as sautéed onions and mushrooms. Add an eclectic jukebox to all of the above and you've got a great burger experience. **Family Matters:** Kids enjoy shucking the peanuts here, and of course the reliable troika of hot dogs, hamburgers, and grilled-cheese. ✉1335 Wisconsin Ave. NW, Georgetown 20007 ☏202/337–0400 ▭AE, MC, V.

¢ ✕ **Georgetown Cupcake.** *Bakery.* Founded by two sisters in 2008, this tiny bakery already has a loyal following, particularly with the after-school crowd. Most children choose basic vanilla and chocolate with baby blue or bubblegum pink icing, but the sisters offer more sophisticated flavors, including mocha and chocolate hazelnut. Milk choices range from organic and soy to chocolate. Cupcakes are cheaper by the dozen. **Family Matters:** One table seats only three, but the C&O Canal with its grassy patches in the shade is only a few blocks away. ✉1209 Potomac St. NW, between Prospect and M Sts., Georgetown ☏202/333–8448 ▭AE, D, MC, V.

$$ ✕ **Leopold's Kafe & Konditorei.** *Austrian.* Forget all the clichés about heavy Austrian fare served by waiters in lederhosen. Leopold's is about as Euro trendy as it gets, with an all-day coffee and drinks bar, an architecturally hip dining space, and a chic little patio complete with a spewing minifountain. Food is pared down Mitteleuropean: wine soup, crisp Wiener schnitzel paired with peppery greens, a spaetzle casserole that tastes like luxe mac 'n' cheese. In the middle of design-obsessed Cady's Alley, the café draws both an artsy city crowd that's content to sit and watch the scene evolve, just as it's done in Europe. **Family Matters:** A good place for sweet treats and hot chocolate (but don't expect marshmallows). Lemon soufflé pancakes, Belgian waffles, and other breakfast foods are served until 4 every day. Enter through Cady's alley. ✉3318 M St. NW, Georgetown 20007 ☏202/965–6005 ▭AE, DC, MC, V.

$$$ ✕**Mie n Yu.** *Chinese.* Exotic romance abounds at this palatial retreat inspired by the Europe-to-Asia journey of explorer Marco Polo. The menu matches Polo's route along the Silk Road and takes on multiple ethnic personalities: nowhere else in the capital can you find a Thai pu-pu platter of beef satay and sugarcane pork alongside Chinese prawn toast and Indian-inspired banana hummus with naan bread. If you'd like to take your dining adventure even further, try the chef's tasting menu and take your seat inside a giant birdcage at the center of the dining room where chic couples head for special nights. Restaurants don't get more memorable than Mie n Yu. **Family Matters:** ✉*3125 M St. NW, Georgetown* ☎*202/333-6122* ▭ *AE, DC, MC, V.* ☉*Closed for lunch Mon. and Tues.*

$$ ✕**Old Glory.** *American.* This all-American barbecue pub is known for its sauces—six of them lined up in easy squirt bottles on each table. Side dishes for the pulled chicken, pork, ribs, and catfish include collard greens, mashed potatoes, and creamed succotash. The kids' menu is more extensive than most and in lieu of fries, kids can order carrots. The friendly waitstaff is as generous with its crayons as it is with its disposable hand towels. Everyone ends the meal with a lollipop. **Family Matters:** Kids meals come with free ice cream sundaes and drinks. Kids eat free with any adult entrée purchased on Sunday and Monday nights from 4 to 9. But you wouldn't want to be here past 9, as bar hoppers gather to sample the more than 80 bourbons. ✉*3139 M St., NW, Georgetown* ☎*202/337–3406* ▭*AE, D, MC, V.*

★ **Fodor's**Choice ✕**Tackle Box.** *Seafood.* Next to Hook, a seafood
$$$ restaurant lauded for its commitment to the "sustainable seafood" movement, this casual seafood joint offers some of the same fish caught using environmentally friendly methods, but the atmosphere is casual. Order your meal at the counter and spread out on long picnic tables, or grab a bar stool at the front and watch the folks strolling around Georgetown. Fish is served grilled or crispy. **Family Matters:** Lobster pots are available to eat in or out. The utensils are biodegradable. ✉*3245 M St. NW, Georgetown* ☎*202337–8269* ▭*AE, MC, V* ☉*No lunch Mon.*

$ ✕**Thomas Sweet.** *American.* This sweet spot has the look of an old-fashioned malt shop. All selections of sandwiches and desserts are posted above the counter, but the most popular is the Blend-in, a mixture of yogurt or ice cream with three toppings (cookies, candies, and fresh fruit). ✉*3214 P St. NW, Georgetown* ☎*202/337–0616* ▭*No credit cards.*

DUPONT CIRCLE

Dupont Circle, which lies south of U Street and north of K Street, is dense with restaurants and cafés, many with outdoor seating. Chains such as Starbucks have put fancy coffee on every corner, but homegrown lunch and coffee spots, from the 24-hour Kramerbooks & Afterwords to Teaism to the Bread Line, have more character and are more interesting for breakfast and light or late fare.

★ Fodor'sChoice ✕ **Hank's Oyster Bar.** *Seafood.* The watchword
$–$$ is simplicity at this popular and chic take on the shellfish shacks of New England. A half-dozen oyster varieties are available daily on the half shell, both from the West Coast and local Virginia waters, alongside another half-dozen daily fish specials. An amuse-bouche of cheddar Goldfish crackers adds a touch of whimsy. Don't be shy about asking for seconds on the complimentary baking chocolate presented along with your check—the kitchen doesn't serve sweets, but it doesn't need to. **Family Matters:** No kids' menu, but popcorn shrimp and macaroni and cheese and even Old Bay fries might satisfy young ones. When pasta's on the menu, they'll serve it plain or with butter. Arrive by 6:30 in the winter to avoid lines as all seats move indoors. ⊠ *1624 Q St. NW, Dupont Circle* ☎ *202/462–4265* 🚫 *AE, MC, V* Ⓜ *Dupont Circle.*

¢ ✕ **Hello Cupcake.** *Bakery.* With a pink-and-chocolate-brown decor and a big pink chandelier, this new cupcake place looks more like a boutique than a bakery. Choices vary but you can always count on chocolate and vanilla, carrot cake, peanut butter blossoms and triple coconuts cupcakes, plus one vegan and one gluten-free choice each day. No requests for special toppings. ⊠ *1351 Connecticut Ave. NW, Dupont Circle* ☎ *202/861–2253* 🚫 *AE, D, MC, V* ⊙ *Closed Sun.* Ⓜ *Dupont Circle.*

$ ✕ **Kramerbooks & Afterwords.** *Café.* This popular bookstore-cum-café is a favorite neighborhood breakfast spot. ▇ TIP→ **It's also a late-night haunt on weekends, when it's open around the clock.** There's a simple menu with soups, salads, and sandwiches, but many people drop in just for cappuccino and dessert. The "dysfunctional family sundae"—a massive brownie soaked in amaretto with a plethora of divine toppings—is a local favorite, and especially popular with kids. Catch a live music performance—everything from rock to the blues—here, Wednesday through Saturday from 8 PM to midnight. **Family Matters:** More fun than the after-school special of grilled cheese and soup might be a

Sharezis platter of three appetizers served on a tiered plate rack. You can also buy a children's book at Kramerbooks to enjoy with your breakfast, lunch, or dinner. ✉*1517 Connecticut Ave. NW, Dupont Circle* ☎*202/387–1462* 🚫*AE, D, MC, V* Ⓜ*Dupont Circle.*

$$ ✕**Moby Dick House of Kabob.** *Iranian.* For two decades, D.C. residents have flocked to these fast-food Iranian restaurants that serve kebabs, of meat, swordfish, and chicken, but it's the fresh pita with yogurt sauce and hummus for dipping that kids find most fun. **Family Matters:** Sandwiches are large enough to feed two children. Twelve area locations in D.C., Maryland, and Virginia. ✉*1300 Connecticut Ave. NW,Dupont Circle* ☎*202/833–9788* 🚫*MC, V* Ⓜ*Dupont Circle.*

$ ✕**Pizzeria Paradiso.** *Italian.* A trompe l'oeil ceiling adds space and light to a simple interior at the ever-popular Dupont Circle Pizzeria Paradiso. The restaurant sticks to crowd-pleasing basics: pizzas, panini, salads, and desserts. Although the standard pizza is satisfying, you can enliven it with fresh buffalo mozzarella or unusual toppings such as potatoes, capers, and mussels. Wines are well chosen and well priced. The intensely flavored gelato is a house specialty. At the larger location in Georgetown, a new Rathskeller-style beer pub on the lower level opened in 2006. **Family Matters:** Good choice for kids looking to try unusual toppings on their pizza. Watch the chefs in action at the open kitchen. Eat in or take out. No delivery. ✉*2029 P St. NW, Dupont Circle* ☎*202/223–1245* 🚫*DC, MC, V* Ⓜ*Dupont Circle.* ✉*3282 M St. NW, Georgetown* ☎*202/337–1245* 🚫*D, DC, MC, V.*

¢–$ ✕**Sala Thai.** *Thai.* Who says Thai food has to be sweat-inducing? Sala Thai makes the food as spicy as you wish, because this chef is interested in flavor, not fire. Among the subtly seasoned dishes are *panang goong* (shrimp in curry-peanut sauce), chicken sautéed with ginger and pineapple, and flounder with a choice of four sauces. Mirrored walls and warm lights soften this small dining room, as do the friendly service and largely local clientele. The Dupont and U Street locations are most popular, but Arlington, Bethesda, and the Upper Northwest neighborhood all host winning Sala locations. **Family Matters:** For less adventurous young diners, the waitstaff is happy to bring out unseasoned chicken and rice, and if your kids don't want to end a meal with fried bananas like kids in Thailand, they can order a scoop of vanilla ice cream. ✉*2016 P St.*

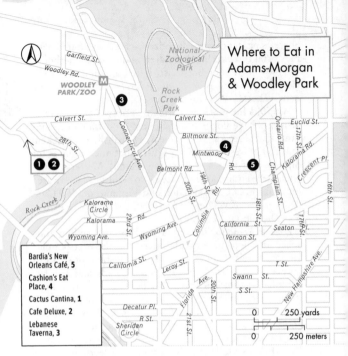

Where to Eat in Adams-Morgan & Woodley Park

Bardia's New Orleans Café, 5

Cashion's Eat Place, 4

Cactus Cantina, 1

Cafe Deluxe, 2

Lebanese Taverna, 3

NW, Dupont Circle 20036 ☎202/872–1144 ▤*AE, D, DC, MC, V* Ⓜ*Dupont Circle.*

ADAMS-MORGAN

Wall-to-wall restaurants line 18th Street NW, which extends south from Columbia Road. In this section of Adams-Morgan, small ethnic spots open and close frequently; it's worth taking a stroll down the street to see what's new and interesting. Although the area has retained some of its Latin American identity, the newer eating establishments tend to be Asian, contemporary, Italian, and Ethiopian. Parking can be impossible on weekends. You can walk from the nearest Metro stop, Woodley Park/Zoo, in 10 to 15 minutes, but arriving by taxi is recommended before the streets crowd with revelers every weekend in the premidnight hours.

¢–$ ✕**Bardia's New Orleans Café.** *Southern.* Locals swarm to this cozy café, where great food is accompanied by jazz. Seafood, whether batter-fried, blackened, or sautéed, is always a winner. The house favorite is the blackened catfish. Po'boy sandwiches (subs on French bread) are reasonably priced, fresh, and huge. Breakfast items, served all day, include traditional eggs Benedict or eggs New Orleans, with fried oysters, crabmeat, and hollandaise: they're both delicious. Don't leave without trying the outstanding beignets (fried puffs of dough sprinkled with powdered sugar). **Family Matters:** No kids' menu, but you can request small portions. Three blocks from Woodley Park Metro. ⊠*2412 18th St. NW, Woodley Park* ☎*202/234–0420* ⊟*AE, MC, V* Ⓜ*Woodley Park/Zoo.*

$$–$$$ ╳**Cashion's Eat Place.** *American.* Walls are hung with family photos, and tables are jammed with regulars feasting on up-to-date, home-style cooking. Founder and capital cuisine superstar Ann Cashion recently sold the spot to her longtime sous chef, but the Eat Place has remained a neighborhood favorite. The menu changes daily, but roast chicken, steak, and seafood are frequent choices. Side dishes, such as garlicky mashed potatoes, sometimes upstage the main course. If it's available, order the chocolate terrine layered with walnuts, caramel, mousse, and ganache. ■TIP➔**At Sunday brunch, many entrées are a fraction of the normal price. Family Matters:** The menu can be challenging for children, but the chef will create special meals for kids based on the ingredients available. High chairs available. ⊠*1819 Columbia Rd. NW, Woodley Park* ☎*202/797–1819* ⌂*Reservations essential* ⊟*AE, MC, V* ⊘*Closed Mon. No lunch* Ⓜ*Woodley Park/Zoo.*

$ ╳**Lebanese Taverna.** *Middle Eastern.* Arched ceilings, cedar panels etched with leaf patterns, woven rugs, and brass lighting fixtures give the Taverna a warm yet casual elegance. Start with an order of Arabic bread baked in a wood-burning oven. Lamb, beef, chicken, and seafood are either grilled on skewers, slow roasted, or smothered with a garlicky yogurt sauce. A group can make a meal of the meze platters—a mix of appetizers and sliced *shawarma* (spit-roasted lamb). **Family Matters:** A great stop on the way to the Metro coming from the Zoo. The kids menu offers a trio of miniburgers on pita with fries and hummus for dipping. ⊠*2641 Connecticut Ave. NW, Woodley Park* ☎*202/265–8681* ⊟*AE, MC, V* ⊘*No lunch Sun.* Ⓜ*Woodley Park/Zoo.*

U STREET

The U Street corridor is known for its indie rock clubs, edgy bars, and trendy restaurants. Although the urban hipsterdom is being threatened by skyrocketing rents, you can still find more tattoos and sneakers than pinstripes and pearls here. The neighborhood draws a young and often boisterous crowd day and night. Restaurants stay open late on weekend nights and serve everything from burgers to gourmet pizza and Ethiopian dishes at low prices. Most restaurants don't even bother with a children's menu. There aren't enough families dining in the area to justify one. For families who want to try one of U Street's restaurants, lunch or an early dinner is your best bet.

¢–$ ✕**Ben's Chili Bowl.** *American.* Long before U Street became hip, Ben's was serving chili. Chili on hot dogs, chili on Polish-style sausages, chili on burgers, and just plain chili. Add cheese fries if you dare. The faux-marble bar and shiny red-vinyl stools give the impression that little has changed since the 1950s, but turkey and vegetarian burgers and meatless chili are a nod to modern times. Ben's closes at 2 AM Monday through Thursday, at 4 AM on Friday and Saturday, and at 8 PM Sunday. Southern-style breakfast is served from 6 AM weekdays and from 7 AM on Saturday. **Family Matters:** like sitting at the counter and drawing in the bathroom (chalk provided) at this Washington institution since 1958, but if you're looking for fruits and veggies, it's best to look elsewhere. ⊠*1213 U St. NW* ☎*202/667–0909* ⊟*No credit cards* Ⓜ*U St./Cardozo.*

$$ ✕**Love Café.** *Café.* The sister store to the CakeLove bakery across the street, this is a casual community hot spot. The butter-cream cupcakes are incredibly sweet, and the rosy atmosphere warms you on the inside. **Family Matters:** No kids' menu. Peanut-butter-and-jelly sandwiches and fruit bowls are on the main menu. You can select your own toppings for cupcakes just like at an ice cream shop ⊠*1506 U St. NW* ☎*202/588–7100* ⊟ *AE, MC, V* Ⓜ*U St./Cardozo.*

UPPER NORTHWEST

Many Hill staffers, journalists, and other inside-the-beltway types live along this hilly stretch of Connecticut Ave. Eateries and shops line the few blocks near each of the Red Line Metro stops. Ethnic dining is abundant here, especially in Woodley Park. Tucked into the facades of row houses from the early 20th century are diverse dining options ranging from Afghan to Thai.

¢–$ ✕**2 Amys.** *Pizza.* Judging from the long lines here, the best pizza in D.C. is uptown. Simple recipes allow the ingredients to shine through at this Neapolitan pizzeria. You may be tempted to go for the D.O.C. pizza (it has *Denominazione di Origine Controllata* approval for Neapolitan authenticity), but don't hesitate to try the daily specials. Roasted peppers with anchovies and deviled eggs with parsley-caper sauce have by now become classics. At busy times, the wait for a table can exceed an hour, and the noisy din of a packed house may discourage some diners. **Family Matters:** For a crunchy treat, try the *supli a telefono*, cheesy fried rice ball. Carry out your pizza and lounge on the green grass outside the gorgeous National Cathedral, a 10-minute walk away. ✉ *3715 Macomb St. NW, Glover Park* ☎ *202/885–5700* ⚐ *Reservations not accepted* ▤ *MC, V* ☺ *No lunch Mon.* Ⓜ *Cleveland Park.*

> **WORD OF MOUTH.** "If you do go to the Cathedral, I highly recommend Two Amy's for lunch - fabulous Neopolitan (thin crust) pizza." —beanweb24

¢–$ ✕ **Cactus Cantina.** *Mexican.* Young professionals and families make this a popular spot for Tex-Mex, but this place even gets the presidential seal of approval. President George W. Bush and his wife dined here. He ordered an enchilada; she ordered a fajita. A large display case with antique Stetson hats, a bow and arrow set, a feathered headdress and a long line of cowboy boots can ease waiting for a table on busy weekend evenings. You can also watch the freshly made tortillas constantly roll off a conveyor belt. **Family Matters:** Kids have eight choices on the children's menu, including soft and crispy tacos, quesadillas, and enchiladas. ✉ *3300 Wisconsin Ave. NW, Cleveland Park/Woodley Park* ☎ *202/686–7222* ⚐ *Reservations not accepted* ▤ *AE, MC, V Cleveland Park.*

¢–$ ✕ **Café Deluxe.** *American.* With 2 Amys and Cactus Cantina across the street, some families just wait to see which wait is shortest. The menu here is a basic American mix of comfort foods, such as meat loaf and chicken potpie as well as pan-roasted halibut and grilled salmon niçoise salad. Choose between outdoor seating, booths, and round or rectangular tables. **Family Matters:** The kids' menu could be called parent pleasing with its three vegetable entrées but there's also cheese quesadillas and peanut-butter-and-jelly sandwiches. ✉ *3228 Wisconsin, Ave. NW, Glover Park* ☎ *202/686–2233* ▤ *MC, DC, V* Ⓜ *Cleveland Park.*

$ ✕ **Heritage India.** *Indian.* You feel like a guest in a foreign land dining at this restaurant: there's incredible attention to detail in everything from the tapestried chairs to the paintings of India and the traditional tandoori and curry dishes. *Tahli* is a variety plate of six or seven curry, lamb, or chicken dishes with rice and bread, served in small bowls or compartments on a silver platter. Wine is presented in a small glass pitcher. Whatever you choose, the experience is as fascinating as the meal. **Family Matters:** The chef accommodates children by cooking without spices upon request, but kids often fill up on the six to eight choices of homemade breads. ✉ *2400 Wisconsin Ave. NW, Glover Park* ☎ *202/333–3120* ✍ *Reservations essential* ⊟ *AE, D, MC, V* Ⓜ *Cleveland Park.*

Where to Stay

3

WORD OF MOUTH

"The [Marriott] Residence Inn in Pentagon City will give you lots of space if you have several people in the room (they even have two queen bdrm, two bath suites; studios have 2 doubles and a sofabed)and their price is relatively reasonable for the space and what you get (incl. hot breakfast).

—emd

Updated
by Kathryn
McKay

FROM THE FREE SMITHSONIAN MUSEUMS on the Mall to the cuddly pandas at the National Zoo, D.C. is an eminently family-friendly town. Major convention hotels (and those on the waterfront) don't see many families, so we recommend looking Downtown, in Foggy Bottom, or Upper Northwest, where many hotels offer special panda packages for the zoo-bound. Also, the closer your hotel is to a Metro stop, the more quickly you can get on the sightseeing trail. Consider a stay at an all-suites hotel. This will allow you to spread out and, if you prepare your meals in a kitchenette, reduce your dining costs. It gives the grown-ups the option of staying up past bedtime. A pool may well be essential for a stay with children, especially during D.C.'s notoriously humid summer months, but keep in mind that several hotels are closing their pools in favor of larger fitness centers or spas. Hotel pools tend to be small without any slides, diving boards, and perhaps most importantly, life guards.

A number of well-known chains, including **Embassy Suites, Fairmont, Four Seasons, Ritz-Carlton,** and **St. Regis** also offer special programs for kids and usually can arrange babysitting services. **Holiday Inns** allow kids (typically under 12) to eat free.

If you're looking for *The American President* experience, book a room on Capitol Hill. The Hill will put you in filibuster distance of the Capitol, the National Mall with all its museums, and Union Station. Tony Georgetown, with a Four Seasons and a boutique-style Ritz-Carlton, is another option for an upscale experience. Funky digs like Hotel Monaco in up-and-coming Penn Quarter put you near the International Spy Museum and Museum of Crime and Punishment, high-end restaurants, and shopping. For a quieter stay, try Foggy Bottom, and for the best rates, head over the border to either Bethesda, Maryland, or suburban Virginia. Many of the hotels offer free shuttle services to Metro. New water-taxi service from Old Town Alexandria in Virginia will help make the trip across the Potomac more scenic, not to mention more fun.

Whichever neighborhood you unpack your suitcase in, remember another one is never far away on the Metro. There are many appealing options in places you might not think to look. We've listed them in the pages that follow.

TOP 5 HOTEL EXPERIENCES

■ Kids get a blast from their parents' or even grandparents' past with lava lamps, bunk beds, and a refrigerator full of stuff like Pop Rocks and wax lips at the **Hotel Helix**. Groovy! Or, uhm, peace out!

■ Celebrities aren't the only ones getting red-carpet treatment at the **Four Seasons Hotel**. Tell the staff your kid's age and they aim to please, providing everything from cribs and diapers for babies to teen magazines, popcorn, and other snacks for teenagers.

■ After a day of sightseeing, youngsters can unwind in their kid-size animal print robes courtesy of the **Hotel Palomar**.

■ After a day at the zoo, the **Omni Shoreham** provides plenty of down- or uptime activities such as movies, hammocks, a pool, ghost tours, and more.

■ Children and adults will eat well and play hard in the pool at the **Embassy Suites** on 22nd Street. At 9 AM and 9 PM, kids can feed the huge koi fish swimming in the lobby.

HOTEL PRICES

If you're interested in visiting Washington at a calmer, less-expensive time—and if you can stand semitropical weather—come in August, during the congressional recess. Rates also drop in late December and January, except around an inauguration.

If high-end prices aren't in your vacation budget, don't automatically assume that a stay in a fancy hotel is out of the question. Weekend, off-season, and special rates (such as AARP discounts and Web-only promotions) can make rooms more affordable. A little bit of research can pay off in big savings.

WHAT IT COSTS FOR TWO PEOPLE				
¢	$	$$	$$$	$$$$
under $125	$125–$210	$211–$295	$296–$399	over $400

Prices are for a standard double room in high season, excluding room tax (14.5% in D.C., 12.5% in MD, and 10.15% in VA).

CAPITOL HILL

$$$–$$$$ ☷**Hyatt Regency Washington on Capitol Hill.** A favorite for political events, fundraising dinners, and networking meetings, this property is a solid choice if you're planning on spending a lot of time on the Hill. Expect to find the hotel abuzz with groups getting ready to participate in the political process. The Hyatt often serves as home base for lobbying days, where organizations bring in busloads of people to meet with lawmakers. The hotel is within walking distance of Union Station, home to Amtrak, the Metro, shops, a food court, and restaurants. ■TIP➔**The Old Town Trolley picks you up right in front of the hotel to visit Washington's key tourist destinations.** Pros: Indoor pool; quick walk to Union Station; near the Capitol. Cons: Busy; lots of groups; escalator in lobby. **Family Matters:** You're more likely to find kids playing Marco Polo than adults swimming in the lap pool, which doesn't have a guard on duty. Four blocks from a small grocery store. Children 12 and under may order from a kids' menu or get half off the main menu. ✉ *400 New Jersey Ave. NW, Capitol Hill* ☎*202/737–1234 or 800/233–1234* ⊕*www.washingtonregency.hyatt.com* ⇨*802 rooms, 32 suites* &*In-room: Wi-Fi. In-hotel: restaurant, room service, bar, pool, gym, concierge, laundry service, executive floor, parking (fee), no-smoking rooms* ⊟*AE, D, DC, MC, V* Ⓜ*Union Station.*

$$$ ☷**Washington Court Hotel.** Marble stairs lead you into a contemporary atrium lobby with a skylight, waterfall, and glass elevator. Each deluxe room has a spacious work desk, a lounge chair and ottoman, and marble bathroom. The larger executive king rooms offer expanded sitting areas with a pull-out sofa bed. Convenient to Union Station, the hotel has a wonderful view of the Capitol. **Pros:** Good location; Capitol views from many rooms. **Cons:** Mixed service; expensive parking. **Family Matters:** No deals on meals or microwaves, but you can request a refrigerator at no extra charge and about two-thirds of the rooms can connect with one another. ✉ *525 New Jersey Ave. NW, Capitol Hill* ☎*202/628–2100 or 800/321–3010* ⊕*www. washingtoncourthotel.com* ⇨*252 rooms, 12 suites* &*In-hotel: restaurant, room service, bar, gym, concierge, laundry service, parking (fee), no-smoking rooms* ⊟*AE, D, DC, MC, V* Ⓜ*Union Station.*

DOWNTOWN

$$$–$$$$ 🍴**Capital Hilton.** In close proximity to the best Washington tourist attractions, the Capital Hilton offers you a long list of amenities and access to an 11,000-square-foot health club and day spa. Guest rooms have a neoclassic design with cherry-wood furniture. Babysitting and other child-friendly services are available. The fare at Twigs includes American bistro standards. **Pros:** Family-friendly; a quick walk down 16th Street to the White House. **Cons:** Big hotel with big crowds especially during peak season; no pool. **Family Matters:** In the midst of the business district, but near the National Geographic Museum at Explorers Hall, which opens at 9. Babysitting service arranged through the concierge. ✉*1001 16th St. NW, Downtown* ☎*202/393–1000* ⊕*www.hilton.com* ⊜*544 rooms, 32 suites* ⌂*In-hotel: restaurant, room service, bar, gym, spa, concierge, laundry service, parking (fee), no-smoking rooms* ⊟*AE, D, DC, MC, V* Ⓜ*Farragut N.*

$$$ 🍴**Grand Hyatt Washington.** In this fanciful high-rise hotel's atrium, a player piano sits on a small island surrounded by a waterfall-fed blue lagoon. You can enter Metro Center, the hub of D.C.'s subway system, directly from the lobby. Guest rooms have been upgraded with pillow-top mattresses, thick down comforters, and plush pillows on the beds, and marble baths that offer Portico spa products. Weekend brunch at this giant hotel is very popular. **Pros:** Right at Metro; location great for sightseeing and shopping; often runs good weekend deals. **Cons:** Big business and meeting hotel with a lot going on inside and out; with almost 900 rooms it can feel impersonal. **Family Matters:** Board games at the front desk and half price meals from adult menu in restaurant. No lifeguard at the indoor pool. PlayStation 3 in the bar. Best reasons to book here: location and low rates, as much as two-thirds off when business is slow. ✉*1000 H St. NW, Downtown* ☎*202/582–1234 or 800/233–1234* ⊕*www.grandwashington.hyatt.com* ⊜*851 rooms, 37 suites* ⌂*In-room: Wi-Fi, refrigerator. In-hotel: 4 restaurants, room service, bars, pool, gym, concierge, laundry service, executive floor, parking (fee), public Wi-Fi, no-smoking rooms* ⊟*AE, D, DC, MC, V* Ⓜ*Metro Center.*

¢ 🍴**Hotel Harrington.** One of Washington's oldest continuously operating hotels, the Harrington doesn't offer many frills, but it does have low prices and a location right in the center of everything. It's very popular with springtime high-school bus tours and with families who like the two-

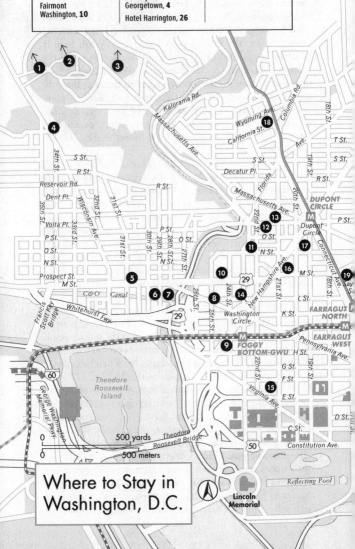

Capital Hilton, **20**	Four Seasons Hotel, **7**	Hotel Helix, **22**
Churchill Hotel, **18**	Georgetown Inn, **1**	Hotel Monaco, **27**
Doubletree Guest Suites, **9**	Georgetown Suites, **6**	Hotel Palomar, **13**
Embassy Suites, **11**	Grand Hyatt Washington, **25**	Hyatt Regency on Capitol Hill, **30**
Embassy Suites at the Chevy Chase Pavilion, **2**	Holiday Inn Capitol, **29**	The Inn at Dupont Circle, **17**
Fairmont Washington, **10**	Holiday Inn Georgetown, **4**	
	Hotel Harrington, **26**	

Where to Stay in Washington, D.C.

J.W. Marriott
Pennsylvania
Avenue, **23**

Marriott
Residence Inn, **12**

Marriott
Wardman Park, **3**

One Washington
Circle Hotel, **14**

Renaissance
Mayflower Hotel, **19**

Renaissance
Washington Hotel, **28**

Ritz-Carlton
Georgetown, **5**

State Plaza Hotel, **15**

St. Gregory, **16**

Washington Court
Hotel, **31**

Washington
Doubletree Hotel, **21**

Washington Suites
Georgetown, **8**

Willard
Inter-Continental, **24**

New Hampshire Ave.

U ST.-
CARDOZO Ⓜ

U St.

16th St.

15th St.

14th St.

T St.

S St.

R St.

Vermont Ave.

10th St.

Ⓜ SHAW-HOWARD
UNIVERSITY

Rhode Island Ave.

S St.

R St.

Florida Ave.

New Jersey Ave.

Lincoln Rd.

R St.

Q St.

Corcoran St.

Q St.

Church St.

St.

Logan
Circle

Ⓜ

Ave.

Q St.

O St.

9th St.

7th St.

P St.

Q St.

O St.

Ⓜ Ⓜ
Ⓜ 22

21

Scott
Circle

Rhode Island

13th St.

12th St.

11th St.

N St.

8th St.

6th St.

5th St.

4th St.

3rd St.

New Jersey Ave.

New York Ave.

M St.

Thomas
Circle

Massachusetts Ave.

M St.

50

1st St.

15th St.

14th St.

L St.

Mt. Vernon
Square

0

McPHERSON
SQUARE

H St.

New York Ave.

15th St.

I St.

1

50

Ⓜ MT. VERNON
SQUARE-UDC

28

Massachusetts Ave.

2nd St.

Union
Station

Ⓜ

25

METRO
CENTER

Ⓜ

G St.

Ⓜ GALLERY
PLACE-
CHINATOWN

H St.

395

Ⓜ UNION
STATION

e White
House

24

23

26

F St.

E St.

27

Ⓜ JUDICIARY
SQUARE

31

30

Louisiana Ave.

The
Ⓜlipse

1

FEDERAL
TRIANGLE Ⓜ

Ⓜ

Indiana Ave.

D St.

ARCHIVES-
NAVY MEMORIAL Ⓜ

Pennsylvania Ave.

US
Capitol

National Museum
American History

Madison Dr.

Smithsonian
Institution

THE MALL

National Gallery
of Art

Jefferson Dr.

Vashington
Monument SMITHSONIAN Ⓜ

Independence Ave.

National
Air and Space
Museum

29

bedroom, two-bathroom deluxe suites. **Pros:** Bargain prices; convenient location. **Cons:** No real amenities; shabby but not chic. **Family Matters:** A good bargain if you can over-look scuffed walls and college-dorm-type furniture. ESPN Zone is across the street, and Metro Center is a block away. Some rooms sleep six. Parking fees are substantially lower than at other hotels, but the garage is four blocks away and has a six-foot clearance. ✉*436 11th St. NW, Downtown* ☎*202/628–8140 or 800/424–8532* ⊕*www. hotel-harrington.com* ⇥*250 rooms* ♿*In-room: refrigerator (some). In-hotel: 3 restaurants, room service, bar, laundry facilities, parking (fee), some pets allowed, no-smoking rooms* ⊟*AE, D, DC, MC, V* Ⓜ*Metro Center.*

WORD OF MOUTH. **"The Hotel Harrington is cheap because it's an old tourist class hotel that caters to tour and student groups. Rooms are small and bare bones but the location is great for tourists." —obxgirl**

$$$ **Hotel Helix.** In the District's Logan Circle neighborhood, the Helix combines attitude with colorful hospitality. The theme here is fame, with blown-up photos of pop culture figures ranging from Martin Luther King Jr. to Little Richard. Lava lamps, psychedelic prints, and other objects create a back-to-the-'60s feel. Some suites have bunk beds and flat-screen TVs. Wireless access and an evening champagne hour are included. The Helix Lounge serves American comfort food such as grilled-cheese sandwiches. **Pros:** Funky Brady Bunch vibe makes for a groovy stay; fun extras like Pop Rocks and wax lips in the minibar; good service. **Cons:** A bit of a schlep to the Metro; no pool; small gym. **Family Matters:** Request the bunk beds if you want them. With the "Bring 'em Along" package, kids can have pizza delivered to the room whenever they want. Even pets can have treats delivered to room. Especially cool for teens and tweens. ✉*1430 Rhode Island Ave. NW, Downtown* ☎*202/462–9001 or 866/508–0658* ⊕*www.hotelhelix.com* ⇥*160 rooms, 18 suites* ♿*In-room: safe, DVD, Wi-Fi. In-hotel: restaurant, room service, bar, gym, laundry service, Wi-Fi, concierge, parking (fee), some pets allowed, no-smoking rooms* ⊟*AE, D, DC, MC, V* Ⓜ*McPherson Sq.*

WORD OF MOUTH. **"If you're looking for a memorable hotel, try exploring the Kimpton chain. They are all near metro, pretty afforable (for DC!) and everyone I've known who's stayed at them has raved—definitely memorable. This would include, Hotel**

George, Hotel Rouge, Hotel Topaz, Hotel Helix, Hotel Madeira, etc." —DoctorCarrie

$$$ ☷**Hotel Monaco.** The 1839 Tariff Building, originally designed by Robert Mills (of Washington Monument fame), was one of the leading neoclassical buildings of its day. The brilliantly restored interior introduces a colorful, playful design to the landmark edifice. Rooms have 15-foot vaulted ceilings, eclectic furnishings, and minibars with martini kits; the "Monte Carlo Tall Rooms" accommodate those needing extra bed space. Upon request, the hotel will deliver companion goldfish to your room for the duration of your stay. The fashionable Poste Brasserie serves contemporary American cuisine, and the Verizon Center is right across the street. **Pros:** Fun location next to Spy Museum; near great restaurants and shops and Metro. **Cons:** Not a quiet part of town; pricey; no pool. **Family Matters:** Close to attractions that tweens and teens like but require admission such as the Museum of Crime and Punishment, Madame Toussauds, and the Spy Museum. Children under 16 stay for free. No adjoining rooms, but rollaway beds available for a fee. Gifts at check-in, complimentary fresh cookies usually disappear in 30 minutes. ✉*700 F St. NW, Penn Quarter* ☎*202/628–7177 or 877/202–5411* ⊕*www.monaco-dc. com* ⇦*167 rooms, 16 suites* &*In-room: safe, DVD, Wi-Fi. In-hotel: restaurant, room service, gym, concierge, laundry service, parking (fee), some pets allowed, no-smoking rooms* ▤*AE, D, DC, MC, V* Ⓜ*Gallery Pl./Chinatown.*

WORD OF MOUTH. "When staying at the Hotel Monaco, near Gallery Place, you can request a pet goldfish for your room. They will feed and clean the bowl, so all you have to do is stare at the fish."—mcnyc

$$$$ ☷ **JW Marriott Pennsylvania Avenue.** From the location near the White House to the (literally) monumental views from the top floors, it's hard to forget you are in the nation's capital when you stay here. A recent room renovation in 2007 brought with it plush linens, new signature beds, and modern technology that will keep business travelers plugged in. The lobby is also new following a $20 million face-lift in 2008. **Pros:** In the heart of town; recently updated rooms, elevators, and lobby. **Cons:** With more than 700 rooms not an intimate hotel, pricey. **Family Matters:** Families reaping the rewards of Marriott points can't beat the monumental location near where the Mar-

---

ABOUT THE MAYFLOWER

■ President Franklin D. Roosevelt wrote, "The only thing we have to fear is fear itself" in room 776.

■ J. Edgar Hoover ate lunch at the Mayflower restaurant almost every weekday for 20 years. He almost always brought his own diet salad dressing.

■ Walt Disney once dined on the Mayflower's roof.

■ The state dinner celebrating the 1979 Arab-Israeli peace treaty was held here.

■ Winston Churchill sat for a portrait here.

■ Members of the House interviewed Monica Lewinsky in the 10th-floor presidential suite while pursuing the impeachment of President Bill Clinton.

■ Former New York Governor Eliot Spitzer (aka "Client 9") was allegedly visited by high-price call girl "Kristen" in room 871 on February 13, 2008. The resulting scandal caused him to resign.

---

riotts opened their first business: a root beer stand in 1927. More luxurious than most Marriott hotels, the JW brand is considered one level below their Ritz-Carlton line. Connected to the Shops at National Place with a food court and anchored by Filene's Basement, the famed discounter that opened in Boston in 1909. ⊠ *1331 Pennsylvania Ave. NW, Downtown* ☏ *202/393–2000 or 800/228–9290* ⊕ *www.jwmarriottdc.com* ↬ *729 rooms, 33 suites* ♿ *In-room: safe, Internet, Wi-Fi. In-hotel: 2 restaurants, room service, bars, pool, gym, concierge, laundry service (fee), executive floor, parking (fee), no-smoking room* ⊟ *AE, D, DC, MC, V* Ⓜ *Metro Center.*

$$$ ☒ **Renaissance Mayflower Hotel.** The magnificent block-long lobby with its series of antique crystal chandeliers and gilded columns is a destination in and of itself. Guest rooms at this grande dame hotel, which opened its doors in 1925 for Calvin Coolidge's inauguration, have been treated to a recent makeover and are done in soothing yellows, greens, tans, and blues. Town and Country, the hotel's inside-the-Beltway power bar, has been a place for political wheeling and dealing for nearly as long as the hotel. Sam the bartender mixes up 101 martinis to keep guests happily in the drink. Work off the booze and the crab cakes, a favorite on the menu at the hotel's elegant Café Promenade, in the new spalike fitness center. **Pros:** Gorgeous lobby; new fitness center with natural light and new equipment; a few steps from the Metro. **Cons:** Rooms vary in size; recent

upgrade stopped short of flat-screen TVs and Wi-Fi in the guest rooms; no pool. **Family Matters:** The grande dame of Marriott's Renaissance line caters to business types but welcomes families. Guests have access to the local YMCA, which has a 25-meter pool. ⊠*1127 Connecticut Ave. NW, Downtown* ☎*202/347–3000 or 800/228–9290* ⊕*www.marriott.com* ⌁*580 rooms, 74 suites* ⚿*In-room: Internet. In-hotel: Wi-Fi, restaurant, room service, bar, gym, concierge, laundry service, executive floor, parking (fee), no-smoking rooms* ☰*AE, D, DC, MC, V* Ⓜ*Farragut N.*

$$ ▦**Renaissance Washington D.C. Hotel.** Close to the Washington Convention Center and MCI Center, the Renaissance offers extensive business services and guest rooms with special mattresses and linens to help you get a good night's rest. The hotel includes a 10,000-square-foot fitness center and indoor lap pool. The casual restaurant, 15 Squares, serves regional American food; the Presidents' Sports Bar is decorated with black-and-white photos of U.S. presidents at play; Starbuck's serves its signature brew in the lobby. **Pros:** Convenient to convention center; near Metro; guest rooms updated in 2006. **Cons:** Big hotel, busy convention hotel. **Family Matters:** A good location and a staff that will accommodate a family with two adults and three kids in one room may offset the lack of family-friendly amenities such as a pool. ⊠*999 9th St. NW, Downtown* ☎*202/898–9000 or 800/228–9898* ⊕*www.marriott.com* ⌁*775 rooms, 26 suites* ⚿ *In-hotel: Wi-Fi, 2 restaurants, room service, bar, pool, gym, concierge, laundry service, parking (fee), some pets allowed, no-smoking rooms* ☰*AE, D, DC, MC, V* Ⓜ*Gallery Pl./Chinatown.*

$ ▦**Washington Doubletree Hotel.** Just off Scott Circle, the Doubletree offers spacious guest rooms that are up for renovation in October 2008, with comfortable beds, well-equipped workstations, CD players, coffeemakers, and robes. An American bistro, 15 Ria, brings a New York sensibility to the hotel, which is only six blocks from the White House. **Pros:** Child-friendly; good location; fitness center. **Cons:** No pool; limited street parking at times. **Family Matters:** Right between Metro's orange and red lines. Cookies at check-in. No microwaves. Refrigerators upon request for a fee. One block from Starbucks and Caribou Coffee. ⊠*1515 Rhode Island Ave. NW, Downtown* ☎*202/232–7000 or 800/222–8733* ⊕*www.washington.doubletree.com* ⌁*181rooms, 39 suites* ⚿*In-room: safe, Internet, refrigerator. In-hotel: Wi-Fi, restau-*

rant, gym, concierge, parking (fee) ⊟*AE, D, DC, MC, V* Ⓜ*Dupont Circle.*

$$$-$$$$ 🏨**Willard InterContinental.** The historic Willard has long been a favorite of American presidents and other newsmakers. Superb service and a wealth of amenities are hallmarks of the hotel, two blocks from the White House. The spectacular beaux arts lobby showcases great columns, sparkling chandeliers, mosaic floors, and elaborate ceilings. Period detail is reflected in the rooms, which have elegant, Federal-style furniture and sleek marble bathrooms. The hotel's formal restaurant, the Willard Room, has won nationwide acclaim for its modern take on French and American dishes. The Willard has opened its own history gallery, which chronicles the hotel's legendary past with photos, newspaper articles, and artifacts. There's also an outstanding spa and fitness center. **Pros:** Luxurious hotel; great location; noted restaurant. **Cons:** Expensive; no pool. **Family Matters:** Washington's most famous hotel might be fancy, but its location and service are fabulous. Holiday decorations are some of best in D.C. Children can order "kidtails" that go way beyond Shirley Temples. Martin Luther King Jr. drafted his "I Have a Dream" speech here. ⊠*1401 Pennsylvania Ave. NW, Downtown* ☎*202/628–9100 or 800/827–1747* ⊕*www.washington.interconti.com* ⊅*292 rooms, 40 suites* ⌂*In-room: safe, Internet. In-hotel: 2 restaurants, room service, bar, gym, concierge, laundry service, parking (fee), some pets allowed, no-smoking rooms* ⊟*AE, D, DC, MC, V* Ⓜ*Metro Center.*

DUPONT CIRCLE

$$ 🏨**Churchill Hotel.** This historic beaux arts hotel offers comfort and elegance right outside Dupont Circle. Spacious rooms have recently gotten a face-lift and include a small work and sitting area. The building's hilltop location means that many guest rooms have excellent views of Washington. The staff goes out of its way to be helpful. **Pros:** Friendly service; good-size rooms; frequent guest program. **Cons:** Far walk to Metro; uphill from Metro to hotel; elevators sometimes run slow. **Family Matters:** Tables in suites are large enough to accommodate a family of four; request extra chairs. Refrigerators in all rooms; microwaves upon request. Discount trolley tickets at front desk. ⊠*1914 Connecticut Ave. NW, Dupont Circle* ☎*202/797–2000 or 800/424–2464* ⊕*www. thechurchillhotel.com* ⊅*91 rooms, 82 suites* ⌂*In-room: kitchen (some), Wi-Fi. In-hotel: Wi-Fi, restaurant, room*

service, bar, gym, concierge, laundry service, parking (fee) ⊟AE, D, DC, MC, V ⓂDupont Circle.

$$$$ ☷**Hotel Palomar.** The Palomar is winning hearts and minds with space, style, and a pro-pets policy. Perhaps accordingly, standard rooms here are some of the largest in town. Kimpton's signature animal prints make the scene in leopard-stripe robes, crocodile-pattern carpets, and faux-lynx throws; plush purple and fuschia furnishings splash color on muted chocolate-beige rooms. Although some bathrooms are surprisingly small, L'Occitane toiletries ease the blow; other up-to-the-minute details include laptop-size safes and iPod docking stations. **Pros:** Spacious rooms; outdoor pool; fun extras. **Cons:** Smallish baths; busy public areas not cozy for sitting. **Family Matters:** Upon arrival, kids select a toy from a treasure box. At the on-site restaurant, kids can watch their pizza's creation. Water toys and a lifeguard are at the pool from 10 to 8, but kids must have an adult with them. Dancers of all ages ask about the Ballet Suite with its bar and mirror. Milk and cookies delivered once a day when kids want them. The largest Kimpton in the city has more flexibility with rates particularly in the late summer. ✉2121 P St. NW, Dupont Circle ☎202/448–1800 ⊕www.hotelpalomar-dc.com ⌖315 rooms, 20 suites ♿ In-room: safe, refrigerator, DVD, Internet, Wi-Fi. In-hotel: restaurant, room service, bar, pool, gym, laundry service, parking (fee), pets allowed, no-smoking rooms ⊟AE, D, DC, MC, V ⓂDupont Circle.

★ Fodor'sChoice ☷**The Inn at Dupont Circle South.** This is the inn
$ where everybody knows your name. Innkeeper Carolyn jokes that her guests are "her babies," and the personal attention shows: there are many repeat customers here, and some keep in touch even when they are not in town. Most rooms have private baths; all have TVs, featherbeds, and typical inn decor complete with doilies, bric-a-brac, and Impressionist posters. Carolyn serves a hot breakfast in the parlor or on the sun porch. ▪TIP→ **The Nook Room is aptly named and budget friendly at $95 per night.** **Pros:** Personable innkeeper; personalized service; great Dupont location across from Metro; children welcome. **Cons:** Older home complete with creaking floors; no elevator; not all rooms have private baths. **Family Matters:** Cribs available upon request as are chocolate-chip pancakes in the morning if you ask the night before. ✉1312 19th St. NW, Dupont Circle ☎202/467–6777 or 866/467–2100 ⊕thedupont-collection.com ⌖8 rooms ♿In room: safe, refrigerator, Wi-Fi. In-hotel: no elevator, laundry facilities, Wi-Fi, airport

shuttle, parking (fee), no-smoking rooms ⊟ *AE, MC, V* ⊙*BP* Ⓜ*Dupont Circle.*

$$$ 🖼**Marriott Residence Inn.** It's remarkable that a commercial chain can feel so cozy, but this Residence Inn does just that by offering a small fireplace sitting room right off the lobby. The hotel has studios and one- and two-bedroom suites, excellent for business travelers or families. An evening reception (Monday through Thursday) is offered with complimentary snacks, and STARS Bistro and Bar next door has an innovative bar with piano and cabaret-style singing on weekends and half-price wine nights on Monday and Tuesday. **Pros:** Breakfast buffet included; good choice for families. **Cons:** Standard chain hotel; no unique touches. **Family Matters:** In the midst of cafés and restaurants. Metro is two blocks away. Pet-friendly. ⊠*2120 P St. NW, Dupont Circle* ☎*202/466–6800 or 800/331–3131* ⊕*www. marriott.com/wasri* ⇨*107 suites* ⌂*In-room: kitchen, Internet. In-hotel: Wi-Fi, restaurant, room service, gym, laundry facilities, parking (fee), no-smoking rooms* ⊟*AE, D, DC, MC, V* ⊙*CP* Ⓜ*Dupont Circle.*

GEORGETOWN

★ Fodor'sChoice 🖼**Four Seasons Hotel.** Having completed a whopping $40 million renovation in 2005, the Four Seasons has
$$$$ reasserted its role as Washington's leading hotel. Impeccable service and a wealth of amenities have long made this a favorite with celebrities, hotel connoisseurs, and families. Luxurious, ultramodern rooms offer heavenly beds, flat-screen digital TVs with DVD players, and French limestone or marble baths with separate showers and sunken tubs. A 2,000-piece original art collection graces the walls, and a walk through the corridors seems like a visit to a wing of the MoMA or the Met. The formal Seasons restaurant offers traditional dishes with an elegant twist, as well as a popular Sunday brunch. The sophisticated spa here is one of the best in town. **Pros:** Edge of Georgetown makes for a fabulous location; lap of luxury feel; Four Seasons service. **Cons:** Expensive; challenging street parking, expensive ($42 a night) valet service. **Family Matters:** Service begins with babies who are set up with cribs complete with sheets and bumper pads; and keeps going for toddlers who get a personalized cookie, balloons, and bath toy; and continues for teenagers who will find magazines, popcorn, and other snacks in the room. ⊠*2800 Pennsylvania Ave. NW, Georgetown* ☎*202/342–0444 or 800/332–3442* ⊕*www.*

fourseasons.com/washington ⇨*160 rooms, 51 suites* ☆*In-room: safe, Internet. In-hotel: restaurant, room service, bar, pool, gym, concierge, children's programs (ages 5–16), parking (fee), some pets allowed, no-smoking rooms* ⊟*AE, D, DC, MC, V* Ⓜ*Foggy Bottom.*

$ ☒**Georgetown Inn.** Reminiscent of a gentleman's sporting club, this quiet, Federal-era, redbrick hotel seems like something from the 1700s. The spacious guest rooms are decorated in a colonial style. The hotel, in the heart of historic Georgetown, lies near shopping, dining, galleries, and theaters. The publike Daily Grill restaurant serves American cuisine. **Pros:** Shoppers will love the location; good price for the neighborhood. **Cons:** A hike to Metro; crowded area. **Family Matters:** On weekends the inn caters to many families visiting Georgetown University students. Some rooms with two queen-size beds and sleeper sofas can accommodate six people. Complimentary coffee in the morning and a beverage such as lemonade or hot chocolate in the afternoon. Good choice for teens and tweens who like to shop. Perhaps too far from Metro to be a great option for those with younger children ✉*1310 Wisconsin Ave. NW, Georgetown* ☎*202/333–8900 or 800/368–5922* ⊕*www.georgetowncollection.com* ⇨*86 rooms, 10 suites* ☆*In-room: Wi-Fi. In-hotel: Wi-Fi, restaurant, room service, bar, gym, parking (fee)* ⊟*AE, D, DC, MC, V* Ⓜ*Foggy Bottom.*

$–$$ ☒**Georgetown Suites.** If you consider standard hotel rooms cramped and overpriced, you'll find this establishment a welcome surprise. Consisting of two buildings a block apart in the heart of Georgetown, the hotel has suites of varying sizes. All have fully equipped kitchens and separate sitting rooms, and include free local calls and continental breakfast. **Pros:** All suites; good price; good choice for a family that wants to spread out. **Cons:** Parking can be challenging at times; not a lot of character. **Family Matters:** Free Wi-Fi, flat-screen TVs, coin-operated laundry machines. The circulator bus that goes downtown stops a block away. ✉*1111 30th St. NW, Georgetown* ☎*202/298–7800 or 800/348–7203* ⊕*www.georgetownsuites.com* ⇨*216 suites* ☆*In-room: kitchen, Wi-Fi. In-hotel: gym, laundry facilities, laundry service, public Wi-Fi, parking (fee), no-smoking rooms* ⊟*AE, D, DC, MC, V* ⦿*CP* Ⓜ*Foggy Bottom.*

$–$$ ☒**Holiday Inn Georgetown.** On the edge of Georgetown, this Holiday Inn is a short walk from dining, shopping, Dumbarton Oaks, the National Cathedral, and Georgetown University. Many guest rooms offer a scenic view of the Washington skyline. There's a free shuttle service to the Metro. ■TIP→**Kids under 12 eat free, and rooms offer video games. Pros:** Quiet neighborhood; walk to Whole Foods and a selection of restaurants. **Cons:** Not near a Metro; a bit off-the-beaten path for downtown sightseeing. **Family Matters:** Microwave and refrigerator upon request. Quarter mile from Whole Foods and half mile from Montrose Park. ✉*2101 Wisconsin Ave. NW, Georgetown* ☎*202/338–4600 or 800/465–4329* ⊕*www.higeorgetown. com* ⮑*281 rooms, 4 suites* ⌂*In-room: Internet. In-hotel: restaurant, room service, bar, pool, gym, laundry facilities, parking (fee), no-smoking rooms* ▤*AE, D, DC, MC, V* Ⓜ*Foggy Bottom.*

$$$$ ▧**Ritz-Carlton Georgetown.** D.C.'s second Ritz-Carlton is smaller than its Foggy Bottom sister and a complete departure from the traditional style typical to the chain. Opened in 2003, this understated yet sophisticated Ritz is adjacent to the C&O Canal and built on the site of Georgetown's 1932 incinerator. The contemporary hotel is a stone's throw from the waterfront and a block from M Street, Georgetown's main shopping street. Guest rooms are connected by brick hallways with carefully chosen pieces from regional American artists. The upper-level rooms and suites facing south have amazing views of the Potomac, and all have feather duvets, goose-down pillows, marble baths and access to a personal concierge. The hotel's sexy Fahrenheit Restaurant serves contemporary American cuisine. **Pros:** Quaint luxury boutique hotel; steps away from Georgetown restaurants and shopping; refined service. **Cons:** Not on the Metro; expensive. **Family Matters:** You won't find Ritz Kids specials in D.C. but family packages might include treasure hunts, walking tours and history books. Ben & Jerry's and Häagen-Dazs ice cream parlors and two bakeries, Georgetown Cupcake and Baked and Wired, are within an easy walk of this sweet spot in the city. ✉*3100 South St. NW, Georgetown,* ☎*202/912–4200 or 800/241–3333* ⊕*www. ritzcarlton.com/hotels/georgetown* ⮑*86 rooms, 29 suites* ⌂*In-room: safe, Wi-Fi. In-hotel: restaurant, room service, bar, gym, concierge, laundry service, Wi-Fi, parking (fee), no-smoking rooms* ▤*AE, D, DC, MC, V.*

$$ ▧**Washington Suites Georgetown.** Just outside the center of Georgetown, this older all-suites accommodation offers families and long-term-stay travelers an alternative to standard hotel rooms. Each suite has a fully equipped kitchen, a small living and dining area, and a separate bedroom and bath. ■TIP→**Stock your fridge at the Trader Joe's across**

the street. Fresh pastries, juices, and cereal are served each morning in the breakfast room. Many of the staff members have worked at the hotel for years and know regular guests by name. **Pros:** Friendly staff; good for long-term stays; good value. **Cons:** No-frills; breakfast room can be crowded when hotel is full. **Family Matters:** Bag of cookies at check-in. Receptions on Tuesday from 6 to 7 catered by Red, Hot and Blue barbecue during the summer and other restaurants the rest of the year. Pet-friendly. Just outside of Georgetown. ⊠ *2500 Pennsylvania Ave. NW, Georgetown* ☎ *202/333–8060 or 877/736–2500* ⊕ *www.washingtonsuitesgeorgetown.com* ⟿ *124 suites* ₲ *In-room: kitchen, Internet. In-hotel: gym, laundry facilities, parking (fee), no-smoking rooms* ⊟ *AE, D, DC, MC, V* ◎ *CP* Ⓜ *Foggy Bottom.*

SOUTHWEST

$–$$ 🏨 **Holiday Inn Capitol.** One block from the National Air and Space Museum, this family-friendly hotel is also well equipped for business travelers, including free Wi-Fi. Rooms were upgraded in 2005 with new beds, granite vanities in the bathrooms, and include coffeemakers and hair dryers. The downtown sightseeing trolley stops here, and you can buy discount tickets for the National Air and Space Museum's IMAX movies at the front desk. Kids under 19 stay free, and those under 12 eat for free at Smithson's Restaurant. **Pros:** Family-friendly; rooftop pool; close to museums. **Cons:** Limited restaurants nearby; not much going on in the neighborhood at night. **Family Matters:** Rooftop outdoor pool may open as early as mid-May and stay open as late as October, weather permitting. Refrigerators in all rooms. Train traffic near the back of the hotel may disturb light sleepers. Near fast-food restaurants, including McDonald's and Quiznos. ⊠ *550 C St. SW, Southwest* ☎ *202/479–4000 or 877/477–4674* ⊕ *www.holidayinncapitol.com* ⟿ *532 rooms, 13 suites* ₲ *In-room: Internet, Wi-Fi. In-hotel: restaurant, room service, bar, pool, gym, laundry facilities, parking, no-smoking rooms (fee)* ⊟ *AE, D, DC, MC, V* ◎ *BP* Ⓜ *L'Enfant Plaza.*

WEST END & FOGGY BOTTOM

$$–$$$ 🏨 **Doubletree Guest Suites.** Among the row houses on this stretch of New Hampshire Avenue, you might not realize at first how close you are to the Kennedy Center and Georgetown. This all-suites hotel has a tiny lobby, but its

roomy one- and two-bedroom suites have full kitchens and living-dining areas with desks, dining tables, and sofa beds. The rooftop pool provides a place to relax after summertime sightseeing. You receive chocolate-chip cookies upon arrival. **Pros:** Near Metro and supermarket; quiet neighborhood; good online deals sometimes available. **Cons:** Far from the museums and major attractions. **Family Matters:** Like many D.C. hotels, it's been renovated in 2008 in preparation for the presidential inauguration. Not near kid-friendly restaurants and the pool is only open from Memorial Day through Labor Day. ⊠ *801 New Hampshire Ave. NW, Foggy Bottom* ☎ *202/785–2000 or 800/222–8733* ⊕ *www.doubletree.com* ⟿ *105 suites* ⌂ *In-room: kitchen, Wi-Fi. In-hotel: room service, pool, laundry facilities, laundry service, Wi-Fi, parking (fee), some pets allowed, no-smoking rooms* ⊟ *AE, D, DC, MC, V* Ⓜ *Foggy Bottom/GWU.*

$$–$$$ 🏨 **Embassy Suites.** Plants cascade over balconies beneath a skylight in this modern hotel's atrium, which is filled with classical columns, plaster lions, wrought-iron lanterns, waterfalls, and tall palms. Within walking distance of Georgetown, the Kennedy Center, and Dupont Circle, the suites here are suitable for both business travelers and families. Beverages are complimentary at the nightly manager's reception, and the rate includes cooked-to-order breakfast. There's a kids' corner with movies and games, and the Italian restaurant, Trattoria Nicola's, serves lunch and dinner. **Pros:** Family-friendly; all suites; pool to keep the little ones—and sweaty tourists—happy. **Cons:** Not a lot of character; museums not in walking distance. **Family Matters:** Practical for parents. TVs in both rooms of suites, near a Walgreens and Trader Joe's. Family fun includes a game room with air hockey, pinball machines, and Pac-Man. One of 10 hotels in the city to offer a Panda package. At 9 AM and 9 PM daily, kids feed the huge koi fish in the lobby. ⊠ *1250 22nd St. NW, West End* ☎ *202/857–3388 or 800/362–2779* ⊕ *www.embassysuites.com* ⟿ *318 suites* ⌂ *In-room: refrigerator, Wi-Fi. In-hotel: restaurant, room service, bar, pool, gym, laundry service, parking (fee), no-smoking rooms* ⊟ *AE, D, DC, MC, V* ⏚ *BP* Ⓜ *Foggy Bottom/GWU or Dupont Circle.*

$$$$ 🏨 **Fairmont Washington.** The large, glassed-in lobby and about a third of the bright, spacious rooms overlook the Fairmont's central courtyard and gardens. Rooms are comfortable, if not the city's most modern. The informal Juniper restaurant serves mid-Atlantic fare and has courtyard dining; there's a champagne brunch on Sunday in the Colonnade Room. ■TIP→The health club is one of the best in the city. Families have access to the pool, kids' menus and crayons in the restaurant, and a babysitting referral service. The Fairmont also offers family packages, such as the Panda Package, a trip to visit the pandas at the National Zoo. **Pros:** Fitness-focused guests will love the health club; lots of kid-friendly features. **Cons:** Pricey; not many attractions in walking distance. **Family Matters:** At 50 feet long, the pool is one of the largest hotel pools in the city. Every fourth Sunday is a chocolate lovers' brunch. December is chockfull of activities for children, from cookie decorating to Santa visits. ⊠*2401 M St. NW, Foggy Bottom* ☎*202/429–2400 or 877/222–2266* ⊕*www.fairmont.com* ↩*406 rooms, 9 suites* ♿*In-room: safe, Internet. In-hotel: restaurant, room service, bar, pool, gym, concierge, executive floor, parking (fee), some pets allowed, no-smoking rooms* ▭*AE, D, DC, MC, V* Ⓜ*Foggy Bottom/GWU.*

$$ ⛫**One Washington Circle Hotel.** Given its location near the State Department and George Washington University, this all-suites business hotel is a relative bargain. The suites have modern, vibrant furnishings and feature separate bedrooms, living rooms, dining areas, and walk-out balconies; some have full kitchens. The American-style Circle Bistro is popular with locals. **Pros:** All suites; balconies; near Metro. **Cons:** Some street noise; small bathrooms. **Family Matters:** Different configurations of suites that range from 400 to 700 square feet. Cots are an extra \$25 per day. Less than a block from Foggy Bottom Metro. ⊠*1 Washington Circle NW, Foggy Bottom,* ☎*202/872–1680 or 800/424–9671* ⊕*www.thecirclehotel.com* ↩*151 suites* ♿*In-room: kitchen, Internet. In-hotel: Wi-Fi, restaurant, room service, bar, pool, gym, laundry facilities, laundry service, parking (fee), no-smoking rooms* ▭*AE, D, DC, MC, V* Ⓜ*Foggy Bottom/GWU.*

$$–$$$ ⛫**St. Gregory.** Once the FCC building, the handsome St. Gregory caters to business and leisure travelers who appreciate the spacious accommodations that include fully stocked kitchens. All rooms include turndown service, a newspaper, and shoe shine. The modern lobby, which has a sculpture of Marilyn Monroe in her *Seven Year Itch* pose, connects to the M Street Bar & Grill. **Pros:** Big rooms; good for long-term stays. **Cons:** Far from the Mall and museums; area is sleepy at night. **Family Matters:** Pantry kitchens with refrigerators, microwaves, and stoves are in 85 of the 100 suites. Up to two adults and three children

up to age 13 per room or suite. Stock up the refrigerator from Trader Joes, four blocks away. ⊠*2033 M St. NW, West End,* ☎*202/530–3600 or 800/829–5034* ⊕*www. stgregoryhotelwdc.com* ⇨*54 rooms, 100 suites* ⌂*In-room: kitchen (some), Internet. In-hotel: restaurant, room service, gym, concierge, laundry service, executive floor, parking (fee), no-smoking rooms* ⊟*AE, D, DC, MC, V* Ⓜ*Dupont Circle.*

$$ ▦**State Plaza Hotel.** No Washington hotel gets you quicker access to the State Department, which sits across the street. There's nothing distinguished about the lobby, but the spacious guest rooms have kitchenettes and lighted dressing tables, and the hotel staff is friendly and attentive. Guests receive a complimentary newspaper and a shoe shine. Nightly turndown service is provided. **Pros:** All suites; free Internet access; walk to Metro. **Cons:** Far from museums; not a lot of character. **Family Matters:** Close to the beloved Albert Einstein Memorial, the 7,000-ton tribute to *Time* magazine's person of the century, welcomes kids of all ages in his lap. Microwaves available by request for rooms that don't have them. Monumental Package includes T-shirts, water bottles, camera, and continental breakfast for every day of stay. ⊠*2117 E St. NW, Foggy Bottom* ☎*202/861–8200 or 800/424–2859* ⊕*www.stateplaza.com* ⇨*214 rooms, 16 suites* ⌂*In-room: kitchen, Internet. In-hotel: restaurant, room service, gym, laundry service, parking (fee), no-smoking rooms* ⊟*AE, D, DC, MC, V* Ⓜ*Foggy Bottom/GWU.*

WOODLEY PARK & UPPER NORTHWEST

$–$$ ▦**Embassy Suites.** You can feel good about your carbon footprint as you enjoy the newly renovated suites at this green hotel. The hotel cut its energy usage by a third in 2007 and boasts efficient heating and cooling systems in every suite, energy star appliances, a saline pool, and even prints with soy-based ink. Families will love the free breakfast and afternoon reception, two-room suites, and being attached to two shopping malls complete with dining and movie theaters. You can hop on the Metro without ever stepping outside. **Pros:** Bethesda, with more than 150 restaurants and 20 art galleries, is one Metro stop away in MD. **Cons:** The 6-foot 3-inch garage might be too short for some minivans. Must be at least 18 to use the exercise room. **Family Matters:** Most of the nearby Mall stores cater to adults with two notable exceptions. Borders Books has an extensive children's department, and the World Market sells novelty candy, such as 10-inch gummy gators, and craft kits, but lots of family-friendly restaurants are nearby, including the Cheesecake Factory, the Corner Bakery, and Booeymongers. ⊠*4300 Military Rd., Upper Northwest* ☎*202/362–9300 or 800/760–6120* ⊕*www.embassysuitesdc.com* ⇆*198 suites* �*In-room: refrigerator, Internet. In-hotel: room service, bar, pool, gym, laundry service, parking (fee), no-smoking rooms* ⊟*AE, D, DC, MC, V* ⊚*BP* Ⓜ*Friendship Heights.*

$$$ 🖼**Marriott Wardman Park.** You almost get the sense that you stepped into a minicity when you first enter the Marriott Wardman Park. The hotel, housed in a hard-to-miss redbrick Victorian building behind the Woodley Park Metro, just got a $100 million upgrade, leaving all guest rooms with splashes of bright colors typical of many a Marriott these days. Rooms in the decidedly quieter 1918 Wardman Tower have not been renovated yet, but some will prefer its lower-key energy. The hotel's ground level has tons of seating, food choices, a full-service Starbucks, and lots of places to plug in. Kids will love the outdoor pool and the proximity to the pandas. **Pros:** On top of Metro; light-filled sundeck; pretty residential neighborhood with some good ethnic restaurants. **Cons:** Busy; loud; lines at restaurants when hotel is at capacity. **Family Matters:** The nearby Omni Shoreham has more family-friendly amenities but Marriott offers a Panda Package that includes hotel parking, a stuffed panda, and a donation to a panda conservation fund. The gardens are gorgeous in the spring, when more than 44,000 tulips emerge. ⊠*2660 Woodley Rd. NW, Woodley Park* ☎*202/328–2000 or 800/228–9290* ⊕*www.marriott.com* ⇆*1,171 rooms, 145 suites* �*In-room: safe, kitchen (some),refrigerator (some), Internet. In-hotel: 2 restaurants, room service, 3 bars, pool, gym, spa, laundry service, concierge, executive floor, Wi-Fi, parking (fee), some pets allowed, no-smoking rooms* ⊟*AE, D, DC, MC, V* Ⓜ*Woodley Park/Zoo.*

★ Fodor'sChoice 🖼**Omni Shoreham Hotel.** A $15-million face-lift
$$$–$$$$ has enhanced this already elegant hotel overlooking Rock Creek Park, and the historic property is aging gracefully. The light-filled guest rooms have a soothing garden palette and feature flat-screen TVs and marble bathrooms. The vast art deco-and-Renaissance–style lobby welcomes visitors, who in the past have ranged from the Beatles to heads of state (the hotel has played host to inaugural balls since its 1930 opening). There is even a resident ghost said to haunt

Suite 870. Families will love the larger-than-typical guest rooms, kiddie pool, bird-watching, bike rentals, and movie nights. ■TIP→**Parents: Ask the concierge about story time and cuddles with the guide dog for the blind who trains at the hotel. Pros:** Newly renovated historic property; great outdoor pool and sundeck; good views from many rooms. **Cons:** Not downtown; big. **Family Matters:** Fun begins at check-in when children receive a bag of trinkets. After a day at the nearby zoo, kids bird-watch with binoculars, play croquet, or swing on hammocks—all within eyesight of parents on the patio or in the gardens. Summer movie nights are held the same night as all-adult happy hours. Ghost tours on weekends in October and Christmas trees line the hallways in December. Photos with Santa cost $1 with proceeds benefiting the Special Olympics. ✉*2500 Calvert St. NW, Woodley Park* ☎*202/234–0700 or 800/545–8700* ⊕*www. omnihotels.com* ➩*818 rooms, 16 suites* ⌂*In-room: safe, refrigerator (some), DVD (some), VCR (some), Wi-Fi. In-hotel: restaurant, room service, bar, pool, gym, spa, bicycles, children's programs (ages 3–13), concierge, laundry service, parking (fee), some pets allowed, no-smoking rooms* ⊟*AE, D, DC, MC, V* Ⓜ*Woodley Park/Zoo.*

SUBURBAN MARYLAND

Hopping on the Metro from downtown Bethesda is easy. You can either walk or take a free trolley. With more than 100 restaurants, you can nibble your way around the world in this town, which has become a dining destination. Every Wednesday and weekend in a low white building on Wisconsin Avenue in the midst of high-rise buildings, the Montgomery Women's Cooperative sells baked goods, fresh fruits, and crafts, a tradition since the early 1930s.

$–$$ ▧**Bethesda Court Hotel.** Bright burgundy awnings frame the entrance to this comfortable, intimate, three-story inn, where there's a lovely, well-tended courtyard. The relaxed hotel is two blocks from the Bethesda Metro and set back from busy Wisconsin Avenue. Nearby downtown Bethesda is home to restaurants, shops, and an independent movie theater. ■TIP→**Evening tea with cookies is complimentary, as are limousine service and shuttles to the National Institutes of Health. Pros:** Free Wi-Fi; close to Metro; basic continental breakfast included. **Cons:** Far from downtown and major attractions; small rooms; no room service. **Family Matters:** Free limousine service extends to destinations within 3 mi, including three large shopping malls. Complimentary breakfast includes pastries, fruit, and cold cereal. Rollaway beds, refrigerators and microwaves available at no extra charge, but the snacks at the front desk will set you back a dollar. ⊠ *7740 Wisconsin Ave., Bethesda, MD* ☎ *301/656–2100 or 800/874–0050* ⊕ *www.bethesdacourtwashdc.com* ⇴ *74 rooms, 1 suite* ♿ *In-room: safe, refrigerator, Wi-Fi. In-hotel: Wi-Fi, gym, laundry facilities, parking (fee)* ☐ *AE, D, DC, MC, V* ⊙ *CP* Ⓜ *Bethesda.*

$$–$$$ 🖳 **Doubletree Hotel Bethesda.** Newly renovated in 2007, the Doubletree has guest rooms that are larger than those at comparable hotels, with firm, comfortable beds, ample working space, and free morning newspaper delivery. The hotel caters to business travelers with a free shuttle to the nearby Metro (about five blocks on foot), the National Institutes of Health, and the Naval Medical Center. **Pros:** Rooftop pool; hypoallergenic rooms available with allergy-free pillows and bedding; in-room air purification systems; unscented and antimicrobial products used; good value. **Cons:** Outside the city; far from major attractions; a bit of a walk to Metro and downtown Bethesda. **Family Matters:** The good news for gamers is that you can get X-Box turned on at 4 PM; the bad news is that it's in the lobby. Imagination Stage for children is three blocks away. Weekend rates are usually lower. ⊠ *8120 Wisconsin Ave., Bethesda, MD* ☎ *301/652–2000 or 888/465–4329* ⊕ *www. doubletreebethesda.com* ⇴ *269 rooms, 7 suites* ♿ *In-room: safe, Wi-Fi. In-hotel: restaurant, bar, pool, gym, laundry facilities, laundry service, parking (fee)* ☐ *AE, D, DC, MC, V* Ⓜ *Bethesda.*

$$$ 🖳 **Hyatt Regency Bethesda.** This hotel stands atop the Bethesda Metro station on Wisconsin Avenue, the main artery between Bethesda and Georgetown; downtown Washington is a 15-minute Metro ride away. Well-equipped guest rooms have sleigh beds and mahogany furnishings, as well as large workstations for business travelers. They also include 32-inch TVs and marble baths. The rooftop fitness center and indoor pool are welcome retreats from a busy day in the city. **Pros:** On top of Metro; walk to dozens of restaurants and two movie theaters; indoor pool. **Cons:** Reports of noise traveling up from the atrium. **Family Matters:** The whirlpool next to the covered pool allows adults to keep an eye on kids while relaxing. Complimentary continental breakfast for AAA members. Sculptures and a waterfall make the plaza at the Bethesda Metro a nice place to hang out in the early evening. ⊠ *1 Bethesda Metro Center, 7400 block of Wisconsin Ave., Bethesda,*

MD ☎*301/657–1234 or 800/233–1234* ⊕*www.bethesda. hyatt.com* ⋑*391 rooms, 7 suites* ⌂*In-room: Wi-Fi. In-hotel: Wi-Fi, 3 restaurants, room service, 2 bars, pool, gym, concierge, laundry service, parking (fee)* ⊟*AE, D, DC, MC, V* Ⓜ*Bethesda.*

$$–$$$ Ⓣ**Marriott Residence Inn Bethesda Downtown.** In the heart of downtown Bethesda, this all-suites hotel caters primarily to business travelers who stay for several nights. If you're looking for an affordable home away from home, this is a sensible option. The comfortably (though slightly blandly) furnished one- and two-bedroom suites come with fully equipped kitchens with a standard-size refrigerator and dishwasher, plates, and utensils. ■TIP➔**The many complimentary services include grocery shopping, a breakfast buffet, and evening cocktail and dessert receptions.** Tons of restaurants are within walking distance. **Pros:** Rooftop pool; large rooms; walk to Metro and restaurants. **Cons:** Far from monuments, museums, and airports. **Family Matters:** You might see as many dogs and cats as kids in this pet-friendly property, but a park with playground equipment and a neighborhood with lots of families are less than a block away. Allergy sufferers may request "pure rooms" with air filtration systems. ✉*7335 Wisconsin Ave., Bethesda, MD* ☎*301/718–0200 or 800/331–3131* ⊕*www. residenceinnbethesdahotel.com* ⋑*187 suites* ⌂*In-room: kitchen, Internet. In-hotel: pool, gym, laundry facilities, parking (fee), no-smoking rooms* ⊟*AE, D, DC, MC, V* ⌷◖*BP* Ⓜ*Bethesda.*

SUBURBAN VIRGINIA

Alexandria can provide a welcome break from the monuments and hustle-and-bustle of the District. Here you encounter America's colonial heritage, and you're 9 mi from Mount Vernon. Many hotels run a shuttle service to the Metro. A free trolley travels on King Street and runs between North Union Street and the King Street Metro station. The city is as dog-friendly as it is family-friendly.

Arlington and other Northern Virginia cities aren't as picturesque as Alexandria, but their hotel options may be more reasonable and still close to the Metro.

$$–$$$ Ⓣ**Embassy Suites Old Town Alexandria.** Adjacent to Alexandria's landmark George Washington Masonic Temple sits this modern all-suites hotel, which is also across the street from the Metro station and around the corner from

the Amtrak station. A free shuttle is available to transport you to the scenic Alexandria riverfront, which has shops and restaurants. The cooked-to-order breakfast is complimentary, as is the reception every evening. There's also a playroom for children. **Pros:** All suites; free made-to-order breakfast; across from Metro station. **Cons:** Outside city; small pool, which is often crowded; popular with school groups. **Family Matters:** Playroom equipped with a little plastic kitchen and tables is best for the under-six set. Indoor pool. Flat-screen TVs. Bedrooms set for renovation in 2009. Hilton points honored. ⊠ *1900 Diagonal Rd., Alexandria, VA* ☎ *703/684–5900 or 800/362-2779.* ⊕ *www. embassysuites.com* ⊅ *268 suites* ⌖ *In-room: kitchen (some), refrigerator, Wi-Fi, Internet. In-hotel: Wi-Fi, restaurant, pool, gym, laundry facilities, laundry service, parking (fee)* ⊟ *AE, D, DC, MC, V* ⍭ *BP* Ⓜ *King St.*

$$$ 🏨 **Hilton Arlington and Towers.** Traveling downtown is easy from this hotel just above a Metro stop. Guest rooms offer "serenity" beds, work desks, and comfy chairs, and the hotel's service is friendly and responsive. An on-site fitness center opened in 2008. The hotel also has direct access via skywalk to the Ballston Common Mall and National Science Foundation. **Pros:** Easy Metro access; big rooms; online check-in for HHonors members. **Cons:** Far from attractions; high-rise building; no pool. **Family Matters:** Walk to the mall and the adjoining skating rink without going outdoors. Within walking distance of dozens of restaurants, a public swimming pool open in the morning and evening and Quincy Park with lighted tennis courts, volleyball nets, and a playground. Refrigerators in rooms available at no charge. ⊠ *950 N. Stafford St., Arlington, VA* ☎ *703/528–6000 or 800/445-8667* ⊕ *www.hiltonarlington. com* ⊅ *204 rooms, 5 suites* ⌖ *In-room: Wi-Fi. In-hotel: Wi-Fi, restaurant, bar, laundry service, concierge, executive floor, parking (fee)* ⊟ *AE, D, DC, MC, V* Ⓜ *Ballston.*

$–$$ 🏨 **Holiday Inn Arlington at Ballston.** You can get in and out of Washington quickly from this hotel three blocks from a Metro station. Especially comfortable for business travelers, rooms have spacious workspaces, plus tea/coffeemakers. Sightseers can take advantage of the hotel's proximity to Arlington National Cemetery and the Iwo Jima and downtown monuments and museums. Kids 12 and under eat free. **Pros:** Free high-speed Internet access; free parking on Friday and Saturday nights; near the Metro. **Cons:** Outside the city; typical chain-style guest rooms. **Family Matters:** A super place to stay for ice skaters and shoppers as a skating rink

ALTERNATIVE LODGINGS

APARTMENT RENTALS

D.C. is a notoriously transient town, with people hopping on and off the campaign trail on a moment's notice, often leaving their apartments in the sublets and long-term rental columns of local newspapers and Web sites. If you can't stomach the idea of another family vacation with you and the kids squeezed into a single hotel room with no kitchen or if you're traveling with others, a furnished rental might be for you. Often these rentals wind up saving you money—especially on meals and snacks. Be warned, the allure of a full kitchen and room to spread out might get you hooked on apartment rentals for life. Here are some Web sites to help you find hotel alternatives, short-term apartment rentals, and apartment exchanges.

⊕www.vrbo.com ⊕www.washingtondc.craigslist.org ⊕thehill.com/classifieds.html ⊕www.militarybyowner.com ⊕www.dcdigs.com ⊕www.remington-dc.com ⊕www.cyberrentals.com ⊕thedupontcollection.com/brookland.html

International Agents Hideaways International (✉767 Islington St., Portsmouth, NH ☎603/430–4433 or 800/843–4433 ⊕www.hideaways.com), membership $185.

Rental Listings Washington Post (⊕www.washingtonpost.com). **Washington City Paper** (⊕www.washingtoncitypaper.com).

B&BS

To find reasonably priced accommodations in small guest houses and private homes, try **Bed and Breakfast Accommodations, Ltd.** (☎413/582–9888 or 877/893–3233 ⊕www.bedandbreakfastdc.com), which is staffed weekdays from 10 to 5. It handles about 45 different properties in the area.

HOME EXCHANGES

If you would like to exchange your home for someone else's, join a home-exchange organization, which will send you its updated listings of available exchanges for a year and include your own listing in at least one of them. It's up to you to make specific arrangements.

Exchange Clubs HomeLink International (☎813/975–9825 or 800/638–3841 ⊕www.homelink.org); $80 for a listing published in a directory and on Web sites. **Intervac U.S.** (☎800/756–4663 ⊕www.intervacus.com); $126 yearly for a listing, online access, and a catalog; $78.88 without catalog.

adjacent to the Ballston Common Mall is open to the public when the NHL Capitals aren't training. A grocery store is a few blocks away. Refrigerators are standard. Request a microwave for $10, regardless of length of stay. ⊠*4610 N. Fairfax Dr., Arlington, VA 22203* ☎*703/243–9800 or 888/465–4329* ⊕*www.hiarlington.com* ⇔*219 rooms, 2 suites* ⬩*In-room: Wi-Fi, Internet. In-hotel: Wi-Fi, restaurant, room service, bar, pool, gym, laundry facilities, parking (fee)* ⊟*AE, D, DC, MC, V* Ⓜ*Ballston.*

$$ ⬛**Hotel Monaco Alexandria.** When you walk into Old Town's new Hotel Monaco you might feel bad for those poor souls who made reservations elsewhere. But don't worry, the Adriatic blue walls, European and Moroccan travel props, and the cheerful and committed staff will cheer you back up in no time. Inviting guest rooms pick up on this Kimpton hotel's theme of "history" with fun details like faux snake-skin walls and chairs done in upholstery with the image of a local vintage map. While the Old Town location puts you outside the District, this historic neighborhood holds its own. Stroll down to the water and admire the D.C. view. ⬛TIP➔ **Water bowls runneth over at the hotel's doggie happy hour on Tuesday and Thursday nights in the summer:** ⊕*www. doggiehappyhour.com.* **Pros:** Hotel restaurant Jackson 20 is getting good early reviews; bend over backward attitude toward service; in the heart of Old Town with its many restaurants, shops, and history. **Cons:** Not in D.C.; long walk to the Metro. **Family Matters:** The restaurant isn't that kid-friendly but "Dive in" movies poolside on Saturday night at 7 and complimentary bikes to borrow on request help make this Kimpton their most popular for families in the D.C. area. ⊠*489 King , Old Town Alexandria* ☎*703/549–6080* ⊕*www.monaco-alexandria.com* ⇔*231 rooms, 10 suites* ⬩*In room: safe, kitchen (some), refrigerator, DVD, Internet, Wi-Fi. In-hotel: restaurant, room service, pool, gym, laundry service, concierge, Wi-Fi, airport shuttle, parking (fee), some pets allowed, no-smoking rooms* ⊟ *AE, D, DC, MC, V* Ⓜ*King Street.*

$$$ ⬛**Key Bridge Marriott.** If you don't mind being across the Potomac, this hotel is a good alternative to downtown. The views from the hotel's Potomac side are camera-phone worthy. Although the property carries a Virginia zip code, you can walk over the Key Bridge into Georgetown, and the Rosslyn Metro is about four blocks away. Added bonus: one of the few hotels in town with an indoor-outdoor pool. **Pros:** Good choice if traveling with kids; can walk across the bridge to Georgetown; about four blocks from

the Metro. **Cons:** Outside the city; not much of note happening in the immediate area, especially at night. **Family Matters:** No flat-screen TVs in the rooms to entertain or distract kids, depending on your point of view, but that may change as rooms are slated for revamping in late 2009. A $35 million renovation of the lobby, meeting rooms and restaurants, included the opening of Revival, which features old Hop Shoppe classics like the Mighty Mo burger and orange freezes. ⊠*1401 Lee Hwy., Arlington, VA* ☎*703/524–6400 or 800/228–9290* ⊕*www.marriott.com/ hotels/travel/waskb-key-bridge-marriott/* ⤳*568 rooms, 14 suites* ⌂*In-room: safe, refrigerator (some,) Internet. In-hotel: 2 restaurants, room service, bar, pool, gym, spa, laundry service, concierge, Wi-Fi, parking (fee), no-smoking rooms* ⊟*AE, D, DC, MC, V* Ⓜ*Rosslyn.*

$$–$$$ ⛲ **Marriott Residence Inn Arlington Pentagon City.** The view across the Potomac of the D.C. skyline and the monuments is magnificent from this all-suites high rise. Adjacent to the Pentagon, it's two blocks from the Pentagon City Fashion Centre mall, which has a food court, 150 shops, and a Metro stop. ■TIP→**All suites include full kitchens with dishwashers, microwaves, stoves (but no ovens), ice-makers, coffeemakers, toasters, dishes, and utensils.** Complimentary services include grocery shopping, daily newspaper delivery, full breakfast, light dinner Monday to Wednesday, and movies, popcorn, and ice cream on Thursday evening. **Pros:** All-suites setup a plus for families; easy walk to Metro. **Cons:** Outside of D.C.; neighborhood dead at night. **Family Matters:** On-call shuttle service between 7 AM and 11 PM to sites within a mile of the hotel, including restaurants such as Champs and Chevys, the Air Force Memorial, and a playground. Two blocks from Harris Teeter grocery stores. Complimentary shuttle to Reagan National Airport. Renovated in 2008 with flat-screen TVs. ⊠*550 Army Navy Dr., Arlington, VA* ☎*703/413–6630 or 800/331–3131* *www.marriott.com/ hotels/travel/waspt-residence-inn-arlington-pentagon-city* ⤳*299 suites* ⌂*In-room: kitchen, Internet. In-hotel: pool, gym, laundry facilities, laundry service, Wi-Fi, airport shuttle, parking (fee), some pets allowed (fee)* ⊟*AE, D, DC, MC, V* ⧖*BP* Ⓜ*Pentagon City.*

The Performing Arts

4

WORD OF MOUTH

"The Kennedy Center offers free shows every night of the year at their Millennium Stage—a different show every night. Get there early because it is very popular."

—Devonmcj

Updated
by Kathryn
McKay

WASHINGTON HAS A LIVELY ARTS scene for young and old alike. The museum community and the John F. Kennedy Center for the Performing Arts serve as a mecca for traveling troupes, and the home-grown talent isn't bad either; children's concerts and plays are entertainment staples for many a Washington family. Museums often host programs related to their exhibitions—African tricksters at the National Museum of Art, for example—and serious groups such as the National Symphony Orchestra have special programs to woo young fans. Check the "For Kids" section in the "Weekend" section of the *Washington Post* for special events that crop up during the year. For example, Wolf Trap Foundation for the Performing Arts hosts the International Children's Festival, with performers from around the world, early each September. The Puppet Company and Adventure Theater in Glen Echo offer performances for children all year round.

PERFORMANCE VENUES

Though most of the very best out-of-town performers flock to the Kennedy Center or the Verizon Center, Washington is also peppered with dozens of small and medium-size venues. Performance halls tend to showcase musicians, but there's no shortage of dance and theater troupes or stand-up comedians. Don't go looking for a theater district: the venues are spread across town and in the Maryland and Virginia suburbs.

Atlas Performing Arts Center. Known as the "People's Kennedy Center," this relatively new performance venue is community-based, encompassing four theaters and three dance studios. In a restored historic movie theater, the Atlas presents performances by the dance troupe Joy of Motion, the light opera company Washington Savoyards, the African Continuum Theatre, and the Capital City Symphony. Atlas is not Metro-accessible; the nearest cab stand is at Union Station, where a free shuttle bus also runs on Friday and Saturday nights. Parking is available on the street. A classical music concert for kids with an instrument petting zoo in November and a holiday sing-along in December are sure bets, but many kids also enjoy the energetic step-dancing performances from Step Afrika every spring. ⊠*1333 H St. NE, Northeast* ☎*202/399–7993* ⊕*www. atlasarts.org.* 7+up

TOP 5 PERFORMING ARTS EXPERIENCES

■ **Kennedy Center.** The nation's performing arts center looks like a place for adults in tuxedos and black dresses, and it is. But the center also rolls out the red carpet for kids.

■ **Puppet Co. Playhouse.** One of the most popular puppet companies in the country, it has been delighting children and parents since 1983.

■ **Discovery Theater.** This small theater on the Mall brings both our national heritage and other cultures to life.

■ **Wolf Trap.** Over a stream and through the forest, you can find Theatre-in-the-Woods, a clearing with a stage and benches where professional children's performers get as many as 800 people clapping, singing, and laughing.

■ **Imagination Stage.** Performances often sell out quickly at this state-of-the-art, 400-seat venue just a few miles outside of D.C.

Center for the Arts. This state-of-the-art performance complex on the suburban Virginia campus of George Mason University satisfies music, ballet, and drama patrons with regular performances in its 1,900-seat concert hall, the 500-seat proscenium Harris Theater, and the intimate 150-seat black-box Theater of the First Amendment. The 9,500-seat Patriot Center, site of pop acts and sporting events, is also on campus. Any show labeled "family-friendly" means all kids 12 and under get half-price tickets. These shows often feature foreign performers such as acrobats from China and Russian ballet dancers or holiday programs. ✉*Rte. 123 and Braddock Rd., Fairfax, VA* ☎*888/945–2468* ⊕*www. gmu.edu/cfa.* 7+up

★ FodorsChoice **John F. Kennedy Center for the Performing Arts.** On the bank of the Potomac River, the gem of the D.C. arts scene is home to the National Symphony Orchestra, the Washington Ballet, and the Washington National Opera. The best out-of-town acts perform at one of three performance spaces—the Concert Hall, the Opera House, or the Eisenhower Theater. Eclectic performers can be found at the Center's smaller venues, including the Terrace Theater, showcasing chamber groups and experimental works; the Theater Lab, home to cabaret-style performances like the audience-participation hit *Sheer Madness*; the KC Jazz Club; and a 320-seat family theater. But that's not all. On the Millennium Stage in the center's Grand Foyer you can

---

FIND OUT WHAT'S HAPPENING

To sift through the flurry of events, check out these resources:

■ The daily "Guide to the Lively Arts" and the Friday "Weekend" sections in the *Washington Post.*

■ The Thursday *Washington Times* "Washington Weekend" section.

■ Online, the *Post* (⊕*www. washingtonpost.com/ cityguide*), *Times* (⊕*www. washingtontimes.com*), and *Washington Parent* (⊕*www. washingtonparent.com*) all publish entertainment guides.

---

catch free performances almost any day at 6 PM. ■TIP→**On performance days, a free shuttle bus runs between the center and the Foggy Bottom/GWU Metro stop.** If your kids need a break, take them out to the balcony for fresh air and a breathtaking view of the Potomac, or pick up a flag sheet from the information desk and start hunting for flags from all over the world. ✉*New Hampshire Ave. and Rock Creek Pkwy. NW, Foggy Bottom* ☎*202/467–4600 or 800/444–1324* ⊕*www.kennedy-center.org* Ⓜ*Foggy Bottom/GWU.* 5+up

Lisner Auditorium. A 1,500-seat theater on the campus of George Washington University in downtown D.C., Lisner hosts pop, classical, and choral music shows, modern dance performances, and musical theater. Christmas Revels rock the house here every December with their audience-participation performances that go beyond sing-alongs. Other kid-pleasing performances include flamingo dancers in February and family shows from the New York City-based Theatreworks USA. ✉*730 21st St. NW, Foggy Bottom* ☎*202/994–6800* ⊕*www.lisner.org* Ⓜ*Foggy Bottom/ GWU.* 5+up

★ Fodor'sChoice **Music Center at Strathmore.** Located ½ mi outside the Capital Beltway in North Bethesda, this concert hall receives praise for its acoustics and its audience-friendly design. Major national folk, blues, pop, jazz, Broadway, and classical artists perform here. The center is home to the Baltimore Symphony Orchestra and the National Philharmonic. More-intimate performances are held in the 100-seat Dorothy M. and Maurice C. Shapiro Music Room. ■TIP→**Consider taking the Metro to Strathmore; the center is less than a block from the Grosvenor Metro station.** Strathmore constantly reaches out to kids with performances ranging from musicians such as Dan Zanes to plays such as Frog and Toad and Flat Stanley. The free film series on Wednesday nights during the summer includes two or three family films. Teddy bear and princess teas and special art tours for kids take place in the mansion built in 1899. Eleven acres includes plenty of lush, green grass for kids to run around before or after performances. ✉*5301 Tuckerman La., North Bethesda, MD* ☎*301/581–5200* ⊕*www.strathmore. org* Ⓜ*Grosvenor/Strathmore.* 3+up

★ **National Gallery of Art.** Since 1942 the National Gallery has offered a variety of music. On Friday from Memorial Day through Labor Day, local jazz groups perform from 5 to 9 PM to a packed Sculpture Garden. Loyal listeners dip their weary feet in the fountain, sip sangria, and let their week wash away. From October to June, free concerts by the National Gallery Orchestra and performances by visiting recitalists and ensembles are held in the West Building's West Garden Court on Sunday night. Entry is first-come, first-served, with doors opening at 6 PM and concerts starting at 6:30 PM. The free Film Program for Children and Teens features recent flicks and classic foreign and domestic films shown in the 500-seat auditorium. Many films such as *The Red Balloon* and *The Buddha Collapsed Out of Shame* appeal to multigenerations. ✉*6th St. and Constitution Ave. NW, The Mall* ☎*202/737–4215* ⊕*www.nga.gov* Ⓜ*Archives/Navy Memorial.* 5+up

★ Fodor'sChoice **Smithsonian Institution.** Jazz, musical theater, and popular standards are performed in the National Museum of American History. In the museum's third-floor Hall of Musical Instruments, musicians occasionally play period instruments from the museum's collection. The Smithsonian's annual Folklife Festival, held on the Mall, highlights the cuisine, crafts, and day-to-day life of several different cultures. The Smithsonian Associates sponsors programs that offer everything from a cappella groups to Cajun Zydeco bands; all events require tickets, and locations vary. Despite the summer heat and humidity, the dancers, demonstrations, animals, and other free attractions make the Folklife Festival one of Washington's most popular events for families. ✉*1000 Jefferson Dr. SW, The Mall* ☎*202/357–2700, 202/633–1000 recording, 202/357–3030 Smithsonian Associates* ⊕*www.si.edu* Ⓜ*Smithsonian.* All ages

Verizon Center. In addition to being the home of the Washington Capitals hockey and Washington Wizards basketball

TICKETS HERE

The Standard Sources:
Tickets to most events are available by calling or visiting the venue's box office or through the following ticket agencies:**Ticketmaster** ☎202/397-7328, 703/573-7328, or 410/547-7328 ⊕www.ticketmaster.com) sells tickets for events at most venues. You can buy by phone, on the Web, in person at Macy's department stores and the D.C. Visitor Information Center. **Tickets.com** ☎800/955-5566 ⊕www.tickets.com) takes online reservations for a number of events around town and has outlets in some Olsson's Books & Records.

On the Cheap: TICKETplace (⊠Old Post Office Pavilion, 407 7th St. NW, Downtown ☎202/842-5387 ⊕www.ticketplace.org ⓜArchives/Navy Memorial) sells half-price, day-of-performance tickets for select shows. They don't operate on Sunday and Monday; tickets for events on those days are sold at the booth on Saturday. The service charge is 12% at the booth and 17% online.

teams, this 19,000-seat arena also plays host to D.C.'s biggest concerts, ice-skating events, and the circus. Parking can be a problem, but several Metro lines converge at an adjacent station. Disney on Ice and the circus usually perform here. Look for special parking areas for strollers. ⊠601 F St. NW, Chinatown ☎202/661-5000 ⊕www.verizoncenter.com ⓜGallery Place/Chinatown. 3+up

Wolf Trap National Park for the Performing Arts. Wolf Trap is the only national park dedicated to the performing arts. June through September, the massive outdoor Filene Center hosts close to 100 performances, ranging from pop and jazz concerts to dance and musical theater productions. In summer, the National Symphony Orchestra is based here, and the Children's Theatre-in-the-Woods delivers 70 free performances. During the colder months, the intimate, indoor Barns at Wolf Trap fill with the sounds of musicians playing folk, country, and chamber music, along with myriad other styles. The park is just off the Dulles Toll Road, about 20 mi from downtown. ■TIP→**When the Filene Center hosts an event, Metrorail operates a $5 round-trip shuttle bus—exact change only—from the West Falls Church Metro station. The bus leaves 20 minutes after the show or no later than 11 pm, whether the show is over or not.** Over a stream and through the woods, you can find a clearing with benches and a stage where the

National Park Service sponsors Theatre-in-the-Woods for at least seven weeks every summer. As many as 800 people per performance come here to see professional children's performers, such as jugglers, clowns, storytellers, and puppeteers. Afterward, romping through the park is encouraged. For one weekend in September, Wolf Trap hosts the International Children's Festival, which features performers from all over the world, many of them children. Keep in mind that for performances at the Filene Center, everyone, even babes in arms, must have a ticket. 3+up ⊠*1645 Trap Rd., Vienna, VA* ☎*703/255–1900, 703/938–2404 Barns at Wolf Trap* ⊕*www.wolftrap.org* Ⓜ*Vienna.*

FOR FREE. The abundance of freebies in Washington extends to the arts. Highlights among the no-charge events include: The **Shakespeare Theatre Free for All**, a two-week run of performances every June. The **Millennium Stage at the Kennedy Center**, where there are free performances daily at 6 PM. The **National Cathedral**, which hosts frequent concerts.

MUSIC

With dozens of acoustically superior venues and majestic backdrops around town, D.C. sets a lofty stage for its musicians, who have the talent to match. Whether it's the four armed-services bands marching in the footsteps of John Philip Sousa, opera singers performing under the direction of Plácido Domingo, or chamber players performing Renaissance pieces on period instruments, this city's musicians consistently lay down a fitting soundtrack.

CHORAL MUSIC

Basilica of the National Shrine of the Immaculate Conception. Choral and church groups occasionally perform at the largest Catholic church in the Americas. Summer recitals on Saturday afternoons with concerts of carillon and organ attract families. ⊠*400 Michigan Ave. NE, Catholic University* ☎*202/526–8300* ⊕*www.nationalshrine.com* Ⓜ*Brookland/CUA.* 7+up

Washington National Cathedral. Choral and church groups frequently perform in this grand church. Admission is usually free. Kids can usually see children their own age perform during Evensong, weekdays at 5:30, as the men and boys choir or the men and girls choir sings for about 45 minutes to an hour. Organ recitals and bell ringing may also be of interest to musically inclined kids. On the last Tuesday of the month, meditators of all ages walk the labyrinth. Parents of little ones who can't be as quiet as church mice during services will find a welcome respite in the walkways and gardens outside. ✉*Massachusetts and Wisconsin Aves. NW, Cleveland Park* ☎*202/537–6207* ⊕*www.cathedral. org/cathedral* Ⓜ*Tenleytown/AU.* 7+up

WORD OF MOUTH. "A concert at the National Cathedral is enthralling and magnificent. On the 4th of July we went to the organ concert there—it was spectacular (and free! . . . we also attended *The Messiah* last December, which was thrilling (but not free)."–vivi

ORCHESTRAS

National Symphony Orchestra. Under the direction of Leonard Slatkin, the NSO performs from September to June at the Kennedy Center Concert Hall. In summer the NSO performs at Wolf Trap and gives free concerts at Rock Creek Park's Carter Barron Amphitheatre. On Memorial and Labor Day weekends and July 4, the orchestra performs on the West Lawn of the Capitol. ✉*New Hampshire Ave. and Rock Creek Pkwy. NW, Foggy Bottom* ☎*202/462–4600* ⊕*www.kennedy-center.org/nso.* All ages

PERFORMANCE SERIES

Armed Forces Concert Series. From June to August, bands from the four armed services perform Monday, Tuesday, Wednesday, and Friday evenings on the East Terrace of the Capitol. Other performances occur at 8 PM from June to August, on Tuesday, Thursday, Friday, and Sunday nights at the **Sylvan Theater** (✉*Washington Monument grounds, 14th St. and Constitution Ave., The Mall* ☎*202/426–6841* Ⓜ*Smithsonian*).Concerts usually include marches, patriotic numbers, and some classical music. The Air Force celebrity series features popular artists such as Earl Klugh and Keiko Matsui on Sunday in February and March at DAR Constitutional Hall. Hour-long free performances usually attract hundreds, but the 1812 Overture draws a crowd of 5,000. ☎*202/767–5658 Air Force, 703/696–3718 Army, 202/433–4011 Marines, 202/433–2525 Navy.* 5+up

Carter Barron Amphitheatre. On weekend nights from June to September this 3,750-seat outdoor theater hosts pop, jazz, gospel, and rhythm-and-blues artists such as Chick Corea and Nancy Wilson. The National Symphony Orchestra also performs here, and for two weeks the Shakespeare Theatre presents a free play. Kids can run wild in the nearby soccer field before or after about a dozen free festivals, including those devoted to Shakespeare, dance, and music from military bands and others. ⊠*Rock Creek Park, 4850 Colorado Ave. NW, Upper Northwest* ☎*202/426–0486* ⊕*www.nps. gov/rocr/cbarron.htm.* 7+up

Washington Performing Arts Society. This nonprofit organization books high-quality classical music, jazz, gospel, modern dance, and performance art into halls around the city. Past artists include the Alvin Ailey American Dance Theater, Yo-Yo Ma, Barbara Cook, Sweet Honey in the Rock, and Joshua Bell. The WPAS-sponsored children's gospel choir and about three other performances for families round out the season, which occasionally offers buy one adult ticket, get one child's ticket free. ☎*202/833–9800* ⊕*www.wpas.org.* 7+up

THEATER & PERFORMANCE ART

Perhaps as a counterbalance to all the political theater in town, D.C.'s playhouses, large and small, have grown into a force to be reckoned with over the past few years. Nearly every major theater in town has recently renovated its performance spaces or is in the process of doing so, and new small theaters are popping up all the time. If all that weren't enough, D.C. often hosts some of the best touring companies from the East Coast and beyond.

LARGE THEATERS

Discovery Theater. In the midst of the mammoth museums on the Mall, kids delight in entertaining and educational performances, such as the antics of a juggler tossing around bowling balls, bananas, and rakes or the more serious historical story of child heroes of the Civil Rights movement. In the S. Dillon Ripley Center west of the Smithsonian Castle, the theater's 130 seats are no more than 10 rows away from the action, which makes encounters between the audience and actors easy. Though most performances are geared to preschoolers through sixth graders, some are for tweens and teens. More popular performances may be held in the 550-seat Baird Auditorium at the Museum of Natural History. One of the most popular months for performances is February, when Black History Month is celebrated. Reservations are recommended. Plan to arrive 15 minutes early. If you're attending a 10 AM show, go around to the west entrance in the Enid A. Haupt garden, where the doors open for Discovery patrons only. ✉ *1100 Jefferson Dr. SW, The Mall* ☎ *202/633–8700* ⊕ *www.discoverytheater.org* Ⓜ *Smithsonian.* 3+up

Ford's Theatre. Looking much as it did when President Lincoln was shot at a performance of *Our American Cousin,* Ford's primarily hosts patriotic musicals, most with family appeal. Dickens's *A Christmas Carol* is staged every year. After undergoing a $50 million renovation, the theater is scheduled to open in February 2009 for the bicentennial of Lincoln's birth. With the exception of *The Christmas Carol,* most performances tend to be best for adults and teens, but a visit here is worth it for most kids about 7 and up. Although they can't sit in the red velvet rocking chair Lincoln sat in when he was shot, they can peer over the ropes and imagine the events of April 14, 1865. ✉ *511 10th St. NW, Downtown* ☎ *202/426–6925* ⊕ *www.fordstheatre.org* Ⓜ *Metro Center.* 7+up

National Theatre. Though once destroyed by fire and rebuilt several times, the National Theatre has operated in the same location since 1835. It now hosts touring Broadway shows, such as *Spamalot* and *Movin' Out.* ■ TIP→ **From September through April, look for free children's shows Saturday morning and free Monday night shows that may include Asian dance, performance art, and a cappella cabarets.** Arrive a half hour prior to free performances for tickets distributed on a first-come, first-served basis, one ticket only per person. Jugglers, magicians, historical interpreters and others amuse kids for 40 minutes on Saturday mornings at 9:30 and 11. The Monday night shows at 6 and 7:30 aren't always for kids, but most are family-friendly. Kids can sit up front on the floor of the 140-seat theater. ✉ *1321 Pennsylvania Ave. NW, Downtown* ☎ *202/783–3372* ⊕ *www.nationaltheatre.org* Ⓜ *Metro Center.* 5+up

★ Fodor'sChoice **Shakespeare Theatre.** This acclaimed troupe, known as one of the world's three great Shakespearean companies, crafts fantastically staged and acted performances of works by Shakespeare and his contemporaries. The theater has undergone an amazing transformation. Complimenting the existing stage in the Lansburgh Theatre is the Sidney Harman Hall, which opened in October 2007.

The new stage provides a 21st-century, state-of-the-art, mid-size venue for an outstanding variety of performances, from Shakespeare's Julius Caesar to the hilarious Abridged History of America. For two weeks in late spring they perform Shakespeare for free at Carter Barron Amphitheatre. A best bet for introducing sophisticated tweens and teens to the Bard, performances have included an all-male cast for *Romeo and Juliet* and *Love's Labor Lost* set in the 1960s. ✉ *450 7th St. NW, Downtown* ☎ *202/547–1122* ⊕ *www. shakespearedc.org* Ⓜ *Gallery Pl./Chinatown or Archives/ Navy Memorial.* 10+up

Warner Theatre. One of Washington's grand theaters, the Warner hosts road shows, dance recitals, pop music, and the occasional comedy act in its majestic art deco performance space. Families often get dressed up to see *The Nutcracker* and the other dozen or so performances specifically for families at this theater one block from Metro Center. ✉ *513 13th St. NW, Downtown* ☎ *202/783–4000* ⊕ *www. warnertheatre.com* Ⓜ *Metro Center.* 5+up

SMALL THEATERS & COMPANIES

Often performing in churches and other less-than-ideal settings, Washington's small companies present drama that can be every bit as enthralling as—and often more daring than—that offered by their blockbuster counterparts. No matter the size, all companies in town compete fiercely for the Helen Hayes Award, Washington's version of the Tony.

Adventure Theatre. Entertaining children since 1951, the oldest children's theater in Washington has been housed at the old Penny Arcade at Glen Echo since 1971. The majority of performances are geared toward two- to five-year olds. The 2008–09 schedule included mostly plays based on children's literature such as *If you Give Mouse a Cookie*, *Harold and the Purple Crayon*, and *Holes*. Benches in the 185-seat theater keep kids close to the action and each other. ✉ *7300 MacArthur Blvd., Glen Echo, MD 20812* ☎ *301/634–2270* ⊕ *www.adventuretheatre.org.* 3+up

Folger Shakespeare Library. The library's theater, a 250-seat re-creation of the inn-yard theaters with seating in the balcony popular in Shakespeare's time, hosts three to four productions a year of Shakespeare or Shakespeare-influenced works. Though the stage is a throwback, the sharp acting and staging certainly push the envelope. Best for adults with one big exception: The bard's birthday on the Sunday closest to April 23 is celebrated as vigorously as any kid's birthday with free Elizabethan arts and crafts, portrait contests, dramatic readings, street performers, scavenger hunts, and, of course, cake. ✉ *201 E. Capitol St. SE, Capitol Hill* ☎ *202/544–7077* ⊕ *www.folger.edu* Ⓜ *Union Station or Capitol S.* 7+up

Gala Hispanic Theatre. This company attracts outstanding Hispanic actors from around the world, performing works by leading Latino playwrights, such as Federico García Lorca and Mario Vargas Llosa. Plays are presented in English or in Spanish with instant English translations supplied through earphones. The company performs in the newly renovated Tivoli Theatre in Columbia Heights, a hot spot for Latino culture and cuisine. Child-oriented, family series are performed throughout the year. The three kings festival in January is wildly popular. ✉ *Tivoli Sq., 3333 14th St. NW, 14th and Park Rd., Columbia Heights* ☎ *202/234–7174* ⊕ *www.galatheatre.org* Ⓜ *Columbia Heights.* 7+up

Glen Echo Park. The National Park Service has transformed this former amusement park into a thriving arts center. Every weekend the Adventure Theater puts on traditional plays and musicals aimed at children ages four and up. Families can spread out on long benches. At the Puppet Company Playhouse, skilled puppeteers perform classic stories Wednesday through Sunday. The arts thrive at this historic park on the D.C. border. Whatever event you're going to, allow an extra 30 minutes. Just stomping over the bridge leading to the park takes time. You may also want to act out the Norwegian folktale of Billy Goats Gruff, toss stones in the creek, and take a spin around the Denzel carousel. ✉ *7300 MacArthur Blvd., Glen Echo, MD* ☎ *301/634–2222, 301/320–5331 Adventure Theater, 301/320–6668 Puppet Co.* ⊕ *www.glenechopark. org.* 4+up

Imagination Stage. Shows like Roald Dahl's classic story *The BFG,* and original fare such as Karen Zacarias and Deborah Wicks LaPuma's *Cinderella Likes Rice and Beans* are produced here for children ages four and up. The state-of-the-art center in Bethesda includes two theaters and a digital media studio. Make reservations in advance. Kids (and their parents) who can't keep quiet can still enjoy the show from a soundproof room in the back of this nearly

400-seat theater. An outdoor intermission terrace with bright-color geometric shaped sculptures adds to the fun. The gift shop, stocked with reasonably priced costumes, puppets, and fashion shades, is near the front of the theater but you don't have to walk through it to enter or leave. Booster seats available, but kids under two can qualify for a $5 lap ticket. Admission for everyone else ranges $10–$21. On weekends, parking is free in the garage next door. Located a half-mile from the Bethesda Metro station. ✉ *4908 Auburn Ave., Bethesda, MD* ☎ *301/961–6060* ⊕ *www.imaginationstage.org.* 3+up

Puppet Co. Skilled puppeteers manipulate a variety of puppets in classic plays and stories in a theater that was built specifically for puppet shows. Twice a month, the Playhouse hosts Tiny Tots for wee ones up to four years old ($5 for all ages). *The Nutcracker,* in winter, is one of the most popular productions. Sometimes puppeteers greet children after the shows. Reservations are recommended for this popular puppet place that seats 250. ✉ *7300 MacArthur Blvd., Glen Echo, MD* ☎ *301/320–6668* ⊕ *www.thepuppetco. org.* All ages

Teatro de la Luna. Founded in 1991 to provide D.C. with theater from a Latin American perspective, this enthusiastic arts organizations presents a traditional repertoire of plays for children, such as *Sleeping Beauty, Hansel and Gretel,* and *Pinocchio,* performed in Spanish, but performances for families during their six-week international festival of Hispanic theater usually include live English dubbing or written translations. Venues include their space in Arlington, the Mexican Cultural Institute, and Latin American embassies. ✉ *Tivoli Sq., 2700 S. Lang St, Arlington, VA* ☎ *703/548–3092* ⊕ *www.teatrodelaluna.org.* 5+up

SONG & DANCE

The solid performances of the Washington Ballet, generally considered one of the better troupes in the U.S., and those of smaller companies around town are complemented by frequent visits from some of the world's best companies, including the Kirov Ballet and the Alvin Ailey American Dance Theater. Washington is also host to many festivals, and dance is often highlighted. The traditional Japanese dance featured during the Cherry Blossom Festival and the varied styles that come to town during the Smithsonian Folklife Festival are particular treats.

Dance Place. This studio theater showcases the best local dance talent in an assortment of modern and ethnic shows; performances take place most weekends. It also conducts dance classes daily. One child attends free with a paying adult during target family performances once a month. The neighborhood can be a bit sketchy at night. ✉ *3225 8th St. NE, Catholic University* ☎ *202/269–1600* ⊕ *www. danceplace.org* Ⓜ *Catholic University.* 5+up

★ **Washington Ballet.** Between September and May, this company presents classical and contemporary ballets, including works by choreographers such as George Balanchine, Choo-San Goh, and artistic director Septime Webre. Its main shows are mounted at the Kennedy Center. Each December the Washington Ballet performs *The Nutcracker* at the Warner Theatre. Shows specifically for families are usually held three times a year. Recent examples include *Peter Pan, Cinderella,* and *Where the Wild Things Are.* ☎ *202/362–3606* ⊕ *www.washingtonballet.org.* 5+up

FILM

D.C.'s countless foundations, embassies, national museums, and institutions offer the visiting cinephile an unexpected side benefit—quirky, long-forgotten, seldom-seen, and arcane films on as many topics as there are special interests. The most common venues are listed below; more limited engagements are listed in the *Washington CityPaper* or the *Washington Post.* Those looking for selections a little less obscure will likely find what they're looking for in D.C.'s many repertory, independent, and first-run theaters.

AMC Union Station 9. Capitol Hill's AMC Union Station 9 has nine screens showing mainstream, first-run movies; validated, three-hour parking is available at an adjacent lot. With so many choices in Union Station's food court and the Smithsonian Postal Museum across the street, families will find a lot to do before or after a movie. ✉ *Union Station, 50 Massachusetts Ave. NE, Capitol Hill* ☎ *202/842–3757* Ⓜ *Union Station.*

★ FodorsChoice **American Film Institute Silver Theatre and Cultural Center.** This three-screen, state-of-the-art center for film is a restoration of architect John Eberson's art deco Silver Theatre, built in 1938. The AFI hosts film retrospectives, festivals, and tributes celebrating artists from Jeanne Moreau to Russell Crowe. The AFI Silver also hosts the annual Silver Docs festival, which features some of the world's best documentaries and appearances by some of the greatest filmmakers, such Martin Scorsese. Families serious about film will appreciate the in-depth series. A recent slate of muppet movies included rarely viewed clips. ✉8633 Colesville Rd., Silver Spring, MD ☎301/495–6700 ⊕www.afi.com/silver Ⓜ Silver Spring. 10+up

Loews Cineplex Uptown 1. Featuring the largest movie screen in town, the Uptown is a true movie palace with art deco flourishes, a wonderful balcony, and—in one happy concession to modernity—crystal-clear Dolby sound. It's home to Washington's biggest movie premieres. Since opening in 1936, kids and teens have enjoyed the balcony. Allow 15 extra minutes to find a parking space. ✉3426 Connecticut Ave. NW, Cleveland Park ☎202/966–5400 Ⓜ Cleveland Park.

National Gallery of Art, East Building. Free classic and international films, often complementing the exhibits, are shown in this museum's large auditorium. Pick up a film calendar at the museum or online. Free films for children and teens feature recent flicks and classic foreign and domestic films shown in a 500-seat auditorium. Many titles such as *The Red Balloon* and *The Buddha Collapsed Out of Shame* appeal to multigenerations. ✉Constitution Ave. between 3rd and 4th Sts. NW, The Mall ☎202/842–6799 ⊕www. nga.gov Ⓜ Archives/Navy Memorial. 5+up

Sports & the Outdoors

WORD OF MOUTH

"During the winter, take the kids ice skating at the Sculpture Garden next to the Natl Gallery of Art. During the summer they can kick a ball around the Mall or take a paddle boat ride in the Tidal Basin."

—Devonmcj

Updated
by Kathryn
McKay

WASHINGTONIANS AND THEIR FAMILIES ARE an active bunch. The city's 69 square mi are in part a fantastic recreational backyard, with dozens of beautiful open spaces, and families take full advantage of it, exploring by bike, running amid the monuments, and paddleboating around the Tidal Basin. They're also passionate about their local teams—especially the Redskins, whose games are sold out year after year. Baseball fans have a lot to cheer about with the new stadium that opened in 2008, but in Washington's suburbs, soccer may be even more popular than America's pastime.

Rock Creek Park has miles of wooded trails and paths for bikers, runners, and walkers that extend to almost every part of the city. The National Mall connects the Lincoln Memorial and the Capitol building. With the monuments as a backdrop, you can ride a bike or take a jog. Around the Tidal Basin, see the Jefferson Memorial from a paddleboat or run alongside the Potomac River. Theodore Roosevelt Island, a wildlife sanctuary that deserves to be better known, has several paths for hiking and enjoyable spots for a picnic.

PARKS & NATURE

GARDENS

Constitution Gardens. Many ideas were proposed to develop this 50-acre site near the Reflecting Pool and the Vietnam Veterans Memorial. It once held temporary buildings erected by the Navy before World War I and not removed until after World War II. President Nixon is said to have favored something resembling Copenhagen's Tivoli Gardens. The final design was plainer, with paths winding through groves of trees and, on the lake, a tiny island paying tribute to the signers of the Declaration of Independence, their signatures carved into a low stone wall. In 1986, President Reagan proclaimed the gardens a living legacy to the Constitution; in that spirit, a naturalization ceremony for new citizens now takes place here each year. The paths are quieter here than near the memorials, but walking around the water lengthens the time between memorials. The geese might seem like a nuisance to adults, but kids like tossing them crumbs from the wide, wooden bridge. ⊠*Constitution Ave. between 17th and 23rd Sts. NW* ⊕*www.nps.gov/coga* Ⓜ*Foggy Bottom.* All ages

TOP 5 SPORTS & OUTDOORS EXPERIENCES

■ **Explore the wild side of Washington.** Theodore Roosevelt Island is ideal for kids who believe, as our 26th president did, that "There is delight in the hardy life of the open."

■ **Find plenty of room to run.** The U.S. National Arboretum is not only home to the National Bonsai & Penjing Museum where kids can see old, tiny, and incredibly valuable trees, it's also got wide, open spaces to run, walk, and bike in between gorgeous gardens.

■ **Get a new perspective on the cherry trees.** Take a leisurely trip in a paddleboat around the Tidal Basin, surrounded by the famous blossoms in spring.

■ **Bike the Mall.** Kids can feel like big wheels in Washington biking to monuments and museums.

■ **Cheer on the home team!** Players aren't the only ones running the bases at Nationals Stadium. Ten-foot tall caricatures of the presidents on Mount Rushmore take to the field in the middle of the fourth inning. Who will win? Washington, Jefferson, Lincoln, or Teddy Roosevelt?

NEED A BREAK? At the circular snack bar just west of the Constitution Gardens Lake you can get hot dogs, potato chips, candy bars, soft drinks, and beer at prices lower than those charged by most street vendors.

Dumbarton Oaks. One of the loveliest places for a stroll in Washington is Dumbarton Oaks, the acres of enchanting gardens adjoining Dumbarton House in Georgetown. Planned by noted landscape architect Beatrix Farrand, the gardens incorporate elements of traditional English, Italian, and French styles such as a formal rose garden, an English country garden, and an orangery (circa 1810). A full-time crew of a dozen gardeners toils to maintain the stunning collection of terraces, geometric gardens, tree-shaded brick walks, fountains, arbors, and pools. Plenty of well-positioned benches make this a good place for resting weary feet, too. You enter the gardens at 31st and R streets.

In 1944 one of the most important events of the 20th century took place at **Dumbarton House,** when representatives of the United States, Great Britain, China, and the Soviet Union met in the music room to lay the groundwork for the United Nations. Career diplomat Robert Woods Bliss and his wife, Mildred, bought the property in 1920 and tamed the sprawling grounds and removed later 19th-century additions that had obscured the Federal lines of the 1801 mansion. In 1940 the Blisses gave the estate to Harvard University, which maintains world-renowned collections of Byzantine and pre-Columbian art here. Both collections are small but choice, reflecting the enormous skill and creativity developed at roughly the same time in two very different parts of the world. The Byzantine collection includes beautiful examples of both religious and secular items executed in mosaic, metal, enamel, and ivory. Pre-Columbian works—artifacts and textiles from Mexico and Central and South America by peoples such as the Aztec, Maya, and Olmec—are arranged in an enclosed glass pavilion designed by Philip Johnson. Normally on view to the public are the lavishly decorated music room and selections from Mrs. Bliss's collection of rare illustrated garden books. The lovely gardens may remind nine-year-olds of the classic *Secret Garden*, by Frances Hodgson Burnett. You can't run or toss rocks in any fountains, but many kids still enjoy this outdoor oasis where the Katsura tree's branches at the entrance spread like octopus legs and the outdoor rooms filled with fountains and flowers make a great backdrop for photographs. ⊠ *1703 32nd St. NW, Georgetown* ☏ *202/339–6401 or 202/339–6400* 🖵 *Gardens: Apr.–Oct. $8, $5 ages 2–12; Nov.–Mar. free* ☺ *Gardens: Apr.–Oct., Tues.–Sun. 2–6; Nov.–Mar., Tues.–Sun. daily 2–5.* 5+up

★ **Hillwood Estate, Museum and Gardens.** Cereal heiress Marjorie Merriweather Post purchased the 25-acre Hillwood Estate in 1955. Post devoted equal attention to her gardens as she did to the 40-room Georgian mansion: you can wander through 13 acres of them, including a Japanese rock and waterfall garden, a manicured formal French garden, a rose garden, Mediterranean fountains, and a greenhouse full of orchids. The Lunar lawn, where she threw garden parties that were the most coveted invitation in Washington society, is planted with dogwood, magnolia, cherry, and plum trees, as well as azaleas, camellias, lilacs, tulips, and pansies. The estate is best reached by taxi or car (parking is available on the grounds). It's a 20- to 30-minute walk from the Metro. One of the fanciest houses in Washington hosts family festivals twice a year. In late March or early April, Russian folk dancers and storytellers entertain at the Fabergé Family Festival, which includes, of course, egg decorating. Grandfather Frost and the Russian snow maiden visit during the Russian Winter Festival the second weekend in December. The art activities vary at Family Fun Sundays held sporadically throughout the year. An audio tour for kids, ages 8 to 12, is available at no extra charge. ✉ *4155 Linnean Ave. NW, Northwest* ☎ *202/686–5807 or 202/686–8500* ⊕ *www.hillwoodmuseum.org* ✦ *House and grounds $12; $5 ages 6–18* ☉ *Feb.–Dec., Tues.–Sat. 10–5* Ⓜ *Van Ness/UDC.* 7+up

Tudor Place. A little more than a block from Dumbarton Oaks in Georgetown is this little-known gem, the former home of Martha Washington's granddaughter. The house has 5½ acres of gardens that offer impressive replications of Federal-period gardens and include 19th-century specimen trees and boxwoods from Mount Vernon. Make time for a one-hour tour of the house itself, which features many rare possessions of George and Martha Washington. Call a week in advance and the education staff will arrange a family tour and craft project. Walk-ins can request a detective hunt brochure. Most rooms of the house have touchables such as quills, tea bricks, sugar cones, and games. Young garden detectives (ages 7 to 12) look for lamb's ear plants, goldfish, a fountain of a lion spouting water, and more. ✉ *1644 31st Pl. NW, Georgetown* ☎ *202/965–0400* ⊕ *www. tudorplace.org* ✦ *$6, garden $2; free for children 5 and under, $2 ages 6–12, $3 ages 13–21* ☉ *House tours: Tues.– Fri. 10, 11:30, 1, 2:30, Sat. on the hr 10–3, Sun. on the hr noon–3. Garden: Mon.–Sat. 10–4, Sun. noon–4* ☉ *Closed Jan.* Ⓜ *Woodley Park or Dupont Circle.* 7+up

United States National Arboretum. During azalea season (mid-April through May), this 446-acre oasis is a blaze of color. In early summer, clematis, peonies, rhododendrons, and roses bloom. At any time of year the 22 original Corinthian columns from the U.S. Capitol, reerected here in 1990, are striking. For a soothing, relaxing walk, visit the Cryptomeria Walk and Japanese Stroll Garden, which are part of the Bonsai and Penjing Museum. On weekends a tram tours the Arboretum's curving roadways at 10:30, 11:30, 1, 2, 3, and 4; tickets are $4 for adults and $2 for children. The National Herb Garden and the National Bonsai Collection are also here. You can drive, bike, or walk to the gardens. Walking is pleasant, especially with a stroller, but you can't cover much ground. Whether you come in from New York Avenue or Bladensberg Road, stop by the administration building first, where speckled, bright orange koi flourish in the surrounding pool. Some are as long as a child's arm;

others as little as a finger. Pick up a map inside. You'll need it. At the bonsai museum, kids can find trees much older and smaller than they are. At the National Herb Garden, sniff oregano, basil, and lavender. A Youth Garden features plants grown by local students. ✉*3501 New York Ave. NE, Northeast* ☎*202/245–2726* ⊕*www.usna.usda.gov* ✇*Free* ☼*Arboretum and herb garden daily 8–5, bonsai collection daily 10–3:30* Ⓜ*Weekends only, Union Station, then X6 bus (runs every 40 min); weekdays, Stadium/Armory, then B2 bus to Bladensburg Rd. and R St.* All ages

PARKS

East Potomac Park. This 328-acre finger of land extends from the Tidal Basin between the Washington Channel to the east and the Potomac River to the west. There are playgrounds, picnic tables, tennis courts, swimming pools, a driving range, two 9-hole golf courses, miniature golf, and an 18-hole golf course. Double-blossoming cherry trees line Ohio Drive and bloom about two weeks after the single-blossoming variety that attracts throngs to the Tidal Basin each spring. *The Awakening* sculpture is on Hains Point, at the tip of the park, where the Anacostia River merges with the Potomac. The biggest attraction for kids used to be *The Awakening*, an immense statue of a man half buried in the ground, but in 2007, after 27 years, he was moved to the National Harbor in Prince George's County where families can continue to crawl all over him. The miniature golf course lacks the caves, windmills, and fountains that kids have come to expect, but this course built in the 1920s has native stonework and ponds with goldfish, water lilies and a bridge. Each hole is a par-3. ✉*Maine Ave. SW heading west, or Ohio Dr. heading south, follow signs carefully; Ohio Dr. closed to traffic on summer weekends and holidays 3* PM–*6* AM ☎*202/619–7222* Ⓜ*Smithsonian.* 7+up

Friendship Park. Locals call this neighborhood hangout Turtle Park after the turtle statues near the sandboxes. The park is combination playground, with slides and swings, and in the summer a spray ground, with water for the under six set. Basketball and tennis courts and baseball fields can keep older kids busy. ✉*45th St. and Van Ness Ave. NW, Upper Northwest* ✇*Free* Ⓜ*Tenleytown-AU.* All ages

Montrose Park. Green fields, playground equipment, and a boxwood maze are the draws here, but what will really delight young kids is the park's twist on a touch tank: a creek with crayfish. Tip: To pick up a "crawdad" or "craw-mom" without getting pinched, use thumb and forefinger on the crustacean's midsection. ⊠*3099 R St. NW, Georgetown* ⊠*Free.* All ages

Pershing Park. A quiet, sunken garden honors Gen. John J. "Black Jack" Pershing, the first to hold the title General of the Armies, a rank Congress created in 1919 to recognize his military achievements. Engravings on the stone walls recount pivotal campaigns from World War I, when Pershing commanded the American expeditionary force and conducted other military exploits. Ice skaters glide on the square pool here in winter. Skate to the sounds of pop, disco, oldies, and more. Two-hour sessions cost $6.50 for adults and $5.50 for children 12 and under. Skate rentals run as small as a toddler's size 8. ⊠*15th St. and Pennsylvania Ave., White House area* Ⓜ*McPherson Sq.* All ages

5

Rock Creek Park. The 1,800 acres surrounding Rock Creek have provided a cool oasis for D.C. residents ever since Congress set them aside for recreational use in 1890. Bicycle routes and hiking and equestrian trails wind through the groves of dogwoods, beeches, oaks, and cedars, and 30 picnic areas are scattered about. Rangers at the **Nature Center and Planetarium** (⊠*South of Military Rd.,5200 Glover Rd. NW, Northwest* ☎*202/426–6829*) introduce visitors to the park and keep track of daily events; guided nature walks leave from the center weekends at 2. The center and planetarium are open Wednesday through Sunday from 9 to 5. The nature center brings the outdoors in. Pelts, bones, feathers, and a bird's nest occupy a touch table in the lobby, while another room contains stuffed animals representative of the area and a discovery room is set up with dozens of animal puppets and puzzles. The 75-seat planetarium looks a bit worn, but once the lights go down, you don't notice as it introduces youngsters to the solar system. Children under four may find the shows either boring or scary, but older kids 7 to 10 may enjoy programs that include a Native American legend about a coyote that threw rocks to make pictures in the sky. Outdoors, the short Edge of the Woods trail, a flat asphalt loop leading to a pond the size of a bathtub, is perfect for preschoolers and strollers. The Woodland Trail takes about 40 to 60 minutes, depending on how often you stop to search for animals crawling on the forest floor. The renovated 19th-century **Klingle Mansion**(⊠*3545 Williamsburg La. NW, Northwest*) is used as the National Park Service's Rock Creek headquarters. Also in distant areas of the park are Fort Reno, Fort Bayard, Fort Stevens, and Fort DeRussy, remnants of the original ring of forts that guarded Washington during the Civil War, and the Rock Creek Park Golf Course, an 18-hole public course.

Tidal Basin. This placid pond was part of the Potomac until 1882, when portions of the river were filled in to improve navigation and create additional parkland. At the **Boathouse** (☎202/479–2426), on the northeast bank of the Tidal Basin, you can rent paddleboats during the warmer months. Rental cost is $8 per hour for a two-person boat, $16 per hour for a four-person boat. The boathouse is open from mid-March through October from 10 to 6. One strong adult or teen can provide enough muscle power to motor boats around. Keep in mind that after a certain point, pedaling faster doesn't increase speed. Bring along sunscreen as the cherry blossom trees' branches don't extend far enough to offer shade. Two grotesque sculpted heads on the sides of the Inlet Bridge can be seen as you walk along the sidewalk that hugs the basin. The inside walls of the bridge also sport two other interesting sculptures: bronze, human-headed fish that spout water from their mouths. The bridge was refurbished in the 1980s at the same time the chief of the park, Jack Fish, was retiring. Sculptor Constantine Sephralis played a little joke: these fish heads are actually Fish's head.

Once you cross the bridge, continue along the Tidal Basin to the right. This route is especially scenic when the cherry trees are in bloom. The first batch of these trees arrived from Japan in 1909. The trees were infected with insects and fungus, however, and the Department of Agriculture ordered them destroyed. A diplomatic crisis was averted when the United States politely asked the Japanese for another batch, and in 1912 First Lady Helen Taft planted the first tree. The second was planted by the wife of the Japanese ambassador, Viscountess Chinda. About 200 of the original trees still grow near the Tidal Basin. (These cherry trees are the single-flowering Akebeno and Yoshino variety. Double-blossom Fugenzo and Kwanzan trees grow in East Potomac Park and flower about two weeks after their more famous cousins.)

The trees are now the centerpiece of Washington's two-week **Cherry Blossom Festival,** held each spring since 1935. The festivities are kicked off by the lighting of a ceremonial Japanese lantern that rests on the north shore of the Tidal Basin, not far from where the first tree was planted. The once-simple celebration has grown over the years to include concerts, martial-arts demonstrations, and a parade. Park-service experts try their best to predict exactly when the buds will pop. The trees are usually in bloom for about 10 to 12 days in late March or early April. When winter refuses to release its grip, the parade and festival are held anyway, without the presence of blossoms, no matter how inclement the weather. And when the weather complies and the blossoms are at their peak at the time of the festivities, Washington rejoices. Free concerts, cherry-blossom princesses from each state, and a Japanese lantern lighting ceremony make this one of the best times to be in D.C. despite the crowds. The National Park Service hosts Bloomin' Junior Ranger programs with hands-on activities for kids 6 to 12. Ask at any ranger station about these free activities. ⊠*Bordered by Independence Ave. and Maine Ave., The Mall* ☎202/479–2426 Ⓜ*Farragut W.*

WORD OF MOUTH. **"The National Park Service publishes a very entertaining 'Cherry Blossom Watch', complete with a chart (at the bottom of the page) showing the dates for various stages of blossom for the past 16 years. Peak bloom can be as early as March 15 (1990) and as late as April 18 (1958)." –Anonymous**

West Potomac Park. Between the Potomac and the Tidal Basin, West Potomac Park is best known for its flowering cherry trees, which bloom for two weeks in late March or early April. During the rest of the year, West Potomac Park is just a nice place to relax, play ball, or admire the views at the Tidal Basin.

PARTICIPATION SPORTS

BICYCLING

The numerous trails in the District and its surrounding areas are well maintained and clearly marked.

KEEP IN MIND. **In Washington, D.C., and Maryland, all bicyclists under the age of 16 must wear helmets. In parts of Virginia, including Alexandria, Arlington County, Fairfax County, Falls Church, and Vienna, the law applies to kids 14 and younger.**

For scenery, you can't beat the **C&O Canal Towpath** (⊕*www. nps.gov/choh*), which starts in Georgetown and runs along the C&O Canal into Maryland. You could pedal to the end of the canal, nearly 200 mi away in Cumberland, Maryland, but most cyclists stop at Great Falls, 13 mi from where the canal starts. The occasionally bumpy towpath, made of gravel and packed earth, passes through wooded areas of the C&O Canal National Historical Park. You can see 19th-century locks from the canal's working days, and if you're particularly lucky, you may catch a glimpse of mules pulling a canal barge. The barges now take passengers, not cargo. Picnic tables along this path and historical markers give families good markers for rest stops.

Suited for bicyclists, walkers, rollerbladers, and strollers, the paved **Capital Crescent Trail** (☎202/234–4874 *Capital Crescent Coalition*) stretches along the old Georgetown Branch, a B&O Railroad line that was completed in 1910 and was in operation until 1985. The 7½-mi route's first leg runs from Georgetown near Key Bridge to central Bethesda at Bethesda and Woodmont avenues. At Bethesda and Woodmont, the trail heads through a well-lighted tunnel near the heart of Bethesda's lively business area and continues into Silver Spring. The 3½-mi stretch from Bethesda to Silver Spring is gravel. The Georgetown Branch Trail, as this section is officially named, connects with the Rock Creek Trail, which goes to Rockville in the north and Memorial Bridge past the Washington Monument in the south. On weekends when the weather's nice, all sections of the trails are crowded. The trail can get crowded on weekends as parents with strollers, rollerbladers and dog walkers share the space and during weekday rush hours as commuters bike to work. But the trail is as wide as 12 feet in some places and cyclists tend to know and follow the safety rules for passing. As the trail cuts through downtown Bethesda, you're only a few hundred feet from dozens of restaurants and shops.

Each day, bicyclists cruise the **Mall** amid the endless throngs of runners, walkers, and tourists. There's relatively little car traffic, and bikers can take in some of Washington's landmarks, such as the Washington Monument, the Reflecting Pool, the Vietnam Memorial, and some of the city's more interesting architecture, such as the Smithsonian Castle and the Hirshhorn, the "Doughnut on the Mall." The museums and monuments that seem too far to visit by foot become accessible by bike.

BIKING THE MALL. **A pleasant loop route begins at the Lincoln Memorial, going north past the Washington Monument, and turning around at the Tidal Basin. Along the way are small fountains and parks for water breaks and rests.**

Mount Vernon Trail, across the Potomac in Virginia, has two sections. The northern part, closest to D.C. proper, is 3½ mi long and begins near the causeway across the river from the Kennedy Center that heads to Theodore Roosevelt Island (⇨*Hiking below*). It then passes Ronald Reagan National Airport and continues on to Old Town Alexandria. This section has slight slopes and almost no interruptions for traffic, making it a delightful, but challenging, biking route. Even relatively inexperienced bikers enjoy the trail, which provides wonderful views of the Potomac. To access the trail from the District, take the Theodore Roosevelt Bridge or the Rochambeau Memorial Bridge, also known as the 14th Street Bridge. South of the airport, the trail runs down to the Washington Marina. The final mile of the trail's northern section meanders through protected wetlands before ending in the heart of Old Town Alexandria. The trail's 9-mi southern section extends along the Potomac from Alexandria to Mount Vernon. Be sure to stop at Gravely Point to see, and hear, the jets landing at Ronald Reagan National Airport.

Rock Creek Park covers an area from the edge of Georgetown to Montgomery County, Maryland. The bike path there is asphalt and has a few challenging hills, but it's mostly flat. You can bike several miles without having to stop for cars (the roadway is closed entirely to cars on the weekend). The two separate northern parts of the trail, which begin in Bethesda and Silver Spring, merge around the Washington, D.C., line. Many bikers gather at this point and follow the trail on a path that goes past the Washington Zoo and eventually runs toward the Lincoln Memorial and Kennedy Center. Fifteen miles of dirt trails are also in the park; these are best for hiking. Weekends bring out hundreds of serious bikers who sound like a swarm of wasps when they ride by. The most popular section is the trail along the creek from Georgetown to the National Zoo; about a 4-mi loop. In summer, there's considerable shade, and there are water fountains along the way.

INFORMATION

Washington Area Bicyclist Association (✉*1803 Connecticut Ave., Northwest* ☎*202/518–0524* ⊕*www.waba.org*) lists the latest information about local laws and the trails on their Web site.

RENTALS & TOURS

Big Wheel Bikes, near the C&O Canal Towpath, rents multispeed bikes for $35 per day and $21 for three hours. A second location is near the Capital Crescent Trail. There's also an Alexandria branch if you want to ride the Mount Vernon Trail. One tot trailer that fits two children is available for rent on a first-come, first-served basis. ⊠*1034 33rd St. NW, Georgetown* ☎*202/337–0254* ⊠*3119 Lee Hwy., Arlington, VA* ☎*301/652–0192* ⊠*2 Prince St., Alexandria, VA* ☎*703/739–2300* All ages

Bike and Roll (☎*202/842–2453* ⊕*www.bikethesites.com*) is a tour company that offers three-hour, 8-mi guided tours of downtown Washington and the monuments. Tandem bikes for adults with toddlers and strollers are also available for rent.

The **Boathouse at Fletcher's Cove** (⊠*4940 Canal Rd., at Reservoir Rd., Foxhall* ☎*202/244–0461*), next to the C&O Towpath and Capital Crescent Trail, rents fixed-gear bikes for $8 per hour and $19 per day. Off the beaten path, Fletchers is good for families who also want to rent a canoe or kayak.

Revolution Bikes (⊠*3411 M St. NW, Georgetown* ☎*202/965–3601*), near Georgetown University and Key Bridge by the Potomac River, rents city bikes for $20 per day. They carry 16–inch-wheel bikes on up.

BOATING & SAILING

The Chesapeake Bay is one of the great sailing basins of the world. For scenic and historical sightseeing, take a day trip to Annapolis, Maryland, the home of the U.S. Naval Academy. ∎TIP→**The popularity of boating and the many boating businesses in Annapolis make it one of the best civilian sailing centers on the East Coast.**

Annapolis Sailing School (⊠*601 6th St., Annapolis, MD* ☎*410/267–7205*), the oldest organization of its kind in the United States, is a good choice for lessons and rentals. It's world renowned. Kids five and up have learned to sail through their KidShip program since 1988.

Outdoor Excursions (⊕*Box 24, Boonsboro, MD* ☎*800/775–2925* ⊕*www.outdoorexcursions.com*) organizes trips down the river for first-time or relatively inexperienced rafters. Participants meet just below Great Falls. Children need to be at least eight to participate.

Canoeing, sailing, and powerboating are popular in the Washington, D.C., area. Several places rent boats along the **Potomac River** north and south of the city. You can dip your oars just about anywhere along the river—go canoeing in the C&O Canal or sailing in the widening river south of Alexandria. Experienced kayakers love the raging rapids at Great Falls, a 30-minute drive from the capital.

RENTALS

Belle Haven Marina (⊠*George Washington Pkwy., Alexandria, VA* ☎*703/768–0018*), south of Reagan National Airport and Old Town Alexandria, rents three types of sailboats: Sunfish are $30 for two hours during the week and $35 for two hours on the weekend; Hobie Cat–style sailboats and Flying Scots are $46 for two hours during the week and $54 for two hours during the weekend. Canoes and kayaks are available for rent at $20 for two hours. Rentals are available from April to October. Instruction is available for children eight and up. Parking is free but limited on weekends.

The **Boathouse at Fletcher's Cove** (⊠*4940 Canal Rd., at Reservoir Rd., Foxhall* ☎*202/244–0461*), just north of Georgetown, rents 17-foot rowboats for $11 per hour and $20 per day. Canoes are available for rent at $11 per hour and $21 per day. Off the beaten path (literally the Capital Crescent Trail), Fletchers rents boats and bikes and sells fishing rods. Life vests available for kids 30 pounds and up.

Thompson's Boat Center (⊠*2900 Virginia Ave. NW, Foggy Bottom* ☎*202/333–4861*) is near Georgetown and Theodore Roosevelt Island. The center rents canoes for $8 per hour and $22 per day. Single kayaks are $8 per hour and $24 per day, and double kayaks are $10 per hour and $30 per day. Rowing sculls are also available, but you must demonstrate prior experience and a suitably high skill level. Any child up to 18 must be with an adult. Children must be at least eight and older. During the spring, crowds cheer as crew teams from local high schools, Georgetown University, and George Washington compete.

Tidal Basin (⊠*Bordered by Independence Ave. and Maine Ave., The Mall* ☎*202/479–2426* Ⓜ*Farragut W*), in front of the Jefferson Memorial, rents paddleboats beginning in April and usually ending in September, depending on how cold the water gets. The entrance is at 1501 Maine Avenue SW, on the east side of the Tidal Basin. You can rent two-passenger boats at $8 per hour and four-passenger boats at $16 per hour. Kids must be at least 16 (picture ID required) to venture out alone, but children 1½ years old and up may go out with a parent.

The **Washington Sailing Marina** (⊠*1 Marina Dr., Alexandria, VA* ☎*703/548–9027* ⊕*www.washingtonsailingmarina. com*) rents sailboats from around mid-May to September, or until the water gets too cold. Sunfish are $10 per hour, Island 17's are $17 per hour, and the larger Flying Scots are $19 per hour. There's a one-hour minimum rental for all boats. Sailing camps run throughout the year for kids 9 to15. You must be at least 18 to rent, but children of any age may go out with a parent. Picnic tables and a restaurant nearby with great views and soccer fields offer room to roam.

HIKING

Washington may be a city of museums and monuments, but it's also full of great green spaces for hiking, exploring, and playing.

★ Fodor'sChoice **Theodore Roosevelt Island** (⊠*Foggy Bottom* ☎*703/ 289–2552 or 703/289–2550* ⊕*www.nps.gov/this*), designed as a memorial to the environmentally minded president, is a wildlife sanctuary off the George Washington Parkway on the Virginia side of the city. It can be reached by car by taking the Theodore Roosevelt Bridge or I–66. Hikers and bicyclists can easily reach it by taking the 14th Street Bridge. Many birds and other animals live in the island's marsh and forests. If it weren't for the airplanes from Ronald Reagan National Airport overhead, you might forget you were in D.C. altogether. The 2½ mi of trails crisscross marshland, swampland, and upland forest. To make the most of your visit, pack binoculars, a magnifying glass, a camera, and a plant and animal guide if you have them. Cattails, arrow arum, pickerelweed, willow, ash, maple, and oak all grown on the island that's also home to frogs, raccoons, birds, squirrels, deer, and the occasional fox. Although you won't see the animal most associated with Roosevelt (the bear), a 17-foot bronze statue of this president raises its right hand for emphasis. There's nothing to buy on this island—not even a soda—and public restrooms close between October and early April.

A self-guided nature trail winds through **Woodend** (⊠*8940 Jones Mill Rd., Chevy Chase, MD* ☎*301/652–9188, 301/652–1088 for recent bird sightings* ⊕*www.audubon naturalist.org*), a verdant 40-acre estate, and around the

CLOSE UP

Fun for All Seasons

With every change of the seasons, D.C. offers new pleasures for sports and outdoor enthusiasts:

■ In **winter** you can have an old-fashioned afternoon of ice-skating and hot chocolate in the midst of the National Gallery's sculpture garden, or go to the Verizon Center to see the Wizards play basketball or the Capitals play hockey.

■ Come **spring**, the city emerges from the cold with activities everywhere. Runners become a common sight on the Mall, and boating is available nearby.

■ In **summer,** baseball fans head to new Nationals Park to see the Nationals play, and Washington Redskins fans check out their favorite football stars at training camp in Ashburn, Virginia.

■ When **fall** arrives the seasonal colors of the trees in Rock Creek Park are a spectacular sight for bikers, hikers, and runners. Tickets to see the Redskins at FedEx Field are some of the city's most prized commodities.

5

suburban Maryland headquarters of the local **Audubon Naturalist Society.** The estate was designed in the 1920s by Jefferson Memorial architect John Russell Pope and has a mansion, also called Woodend, on its grounds. You're never far from the trill of birdsong here, as the Audubon Society has turned the place into something of a private nature preserve, forbidding the use of toxic chemicals and leaving some areas in a wild, natural state. Programs include wildlife identification walks, environmental education programs, and a weekly Saturday bird-walk September through June. A bookstore stocks titles on conservation, ecology, and birds. The grounds are open daily sunrise to sunset, and admission is free. No matter what it's like outside there'll be something interesting to see and do at this nature wonderland. From tracking animal tracks in the snow to chasing butterflies in spring. Allowing time to marvel at Mother Nature, you can complete the ¾-mi trail in about one hour. Parents of babies should use a carrier rather than a stroller as most of the trail has wood chips. For smooth, stroller surfaces, head down the driveway from the parking lot. When you reach the huge walnut tree, you're near what some local kids call the secret pond. Ask at the Woodend office to see the library, which contains hundreds of stuffed American birds. During family programs, classes and one-to-two week camps, naturalists unlock nature's mysteries. The bookshop sells puzzles and games with nature themes.

A 1,460-acre refuge in Alexandria, **Huntley Meadows Park** (⊠ *3701 Lockheed Blvd., Alexandria, VA* ☎ *703/768–2525*) is made for birders. You can spot more than 200 species— from ospreys to owls, egrets, and ibis. Much of the park is wetlands, a favorite of aquatic species. A boardwalk circles through a marsh, enabling you to spot beaver lodges, and 4 mi of trails wend through the park, making it likely you'll see deer, muskrats, and river otters as well. The park is usually open daily dawn to dusk. The boardwalk is wide enough to easily accommodate a double stroller but at ½ mi it's short enough for preschoolers. Inside the nature center, a fish tank at eye level for kindergartners and a snake keep youngsters amused. Programs for young nature detectives looking to learn more about fireflies, snakes, and other creatures cater to kids ages three and up.

KITE FLYING. The Smithsonian's annual **Kite festival** (⊠ *Downtown* ☎ *202/357–3030* ⊕ *www.kitefestival.org* Ⓜ *Smithsonian*) at the National Mall gives kids and adults a chance to enjoy a day of kite flying. The granddaddy of kite festivals, held in connection with the Cherry Blossom Festival in April, also features kite battles and incredible kite-flying exhibitions.

HORSEBACK RIDING

Trail rides are available year-round at **Rock Creek Park Horse Center** (⊠ *Military and Glover Rds. NW, Northwest/Upper Connecticut Ave.* ☎ *202/362–0117*). It's the only place in town where kids can take to the saddle. Pony rides (reservations required) take kids as young as 2½, and horseback rides cover trails along some of the same routes that presidents Martin Van Buren, Teddy Roosevelt, and Ronald Reagan once rode.

ICE-SKATING

Area rinks typically charge $4 to $6 for a two-hour session, with slightly lower fees for children and seniors. Skate rentals, available at all the rinks listed, are usually around $2 or $2.50. Some rinks charge a small fee for renting a locker.

The indoor rink at **Cabin John Regional Park** (⊠ *10610 Westlake Dr., Rockville, MD* ☎ *301/365–0585*) is open year-round. Family sessions for children 12 and under are on Sunday from 12:30 to 2:30. Two large rinks and a smaller one for lessons.

The **Mount Vernon Recreation Center** (⊠*2017 Belle View Blvd., Alexandria, VA* ☎*703/768–3222*) has an indoor rink that's open all year. It's convenient if you're staying in the lower half of Washington, D.C. The Center also has an indoor pool in the same building.

The **National Gallery of Art Ice Rink** (⊠*Constitution Ave. NW, between 7th and 9th Sts., Downtown* ☎*202/289–3361* Ⓜ*Navy Memorial/Archives*) is surrounded by the gallery's Sculpture Garden. The art deco design of the rink makes it one of the most popular outdoor winter sites in Washington. In spring the rink becomes a fountain. The rink is illuminated at night, and the Pavilion Café serves hot chocolate.

★ **Fodor'sChoice** The prime location of the **Pershing Park Ice Rink** (⊠*Pennsylvania Ave. and 14th St. NW, Downtown* ☎*202/737–6938* Ⓜ*Metro Center*), a few blocks from the White House, major hotels, and a metro station, makes this rink one of the most convenient spots in Washington for outdoor skating. About two blocks away from the White House and the Ellipse, where the National Christmas Tree stands tall from early December through January 1.

SPECTATOR SPORTS

BASEBALL

Major League Baseball has returned to D.C., where the **Washington Nationals** (⊠*Potomac and First Sts. SW* ☎*202/675–6287* ⊕ *washington.nationals.mlb.com* Ⓜ*Navy Yard*) of the National League play in their new spectacular home, Nationals Park. Tickets range from $5 to $65. Individual game tickets may be purchased at the park or through the team's Web site. ■TIP→ **The Metro is a hassle-free and inexpensive way to get to the ballpark. The closest and most convenient stop is the Navy Yard on the green line.** The Nationals, unofficially nicknamed the Nats, are represented by a group of young adults called the Nat Pack that revs up the crowd and helps give away goodies—T-shirts, pizzas, and magnets. On Sunday after the game, kids take to the field for the diamond dash. Another fun spectacle takes place during the middle of the fourth inning when 10-foot tall

Where the Pros Play

If you're going to a pro sports event, chances are you'll be headed to one of four venues. The perennially popular Redskins play football in the Maryland suburbs at **FedEx Field** (⊠*Arena Dr., Landover, MD*). It's a long walk from the nearest Metro, but parking tends to be expensive at the NFL's largest stadium. The Redskins' home is the largest stadium in the National Football League, seating 91,000. Check the *Washington Post* want ads and Craig's List for tickets for individual games. Parking is a hassle, so arrive several hours early for a game if you don't want to miss the kickoff.

Robert F. Kennedy Stadium (⊠*2400 E. Capitol St. NE, at 22nd St.* Ⓜ*Stadium*). The Redskins' former residence on Capitol Hill, is now home to Major League Soccer's D.C. United. Top soccer teams from Europe and Latin America also play exhibitions there. Not as spiffy as FedEx or Nationals Park, it's easy to get to by car or metro.

Nationals Park (⊠*1500 S. Capitol St. SE 20003* Ⓜ*Stadium*). D.C.'s baseball team, the Nationals, starts its second season in the spacious state-of-the-art ballpark on the Anacostia waterfront in Southwest Washington. The parking lot has limited spaces, making the Metro the best option for getting there. In the Strike Zone, kids 10 and up can test their batting and pitching skills, while younger siblings slide and swing on a jungle gym located past the center outfield. The fireworks that go off after home runs might be too loud for some children.

Verizon Center (⊠*601 F St. NW, between 6th and 7th Sts.* Ⓜ*Gallery Place/Chinatown*) hosts many sporting events, including hockey, basketball, and figure skating. This magnificent downtown facility is very convenient by Metro, and parking around the center is nonexistent. Disney on Ice and the circus usually perform here. Look for a special parking area for strollers.

caricatures of the presidents on Mount Rushmore take to the field.

BASKETBALL

The WNBA's **Washington Mystics** (⊠*6th and F Sts., Downtown* ☎*202/432–7328* ⊕*www.wnba.com/mystics* Ⓜ*Gallery Pl./Chinatown*) play at the Verizon Center in downtown Washington. The Mystics perennially lead the WNBA in attendance, despite a losing record. The games are loud, boisterous events. Ticket prices range from $10 to $60, with courtside tickets for $115. You can buy tickets at the Verizon Center box office, from the team directly through its Web site, or through Ticketmaster. The women's basketball season runs from late May to August. Tickets are easier to come by and cheaper than for the NBA Wizards or the NHL Capitals, which attracts more families. During the games a panda named PAX and Mayhem dancers, ages 7 to 18, cheer on the players and spread high-fives through the crowd.

★ Fodor'sChoice The NBA's **Washington Wizards** (⊠*6th and F Sts., Downtown* ☎*202/432–7328* ⊕*www.nba.com/wizards* Ⓜ*Gallery Pl./Chinatown*) play from October to April at the Verizon Center and feature superstar Gilbert Arenas. Tickets for individual games cost $40 to $850. The team also offers $10 seats in the upper level and courtside seats for a whopping $2,500. Buy tickets from the Verizon Center box office, from Ticketmaster, or directly from the team's Web site. Two big blue mascots get the crowd fired up. Shaggy G-ZWiz says he's 25 Twinkies tall and can hug three fans at once. All muscle G-Man shows off his dunking skills any chance he gets. Dancers and the District Drummers also perform at games. Wiz Kids fan club members get tickets, a backpack, and other promotional goodies.

FOOTBALL

Whatever the vicissitudes of the season, one thing remains the same: tickets to watch the **Washington Redskins** (☎*301/276–6000 FedEx Field stadium* ⊕*www.redskins. com*) are difficult to get. Though FedEx Field is the largest football stadium in the NFL, all 91,000 seats are held by season-ticket holders. Occasionally you can find tickets advertised in the classifieds of the *Washington Post* or on Craigslist, or buy them from online ticket vendors and auction sites—at top dollar, of course. Tickets can range from $175 to $300 for less popular opponents and go as high as $800 for elite teams, such as the New York Giants, or Washington's biggest rival, the Dallas Cowboys. ∎TIP➜ **Tickets are difficult to get, but fans can see the players up close and for free at training camp, held in August.** The Redskins invite the public to attend their training camp in Ashburn, in nearby Loudoun County, Virginia. Camp begins in late July and continues through mid-August. The practices typically last from 90 minutes to two hours. Fans can bring their own chairs, and the players are usually available after practice to sign autographs. Call ahead to make sure the practices are open that day. A practice schedule is on the team's Web site. Tickets are so tough to get that the Skins' games aren't a big draw for families. The best bet to see the players is at their training camp.

HOCKEY

One of pro hockey's better teams, the **Washington Capitals** (⊠ *6th and F Sts., Downtown* ☎ *202/432–7328* ⊕ *www. washingtoncaps.com* Ⓜ *Gallery Pl./Chinatown*), play home games October through April at the Verizon Center and feature one of hockey's brightest new superstars, Alex Ovechkin. Seats on the main level range from $71 to $176, and those in the upper deck range from $10 to $55.50. Tickets are less expensive if you purchase a family pack. Tickets can be purchased at the Verizon Center box office, from Ticketmaster, or directly from the team's Web site. At the Hockey 101 booth, team representatives answer questions from how may sticks do the players use to how players sharpen their skates. (The answer to the latter is they don't. The equipment manager sharpens them.) Kids too young to ask questions might enjoy a hug from Slapshot, the Capitals' mascot whose wingspan is 6 feet.

SOCCER

★ Fodor'sChoice **D.C. United** (⊠ *Robert F. Kennedy Stadium, 2400 E. Capitol St. SE, Capitol Hill* ☎ *202/547–3134* ⊕ *www. dcunited.com* Ⓜ *Stadium*) is one of the best Major League Soccer (U.S. pro soccer) teams. International matches, including some World Cup preliminaries, are often played on RFK Stadium's grass field, dedicated exclusively to soccer play. Games are April through September. You can buy tickets, which generally cost $25 to $65, with discounts for groups, at the RFK Stadium ticket office, through Ticketmaster, or through the team's Web site, which offers package deals for families. Washington, D.C., is a mecca for youth soccer. D.C. United games are called in both English and Spanish. Arrive early to participate in free speed kicks, dribbling contests, and other activities for kids outside the stadium.

Shopping

WORD OF MOUTH

"The best gift shop in DC (IMHO) is in the Building Museum. Every museum has its own gift shop, of course, and the one at the Lincoln Memorial has a good selection of Lincoln mementos. DC's Chinatown is tiny, it doesn't have the kind of shopping you'd find in NYC or on the west coast."

—Anonymous

Updated
by Kathryn
McKay

YOUNG VISITORS CAN LEAVE WASHINGTON loaded down with goodies, from souvenir T-shirts to baseball caps with panda ears to playing cards with presidential portraits. The best places for families to shop are most likely the places you're visiting anyway—most museums offer wonderful selections of merchandise for young and old alike. Prices are usually no higher than you'd find in comparable stores.

Favorite Smithsonian shops include those in the National Museum of American History (books, games), the National Museum of Natural History (dinosaur models, stuffed animals, plastic reptiles), and the National Air and Space Museum, where no kid can resist sampling the astronauts' freeze-dried ice cream in foil pouches, even though they're messy and not particularly tasty. Another bonus: At the Smithsonian shops, there's no tax.

CAPITOL HILL–EASTERN MARKET

As the Capitol Hill area has become gentrified, unique shops and boutiques have sprung up, many clustered around the redbrick Eastern Market. Inside are produce and meat counters, plus the Market Five art gallery. ■TIP→**The flea market, held on weekends outdoors, presents nostalgia and local crafts by the crateful. There's also a farmers' market on Saturday.** Along 7th Street you can find a number of small shops selling such specialties as art books, handwoven rugs, and antiques. Cross Pennsylvania Avenue and head south on 8th Street for historic Barracks Row. Shops, bars, and restaurants inhabit the charming row houses leading toward the Anacostia River. The other shopping lure on the Hill is Union Station, D.C.'s gorgeous train station. Beautifully restored, it now houses both mall shops and Amtrak and commuter trains.

Keep in mind that Union Station and Eastern Market are on opposite sides of the Hill. The Eastern Market Metro stop is the midpoint between the Eastern Market strip and Barracks Row; Union Station is several blocks away. You can certainly walk to Union Station from the Eastern Market stop, but it might be taxing after the time already spent on your feet in the shops. Even the stroller set enjoys the bright colors and lively music of Eastern Market on weekends. Use the Eastern Market Metro stop to leave; Union Station will feel too far for little feet after walking around the market. ⊠*7th and C Sts. SE, Capitol Hill* Ⓜ*Eastern Market or Union Station.*

TOP SHOPS

■ **International Spy Museum Store**. The stuff in the store is almost as cool as the stuff in the museum.

■ **National Air and Space Museum Shops**. The main store has three levels full of space souvenirs and a kiosk sells engraved dog tags. Kids discover that the pens designed for space work well here too but the ice cream tastes different!

■ **National Building Museum Shop**. Known as one of the best museum shops in Washington, their selection ranges from blocks for the bathtub to kits and books for budding architects. They even have blocks for kids who want to build replicas of the U.S. Capitol.

■ **Natural History Museum Shops**. The store outside of Mammal Hall is chock-full of plush and plastic replicas of the real thing. The shop downstairs to the left of the elevator has a huge selection of bag-your-own rocks, dinosaur stuff, and clear, amber-color candy with crickets in it.

■ **American History Museum Shops**. Here you can find all things Americana from playing cards with presidents on them and toy replicas of Lincoln's top hat to goofy, nostalgic toys, including chattering teeth and whoopee cushions.

NEED A BREAK? **The Market Lunch**. Locals line up for pancakes and fried fish at this greasy grill next to the fish counter in Eastern Market's food bazaar. Try their specialty crab-cake sandwiches on Sunday. The casual counter service and informal seating make it ideal for kids. On Saturday you must be in line by noon. Blueberry buckwheat pancakes are especially popular. ⊠*North corner of Eastern Market, 225 7th St. SE, Capitol Hill* ☎*202/547–8444* ⊘*Closed Mon.*

A MARKET & A MALL

Eastern Market. Vibrantly colorful produce and flowers; quality meat, poultry, and fish; fragrant cheeses; and tempting sweets are sold by independent vendors at this D.C. institution. On weekends a flea market and an arts-and-crafts market add to the fun. The redbrick building was gutted by fire in April 2007, but the community rallied around the beloved 134-year-old landmark and restoration work is under way. At this writing, it is scheduled for completion in 2009. In the interim, a temporary structure across the street houses vendors and the lunch counter, the Market

Lunch. Vendors hand out enough samples of seasonal fruits, vegetables, and wedges of cheese to make a meal for some kids. Artists sell tie-dyed onesies, hand-painted sneakers for kids and cloth books that appeal to families. Musicians play anything from the penny whistle to the saxophone. Most vendors only accept cash, but ATMs are nearby. ⊠*306 7th St. SE, Capitol Hill* ⊕*www.easternmarketdc. com* ⊙*Closed Mon.*

Union Station. This group of shops, resplendent with marble floors and gilded, vaulted ceilings, is inside a working train station. Upscale mall retailers include such familiar names as L'Occitane, Ann Taylor, and Nine West, as well as a bookstore, a multiplex movie theater, sit-down restaurants, and a food court. The east hall is filled with vendors of expensive domestic and international wares who sell from open stalls. ■TIP→**There's a tiny outpost of Vacarro's Italian Pastry Shop in the food court. The cannoli and biscotti are to die for.** The Christmas season brings lights, a train display, and seasonal gift shops to Union Station. **Making History** and **America's Spirit** sell a more eclectic selection of souvenirs than you'll find in gift shops at the monuments. **Out of Left Field** features souvenirs from all of Washington's sports teams. Edible Legos, Japanese cream-filled gummy candies and "I love DC" lollipops are just a few of the choices at **Candy Crate.** In late November through early January, one of the world's largest model trains winds through a Norwegian landscape complete with farms, a ski jump, and little trolls. In December, the U.S. Marine Corps kicks off its annual Toys for Tots gift drive for children in the D.C. area. ⊠*50 Massachusetts Ave. NE, Capitol Hill* ☎*202/289–1908* ⊕*www.unionstationdc.com* Ⓜ*Union Station.*

SPECIALTY STORES

BOOKS

Capitol Hill Books. Pop into this three-story maze of books to browse through a wonderful collection of out-of-print history books, political and fiction writings, and modern first editions. The children's book selection is extensive, but they don't host any story hours or activities for families. ⊠*657 C St. SE, Capitol Hill* ☎*202/544–1621* ⊕*www. capitolhillbooks-dc.com* Ⓜ*Eastern Market.*

Fairy Godmother. This specialty store features books for children, from infants through teens, in English, Spanish, and French. It also sells puppets, toys, craft sets, and CDs. Since 1984, families have received personal service at this shop, which has become a must for local families. Toys tend to be traditional as opposed to mechanical and battery operated. ⊠*319 7th St. SE, Capitol Hill* ☎*202/547–5474* ⊘*Closed Sun.* Ⓜ*Eastern Market.*

Trover Shop. A stone's throw from the Capitol, Trover is all about politics. Policy wonks and Hill staffers head to this independent for its excellent selection of political titles and for the book signings. Toys, cards, magazines, and newspapers round out the selection. Note that Trover is close to the Capitol Hill Metro and far from the other shops listed in this section. Stop in here after a visit to the Capitol, the Supreme Court, or the Library of Congress. Stuffed animals and educational toys from Meslissa & Doug round out the more serious stuff in this family-owned and operated store. ⊠*221 Pennsylvania Ave. SE, Capitol Hill* ☎*202/547–2665* ⊕*www.trover.com* Ⓜ*Capitol S.*

CHILDREN'S CLOTHING
Dawn Price Baby. The infant and toddler clothing at this friendly row-house boutique has been carefully selected with an eye for super-comfortable fabrics and distinct designs. They also stock toys, gifts, cribs, bedding, and coveted Bugaboo strollers. This neighborhood store with helpful staff sells baby bibs for young Democrats and Republicans. ⊠*325 7th St. SE, Capitol Hill* ☎*202/543–2920* ⊕*www. dawnpricebaby.com* ⊘*Closed Mon.* Ⓜ*Eastern Market.*

WOMEN'S CLOTHING
Forecast. If you like classic, contemporary styles, Forecast should be in your future. It sells silk sweaters and wool blends in solid, muted tones for women seeking elegant but practical clothing from brands like Yansi Fugel. The housewares and gifts selection on the first floor is colorful and of high quality. ⊠*218 7th St. SE, Capitol Hill* ☎*202/547–7337* ⊘*Closed Mon.* Ⓜ*Eastern Market.*

DOWNTOWN

Downtown D.C. is spread out and sprinkled with federal buildings and museums. Shopping options run the gamut, from the Gallery Place shopping center to small art galleries and bookstores. Gallery Place houses familiar chain stores like Urban Outfitters, Bed, Bath & Beyond, Ann Taylor Loft, and Aveda; it also has a movie theater and a bowling alley. Other big names in the downtown area include Macy's and chain stores like H&M and Banana

D.C.'s Museum Shops

Does someone in your life need a replica of the Hope diamond? It's waiting for you at the gift shop in the National Museum of Natural History. With a wide range of merchandise and price points, from inexpensive postcards to pricey pottery, museum gift shops allow you the flexibility to bring home a small memento of your visit to the nation's capital or to invest in a piece of American art or history. Museum gift shops offer everything from period jewelry reproductions to science kits for kids, not to mention prints and postcards of the masterpiece paintings in the permanent collections. If you don't want to carry around multiple shopping bags, rest assured that most of the items in museum shops can be purchased off the museum's Web site once you return home. Prices are no higher than you'd find in comparable stores. Another bonus: you won't pay tax on anything purchased in a public museum.

Republic. With its many offices, downtown tends to shut down at 5 PM sharp, with the exception of the department stores and larger chain stores. A jolly happy-hour crowd springs up after working hours, and families and fans fill the streets during the weekend sporting events. ⊠*North of Pennsylvania Ave. between 7th and 18th Sts., up to Connecticut Ave. below L St., Downtown* Ⓜ*Archives/Navy Memorial, Farragut N and W, Gallery Pl., McPherson Sq., or Metro Center.*

SPECIALTY STORES

FOOD & WINE

Cowgirl Creamery. A California original, this self-titled cheese shop has an educated staff that can help you find the perfect block (through many taste tests) as well as a matching wine or olive spread. Their artisan cheeses hail from the Bay area, from local cheese makers, and from points beyond. The friendly staff allows you to taste before you buy and encourages kids to help name their stuffed cow and gives kids their cheese labels to use as stickers. ⊠*919 F St. NW, Downtown* ☎*202/393–6880* ⊕*www.cowgirlcreamery.com* ⊙*Closed Sun.* Ⓜ*Gallery Pl.*

MUSEUM

International Spy Museum Store. Tours of the museum end here, but you don't need an admission ticket to get gadgets and gear galore. Fake mustaches are just the beginning.

Kids can eat the evidence with edible spy paper, hide stuff in a book safe, and check what or who's behind them with rearview spyglasses. For $90, kids can even see in the dark with night-vision goggles. ⊠*800 F St. NW, Downtown* ⊕*www.spymuseumstore.com* ☎*202/393–7798* Ⓜ*Gallery Pl./Chinatown*

SHOES

Church's. This top-notch English company's handmade men's shoes are noted for their comfort and durability. ⊠*1820 L St. NW, Downtown* ☎*202/296–3366* ⊗*Closed Sun.* Ⓜ*Farragut N.*

WOMEN'S CLOTHING

Rizik Bros. This tony, patrician Washington institution offers designer women's clothing and expert advice. The sales staff will help find just the right style from the store's inventory, which is particularly strong in formal dresses. Take the elevator up from the northwest corner of Connecticut Avenue and L Street. ⊠*1100 Connecticut Ave. NW, Downtown* ☎*202/223–4050* Ⓜ*Farragut N.*

DUPONT CIRCLE

You might call Dupont Circle a younger, less staid version of Georgetown—almost as pricey but with more apartment buildings than houses. Its many restaurants, offbeat shops, and specialty book and record stores give it a cosmopolitan air. The street scene here is more urban than Georgetown's, with bike messengers and chess aficionados filling up the park. The Sunday farmers' market is a popular destination for organic food, fresh cheese, homemade soap, and handspun wool. To the south of Dupont Circle proper are several boutiques and familiar retail stores close to the Farragut and Farragut North Metro stops. Burberry and Thomas Pink both have stores in this area of Dupont. Teenagers might enjoy shopping here. Families with younger kids will find more on the National Mall. ⊠*Connecticut Ave. between M and S Sts.* Ⓜ*Dupont Circle.*

SPECIALTY STORES

BOOKS

★ Fodor'sChoice **Kramerbooks & Afterwords.** One of Washington's best-loved independents, this cozy shop has a small but choice selection of fiction and nonfiction. Open 24 hours on Friday and Saturday, it's a convenient meeting place. Kramerbooks shares space with a café that has late-night dining and live music from Wednesday to Saturday. ■TIP→**There's a computer with free Internet access available in the bar, though you'll have to stand up to use it.** Serving brunch in the morning, snacks in the afternoon, cocktails in the evening, and coffee all day long, Kramer's is the perfect spot for a break. Try to snag an outside table, drop your shopping bags, and watch the world go by. Children's books range from cloth books for infants to graphic novels that teens read, but there are no toys, no story time, and no changing tables in the rest rooms. ⊠*1517 Connecticut Ave. NW, Dupont Circle* ☎*202/387–1400* ⊕*www.kramers. com* Ⓜ*Dupont Circle.*

Second Story Books. A used-books and -records emporium that stays open late, Second Story may lead bibliophiles to browse for hours. The focus here is on books for adults but they have enough children's books to fill one bookcase. ⊠*2000 P St. NW, Dupont Circle* ☎*202/659–8884* ⊕*www. secondstorybooks.com* Ⓜ*Dupont Circle.*

CHILDREN'S CLOTHING

Kid's Closet. If filling a little one's closet is on your list, stop here for high-quality contemporary infant and children's clothing and toys. They carry sizes 0–7 for boys and 0–16 for girls. Open since 1982, the selection runs from basic brands such as Carters to organic clothes. Gift wrapping available. ⊠*1226 Connecticut Ave. NW, Dupont Circle* ☎*202/429–9247* ⊕*www.kidsclosetdc.com* ⊙*Closed Sun.* Ⓜ*Dupont Circle.*

CRAFTS & GIFTS

Beadazzled. A rainbow of ready-to-string beads fills the cases at this appealing shop. They also stock jewelry as well as books on crafts history and techniques. Check their Web site for a class schedule. Preteens and teens can sign up for the classes. ⊠*1507 Connecticut Ave. NW, Dupont Circle* ☎*202/265–2323* ⊕*www.beadazzled.net* Ⓜ*Dupont Circle.*

The Chocolate Moose. This store is simple, sheer fun for adults and kids alike. Looking for clacking, windup teeth? You can find them here, along with unusual greeting cards, strange boxer shorts, and unique handcrafts. If playing with all those fun toys makes you hungry, you can pick up a select line of premium European chocolates. ⊠*1743 L St. NW, Dupont Circle* ☎*202/463–0992* ⊕*www.chocolatemoosedc. com* ⊙*Closed Sun.* Ⓜ*Farragut N.*

The Written Word. Not just a stationery store, the Written Word is more like a tribute to paper. In addition to a wide variety of handmade papers, there are journals, photo albums, and scrapbooks—all made out of unusual papers—as well as unique greeting cards. It's also one of the few places in D.C. that offer custom letterpress printing. They carry children's stationery, flash cards, and fun coloring books. ✉ *1427 P St. NW, Dupont Circle* ☎ *202/223–1400* ⊕ *www.writtenwordstudio.com* Ⓜ *Dupont Circle.*

HOME FURNISHINGS

Reincarnations. Reincarnations is a neighborhood favorite, partly because of its duo of imposing wooden soldiers at the doorway. It's hard to pinpoint one style that dominates—trendy, antique, funky—and everyone can find something to like here. ✉ *1401 14th St. NW, Logan Circle* ☎ *202/319–1606* ⊕ *www.reincarnationsfurnishings.com/* Ⓜ *Dupont Circle.*

Tabletop. Evoking a museum gift shop, this two-story row house is a delightful place to find bags by Swedish designer Lotta Jansdotter, Marimekko accessories, and daphne olive jewelry, as well as modern furniture, pillows, and rugs. They also carry cloth dolls, knitted monkeys, and art books. ✉ *1608 20th St. NW, Dupont Circle* ☎ *202/387–7117* ⊕ *www.tabletopdc.com* Ⓜ *Dupont Circle.*

KITCHENWARE

Coffee and the Works. Coffee- and tea lovers head to this charmingly cluttered shop for high-end kitchen gadgets, magnets, colorful ceramic pots, and other accessories, as well as the beans and leaves themselves. Made in the USA, mugs with creatures such as dogs, cats, and sea monsters in the bottom might get kids to drink their milk. ✉ *1627 Connecticut Ave. NW, Dupont Circle* ☎ *202/483–8050* Ⓜ *Dupont Circle.*

MEN'S CLOTHING

J. Press. Like its flagship store, founded in Connecticut in 1902 as a custom shop for Yale University, this Washington outlet is resolutely traditional: Shetland and Irish wool sport coats are a specialty. ✉ *1801 L St. NW, Farragut Square* ☎ *202/857–0120* ⊕ *www.jpressonline.com* Ⓜ *Farragut N.*

WOMEN'S CLOTHING

★ Fodor'sChoice **Betsy Fisher.** Catering to women of all ages and sizes in search of contemporary and trendy styles, this store stocks one-of-a-kind accessories, clothes, shoes, and jewelry by well-known designers like Diane Von Furstenberg. A small selection of up-and-coming local designs is also available. ⊠*1224 Connecticut Ave. NW, Dupont Circle* ☎*202/785–1975* ⊕*www.betsyfisher.com* Ⓜ*Dupont Circle.*

★ Fodor'sChoice **Secondi.** One of the city's finest consignment shops, Secondi carries a well-chosen selection of women's designer and casual clothing, accessories, and shoes. The brands carried include Marc Jacobs, Louis Vuitton, Donna Karan, Prada, and Ann Taylor. ⊠*1702 Connecticut Ave. NW, 2nd fl., Dupont Circle* ☎*202/667–1122* ⊕*www.secondi.com* Ⓜ*Dupont Circle.*

GEORGETOWN

Although Georgetown is not on a Metro line and street parking is nonexistent, people still flock here, keeping it D.C.'s favorite shopping area. This is also the capital's center for famous residents, as well as being a hot spot for restaurants, bars, and nightclubs.

National chains and designer shops now stand side-by-side with the specialty shops that first gave the district its allure, but the historic neighborhood is still charming and its street scene lively. In addition to housing tony antiques, elegant crafts, and high-style shoe and clothing boutiques, Georgetown offers wares that attract local college students and young people: books, music, and fashions from familiar names such as Banana Republic, BCBG, Betsey Johnson, Kate Spade, and Urban Outfitters. Most stores lie east and west on M Street and to the north on Wisconsin Avenue. The intersection of M and Wisconsin is the nexus for chain stores and big-name designer shops. The farther you venture in any direction from this intersection, the more eclectic and interesting the shops become. Some of the big-name stores are worth a look for their architecture alone; several shops blend traditional Georgetown town-house exteriors with airy modern showroom interiors.

Shopping in Georgetown can be expensive, but you don't have to add expensive parking-lot fees to your total bill. The nearest Metro, Foggy Bottom/GWU, is a 10- to 15-minute walk from the shops. ■TIP→**The D.C. Circulator is your best bet** for getting into and out of Georgetown, especially if it's hot or if you are laden down with many purchases. This $1 bus runs along M Street and up Wisconsin, passing the major shopping strips. ⊠*Intersection of Wisconsin Ave. and M St., Georgetown* Ⓜ*Foggy Bottom/GWU.*

NEED A BREAK? **DolceZZa.** The handmade gelato and sorbet at this all-white storefront are divine, especially during the heat of summer. The flavors, such as Coconut con Dulce de Leche, are endlessly inventive. Strawberry-, peach-, apple-, and clementine-flavored sorbets are available seasonally. Espresso and churros will warm winter afternoons. ⊠1560 Wisconsin Ave. NW, Georgetown, ☎202/333–4646 ⊕dolcezzagelato.com.

MALL

Shops at Georgetown Park. Near the hub of the Georgetown shopping district is this posh trilevel mall, which looks like a Victorian ice cream parlor inside. The pricey clothing and accessory boutiques and the ubiquitous chain stores draw international visitors in droves. Next door is a branch of the Dean & Deluca gourmet grocery and café. ⊠*3222 M St. NW, Georgetown* ☎*202/298–5577* ⊕*www.shopsat-georgetownpark.com* Ⓜ*Foggy Bottom/GWU.*

SPECIALTY STORES

BOOKS

Bartleby's Books. Be a scholar and surround yourself with rare and precious books in this antiquarian bookstore. The Americana collection—organized by state—is particularly browsable; you might just find an unexpected souvenir from home. Their bookshelf of children's books might include anything from a $5 copy of Charlotte's Web to a $1,000 storybook illustrated by Arthur Rackham. ⊠*1132 29th St. NW, Georgetown* ☎*202/298–0486* ⊕*www.bartlebysbooks. com* ⊙*Closed Sun. and Mon.*

Bridge Street Books. This charming independent store focuses on politics, history, philosophy, poetry, literature, film, and Judaica. A small collection of children's books are in the back corner. ⊠*2814 Pennsylvania Ave. NW, Georgetown* ☎*202/965–5200* ⊕*www.bridgestreetbooks.com* Ⓜ*Foggy Bottom/GWU.*

CHILDREN'S CLOTHING

Magic Wardrobe. This shop caters to kids (or actually their parents) who prefer classic and traditional clothes. Both

American and European designers, plus clothes from their own private label clad kids from newborn to size 16. They also carry shoes. ✉ *1663 Wisconsin Ave. NW, Georgetown* ☎ *202/333–0353* ⊕ *www.themagicwardrobe.com.*

Piccolo Piggies. Chock-full of fun and educational toys as well as classic layette and children's clothing (up to size 14 for girls and 10 for boys), this warm store is a pleasure to browse through—even if you're a bit over the age limit. ✉ *1533 Wisconsin Ave. NW, Georgetown* ☎ *202/333–0123* ⊕ *www.piccolo-piggies.com.*

Tugooh Toys. Like Yiro, its sister store across the street, everything is eco-friendly and free of lead, PVC, and BPA. Nearly everything is made of wood, with most toys imported from Germany, France, and Switzerland. ✉ *1419 Wisconsin St. NW, Georgetown* ☎ *202/333–0032* ⊕ *www. yirostores.com.*

Yiro. One hundred percent organic, Yiro clothing (through age 10) is produced without chemicals and is colored only with natural dyes (and yes, the outfits are soft and attractive). A baby registry will help you pick the perfect gift for the environmentally conscious mom. ✉ *3236 P St. NW, Georgetown* ☎ *202/338–9476* ⊕ *www.yirostores.com.*

HOME FURNISHINGS

★ FodorsChoice **A Mano.** The store's name is Italian for "by hand," and it lives up to its name, stocking colorful hand-painted ceramics, hand-dyed tablecloths, blown-glass stemware, and other home and garden accessories by Italian and French artisans. Items are now also available in their online catalog. Animals appear in everything from kid's cereal bowls to hooded towels. Monogrammed piggy banks can be available within a week. ✉ *1677 Wisconsin Ave. NW, Georgetown* ☎ *202/298–7200* ⊕ *www.amano.bz.*

Theodore's. A Washington institution, Theodore's is the place to visit for ultramod housewares, from stylish furniture to accessories, leather, and upholstery that make a statement. There's an excellent selection of wall-storage units for almost all tastes. ✉ *2233 Wisconsin Ave. NW, Georgetown* ☎ *202/333–2300* ⊕ *www.theodores.com.*

MEN'S & WOMEN'S CLOTHING

Commander Salamander. This funky outpost sells clothes for punk kids and ravers. Retro aficionados will also find clothing and accessories for their wardrobes. Sifting through the assortment of leather, chains, toys, and candy-color makeup is as much entertainment as it is shopping. Teenagers have been flocking here for trendy stuff since it opened in 1979. ⊠*1420 Wisconsin Ave. NW, Georgetown* ☎*202/337–2265* Ⓜ*Foggy Bottom/GWU.*

relish. In the fashionable Cady Alley stretch, this dramatic space holds an expanding men and women's collection hand-picked seasonally by the owner. Modern, elegant, and practical selections include European classics as well as well-tailored modern designers, such as Narciso Rodriguez and Dries Van Noten. ⊠*3312 Cady's Alley NW, Georgetown* ☎*202/333–5343* ⊕*www.relishdc.com* ⊙*Closed Sun.* Ⓜ*Foggy Bottom/GWU.*

SHOES

★ Fodor's Choice **Hu's Shoes.** This cutting-edge shoe store would shine in Paris, Tokyo, or New York. Luckily for us, it brings ballet flats, heels, and boots from designers like Chloé, Schouler, Sonia Rykiel, and Maison Martin Margiela right here to Georgetown. ⊠*3005 M St. NW, Georgetown* ☎*202/342–0202* ⊕*www.hushoes.com* Ⓜ*Foggy Bottom/ GWU.*

Sassanova. There are high-end shoes in this girly shop for every occasion—be it a walk on the beach or through a boardroom. Brands carried include Emma Hope and Sigerson Morrison. Jewelry, bags, and shoes for kids round out the selection. Kids' shoes range from the traditional and trendy from 0 to 6 month size up to size 2. Brands include Jack Rogers, Puddle Jumpers, Primigi, and Treetorn. ⊠*1641 Wisconsin Ave. NW, Georgetown* ☎*202/471–4400* ⊕*www.sassanova.com.*

WOMEN'S CLOTHING

The Phoenix. Here you can find contemporary clothing in natural fibers by designers such as Eileen Fisher and Flax, as well as jewelry and fine- and folk-art pieces from Mexico. Inexpensive finger puppets and dolls may help keep wee ones amused while their mothers shop. ⊠*1514 Wisconsin Ave. NW, Georgetown* ☎*202/338–4404* ⊕*www.the phoenixdc.com.*

Urban Chic. It's hard to imagine a fashionista who wouldn't find something she loved here—whether she could afford it might be another story. Gorgeous suits, jeans, cocktail dresses, and accessories from Catherine Malandrino, Ella Moss, Rebecca Taylor, and Susana Monaco are to be had.

The handbags are a highlight. Kids can stay in style with brands such as Juicy Couture and Splendid in sizes from infant through 14. ✉ *1626 Wisconsin Ave. NW, Georgetown* ☎ *202/338–5398* ⊕ *www.urbanchiconline.com.*

Wink. While the clientele and styles skew toward the young and trendy, women of all ages shop in this subterranean space for coveted jeans and colorful, sparkly tops, dresses, and jewelry. Theory, Diane von Furstenberg, and Development are among the labels carried. ✉ *3109 M St. NW, Georgetown* ☎ *202/338–9465* ⊕ *www.shopwinkdc.com* Ⓜ *Foggy Bottom/GWU.*

FRIENDSHIP HEIGHTS

The major thoroughfare Wisconsin Avenue runs northwest through the city from Georgetown toward Maryland. It crosses the border in the midst of the Friendship Heights shopping district, which is also near Chevy Chase. Expensive department stores and designer shops stand cheek by jowl with major discount chains around the Friendship Heights Metro stop. Other neighborhoods in the District yield more interesting finds and more enjoyable shopping and sightseeing, but it's hard to beat Friendship Heights for sheer convenience and selection. Bloomingdale's is the latest addition to the upscale lineup, which includes Barneys CO-OP, Neiman Marcus, and Saks 5th Avenue. Stand-alone designer stores like Jimmy Choo, Louis Vuitton, Christian Dior, and Cartier up the luxury quotient. Filene's Basement, Loehmann's, and T.J. Maxx hawk the designer names at much lower prices. Lord & Taylor and chains like the Gap, Ann Taylor Loft, and Williams-Sonoma occupy the middle ground.

Tightly packed into a few blocks, the big-name area is self-explanatory. However, there are also a few local gems in the surrounding neighborhood. Some of these small shops are far from Metro stops, so call ahead for directions. The shops with kid-pleasing merchandise are almost all family owned and operated and are known for their quality selection and personalized service. ✉ *Wisconsin Ave. between Jenifer St. NW and Western Ave.* Ⓜ *Friendship Heights.*

SPECIALTY STORES

BOOKS
Politics and Prose. The calendar of this legendary independent is jam-packed with author events and signings, and

their tables are endlessly browsable. There's a coffee shop downstairs where you can debate the issues of the day. The nearest Metro is 15 minutes away. About 25% of the collection is for children and young adults. Monday Morning Storytimes held at 10:30 AM (except in August) draw as many as 50 kids. At least once a month, nationally known children's authors come in to sign books and answer questions. Recent appearances include Christopher Paolini, who wrote the Eragon series; Peter Sis, author of *Madlenka's Dog*; and Nikki Giovanni, author of *Rosa*. The children's booksellers have at least six years of experience in children's literature. ⊠*5015 Connecticut Ave. NW, Friendship Heights* ☎*202/364–1919* ⊕*www.politics-prose. com* Ⓜ*Friendship Heights.*

CHILDREN'S CLOTHING

Full of Beans. Full of children's clothing, largely made in the USA with a growing organic selection. So big kids won't have to walk past baby things, infant outfits are in the back. The owner seeks out colorful, cheerful clothes that, as she says, "have some wit" to them. ⊠*5502 Connecticut Ave. NW, Upper NW* ☎*202/362–8566* Ⓜ*Friendship Heights.*

GIFTS

Periwinkle Inc. Warm and welcoming, Periwinkle offers a panoply of gift options: boutique chocolates, cases of nutty and gummy treats, Stonewall Kitchen snacks, hand-designed wrapping paper, scented bath products, printed note cards, and Voluspa candles. A hutch near the cashier holds puzzles, sketchbooks, and games for kids. ⊠*3815 Livingston St. NW, Friendship Heights* ☎*202/364–3076* Ⓜ*Friendship Heights.*

MEN'S & WOMEN'S CLOTHING

Everett Hall. D.C.'s own Everett Hall designs men's suits that are richly classic in their material and cutting-edge in their design, color, and sensibility. Most suits are $1,000 and up. From NBA and NFL athletes to K Street lawyers, men with verve and a sense of style covet Hall's designs. ⊠*Chevy Chase Pavilion, 5301 Wisconsin Ave. NW, Friendship Heights* ☎*202/362–0191* Ⓜ*Friendship Heights.*

Micmac Bis. Inside this boutique with eye-catching displays are clothes by Issey Miyake and Yohji Yamamoto, and cool Arche shoes. ⊠*5454 Wisconsin Ave. NW, Chevy Chase* ☎*301/654–8686* Ⓜ*Friendship Heights.*

6

Sahba. This avant-garde women's clothing boutique stocks an expertly selected cache of True Religion jeans, Robert Rodriguez tops, and Jamin Peuch handbags. ⊠*5300 Wisconsin Ave. NW, Friendship Heights* ☎*202/966–5080* Ⓜ*Friendship Heights.*

TOY STORES

Child's Play. A favorite among local families since it opened here in 1991, the shop is larger than it appears from the front. You'll find quality toys from Brio, Haba, Playmobil, and Select. plus books and an extensive art section with a wide variety of paints, brushes, and paper. The staff is experienced at suggesting gifts for children with special needs, such as autism. ⊠*5536 Connecticut Ave. NW, Upper NW* ☎*202/244–3602* Ⓜ*Friendship Heights.*

Treetop Toys and Books. One of 10 stores in the D.C. area, the New Mexico Avenue location was the first, opening in 1976. Their biggest business is toys, but you can also find clothes, such as blazers and khakis for boys and fancy dresses for girls. The books tend to be classics, bestsellers, and new titles. During the school year, story times are held throughout the week with special events such as balloon animals and magic shows held most Saturdays. Gift wrapping is free every day. ⊠*3301 New Mexico Ave NW, Upper NW* ☎*202/244-3500* ⊕*www.treetopkids.com* Ⓜ*Cleveland Park.*

FAMILY FUN

Treasure Map
Washington D.C.:
Cash Monuments

Find the monuments of presidents who appear on U.S. money. For each president you locate, add the value of bill and tally the total cash findings for your trip. Give your kids one cent to the dollar for every one they find!

01.	$1	Washington (Massachusetts Ave. & Wisconsin Ave.)
02.	$1	Washington (K Street & 23rd)
03.	$1	Washington (H Street & 23rd)
04.	$5	Lincoln (West Mall)
05.	$2	Jefferson (Tidal Basin)
06.	$1	Washington (Constitution Ave. & 15th)
07.	$20	Jackson (Pennsylvania Ave. & 16th)
08.	$10	Hamilton (E Street & 15th)
09.	$1	Washington (Madison Drive & 14th)
10.	$100	Franklin (Pennsylvania Ave. & 12th)
11.	$5	Lincoln (E Street & 10th-inside Ford's Theater)
12.	$5	Lincoln (D Street between 4th & 5th)
13.	$50	Grant (West side of Capitol)
14.	$2	Jefferson (Library of Congress)

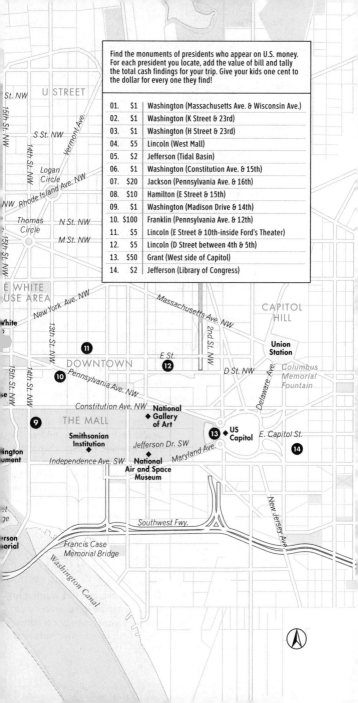

THE CLASSICS

"I'm thinking of an animal . . ."

With older kids you can play 20 Questions: Have your leader think of an animal, vegetable, or mineral (or, alternatively, a person, place, or thing) and let everybody else try to guess what it is. The correct guesser takes over as leader. If no one figures out the secret within 20 questions, the first person goes again. With younger children, limit the guessing to animals and don't put a ceiling on how many questions can be asked. With rivalrous siblings, just take turns being leader. Make the game's theme things you expect to see at your day's destination.

"I see something you don't see and it is blue."

Stuck for a way to get your youngsters to settle down in a museum? Sit them down on a bench in the middle of a room and play this vintage favorite. The leader gives just one clue—the color—and everybody guesses away.

FUN WITH THE ALPHABET

Family Ark

Noah had his ark—here's your chance to build your own. It's easy: Just start naming animals and work your way through the alphabet, from antelope to zebra.

"I'm going to the grocery . . ."

The first player begins, "I'm going to the grocery and I'm going to buy..." and finishes the sentence with the name of an object, found in grocery stores, that begins with the letter "A." The second player repeats what the first player has said, and adds the name of another item that starts with "B." The third player repeats everything that has been said so far and adds something that begins with "C," and so on through the alphabet. Anyone who skips or misremembers an item is out (or decide up front that you'll give hints to all who need 'em). You can modify the theme depending on where you're going that day, as "I'm going to X, and I'm going to see..."

"I'm going to Asia on an ant to act up."

Working their way through the alphabet, players concoct silly sentences stating where they're going, how they're traveling, and what they'll do.

What I See, from A to Z

In this game, kids look for objects in alphabetical order—first something whose name begins with "A," next an item whose name begins with "B," and so on. If you're in the car, have children do their spotting through their own window. Whoever gets to Z first wins. Or have each child play to beat his own time. Try this one as you make your way through zoos and museums, too.

JUMP-START A CONVERSATION

What if . . .?

Riding in the car and waiting in a restaurant are great times to get to know your youngsters better. Begin with imaginative questions to prime the pump.

If you were the tallest man on earth, what would your life be like? The shortest?

If you had a magic carpet, where would you go? Why? What would you do there?

If your parents gave you three wishes, what would they be?

If you were elected president, what changes would you make?

What animal would you like to be and what would your life be like?

What's a friend? Who are your best friends? What do you like to do together?

Describe a day in your life 10 years from now.

Druthers

How do your kids really feel about things? Just ask. "Would you rather eat worms or hamburgers? Hamburgers or candy?" Choose serious and silly topics—and have fun!

Faker, Faker

Reveal three facts about yourself. The catch: One of the facts is a fake. Have your kids ferret out the fiction. Take turns being the faker. Fakers who stump everyone win.

KEEP A STRAIGHT FACE

"Ha!"

Work your way around the car. First person says, "Ha." Second person says, "Ha, ha." Third person says "Ha" three times. And so on. Just try to keep a straight face. Or substitute, "Here, kitty, kitty, kitty!"

Wiggle & Giggle

Give your kids a chance to stick out their tongues at you. Start by making a face, then have the next person imitate you and add a gesture of his own—snapping fingers, winking, clapping, sneezing, or the like. The next person mimics the first two and adds a third gesture, and so on.

Junior Opera

During a designated period of time, have your kids sing everything they want to say.

Igpay Atinlay

Proclaim the next 30 minutes Pig Latin time, and everybody has to talk in this fun code. To speak it, move the first consonant of every word to the end of the word and add "ay." "Pig" becomes "igpay," and "Latin" becomes "atinlay." For words that begin with a vowel, just add "ay" as a suffix.

MORE GOOD TIMES

Build a Story

"Once upon a time there lived . . ." Finish the sentence and ask the rest of your family, one at a time, to add another sentence or two. Bring a tape recorder along to record the narrative—and you can enjoy your creation again and again.

Not the Goofy Game

Have one child name a category. (Some ideas: first names, last names, animals, countries, friends, feelings, foods, hot or cold things, clothing.) Then take turns naming things that fall into that category. You're out if you name something that doesn't belong in the category—or if you can't think of another item to name. When only one person remains, start again. Choose categories depending on where you're going or where you've been—historic topics if you've seen a historic sight, animal topics before or after the zoo, upside-down things if you've been to the circus, and so on. Make the game harder by choosing category items in A-B-C order.

Color of the Day

Choose a color at the beginning of your outing and have your kids be on the lookout for things that are that color, calling out what they've seen when they spot it. If you want to keep score, keep a running list or use a pen to mark points on your kids' hands for every item they spot.

Click

If Cam Jansen, the heroine of a popular series of early-reader books, says "Click" as she looks at something, she can remember every detail of what she sees, like a camera (that's how she got her nickname). Say "Click!" Then give each one of your kids a full minute to study a page of a magazine. After everyone has had a turn, go around the car naming items from the page. Players who can't name an item or who make a mistake are out.

The Quiet Game

Need a good giggle—or a moment of calm to figure out your route? The driver sets a time limit and everybody must be silent. The last person to make a sound wins.

Travel Smart Fodor's Family: Washington, D.C.

WORD OF MOUTH

"Please stay near a Metro line and don't bring the car at all. Parking is expensive and can be difficult to find; traffic is bad and the routes are confusing. Just wear sneakers and enjoy the fact you're burning off pounds."

—Thank you, the Commuters
—kgh8m

GETTING HERE & AROUND

▌ GETTING TO D.C.

Although it may not appear so at first glance, there's a system to addresses in D.C., albeit one that's a bit confusing for newcomers. The city is divided into the four quadrants of a compass (NW, NE, SE, SW), with the U.S. Capitol at the center. Because the Capitol doesn't sit in the exact center of the city, Northwest is the largest quadrant. Northwest also has most of the important landmarks, although Northeast and Southwest have their fair share. The boundaries are North Capitol Street, East Capitol Street, South Capitol Street, and the National Mall. That's where street addresses start and climb as you move up the numbers and alphabet.

If someone tells you to meet them at 6th and G, ask them to specify the quadrant, because there are actually four different 6th and G intersections (one per quadrant). Within each quadrant, numbered streets run north to south, and lettered streets run east to west (the letter J was omitted to avoid confusion with the letter I). The streets form a fairly simple grid—for instance, 900 G Street NW is the intersection of 9th and G streets in the NW quadrant of the city. Likewise, if you count the letters of the alphabet, skipping J, you can get a good approximation of an address for a numbered street. For instance, 1600 16th Street NW is close to Q Street, Q being the 16th letter of the alphabet if you skip J.

As if all this weren't confusing enough, Major Pierre L'Enfant, the Frenchman who originally designed the city, threw in diagonal avenues recalling those of Paris. Most of D.C.'s avenues are named after U.S. states. You can find addresses on avenues the same way you find those on numbered streets, so 1200 Connecticut Avenue NW is close to M Street, because M is the 12th letter of the alphabet when you skip J.

▬ TIP → **Ask the local tourist board about hotel and local transportation packages that include tickets to major museum exhibits or other special events.**

▌ BY AIR

A flight to D.C. from New York takes a little less than an hour. It's about 1½ hours from Chicago, 3 hours from Denver or Dallas, and 5 hours from San Francisco. Those flying from London should expect a trip of about 6 hours. From Sydney it's an 18-hour flight.

▬ TIP → **If you travel frequently, look into the TSA's Registered Traveler program. The program, which is still being tested in several U.S. airports, is designed to cut down on gridlock at security checkpoints by allowing prescreened travelers to pass quickly through kiosks that scan an** iris and/or a fingerprint. How sci-fi is that?

Airlines & Airports **Airline and Airport Links.com** (⊕www.airlineandairportlinks.com) has links to many of the world's airlines and airports.

Airline Security Issues **Transportation Security Administration** (⊕www.tsa.gov) has answers for almost every question that might come up.

Air Travel Resources in Washington, D.C. **U.S. Department of Transportation Aviation Consumer Protection Division** (☎202/366–2220 ⊕www.airconsumer.ost.dot.gov).

AIRPORTS

The major gateways to D.C. are **Ronald Reagan Washington National Airport (DCA)** in Virginia, 4 mi south of downtown Washington; **Dulles International Airport (IAD)**, 26 mi west of Washington, D.C.; and **Baltimore/Washington International–Thurgood Marshall Airport (BWI)** in Maryland, about 30 mi to the northeast.

Reagan National Airport is closest to downtown D.C., and has a Metro stop in the terminal. East Coast shuttles and shorter flights tend to fly in and out of this airport. However, the Mid-Atlantic region is prone to quirky weather that can snarl air traffic, especially at Reagan National. Dulles is configured primarily for long-haul flights. BWI offers blended service, with its many gates for no-frills Southwest Air, as well as international flights. Although the Metro

doesn't serve Dulles and BWI, there is affordable and convenient public transportation to and from each airport. Prices vary between each of the three area airports, so be sure to compare fares before booking your flights.

■TIP➔**Long layovers don't have to be only about sitting around or shopping. These days they can be about burning off vacation calories. Check out ⊕www.airportgyms. com for lists of health clubs that are in or near many U.S. and Canadian airports.**

Airport Information **Baltimore/Washington International–Thurgood Marshall Airport** (☎410/859–7100 ⊕www.bwiairport.com). **Dulles International Airport** (☎703/572–2700 ⊕www.metwashairports.com/Dulles). **Ronald Reagan Washington National Airport** (☎703/417–8000 ⊕www.metwashairports.com/National).

GROUND TRANSPORTATION: REAGAN NATIONAL

By Car: Take the George Washington Memorial Parkway, north, for approximately 1 mi. Exit on I–395 North; bear left onto US-1 North toward downtown. For the city center, turn left on Madison Drive NW and turn right on 15th Street NW. The drive takes 20 to 30 minutes, depending on traffic and your destination.

By Metro: The Metro station is within easy walking distance of terminals B and C, and a free airport bus shuttles between the station and Terminal A. The Metro ride downtown takes about 20 minutes and costs about $1.85, depending on the time of day and your final destination. Up to two children, 4 years and younger, ride free with each adult.

By Shuttle: SuperShuttle, a fleet of bright blue vans, will take you to any hotel or residence in the city. The length of the ride varies, depending on traffic and the number of stops. The approximately 20-minute ride from Reagan National to downtown averages $13.

By Taxi: Expect to pay $10 to $15 to get from National to downtown.

Contacts SuperShuttle (☎800/258-3826 or 202/296-6662 ⊕www.supershuttle.com). **Washington Metropolitan Area Transit Authority** (☎202/637-7000, 202/638-3780 TTY ⊕www.wmata.com).

GROUND TRANSPORTATION: BWI

By Car: Exit BWI and follow I–95 West. Take Exit 2B to MD-295 South for 24 mi; exit on US-50 West toward Washington. Continue on New York Avenue for about 3 mi; continue on Mount Vernon Place NW for 2 mi. Continue on Massachusetts Avenue NW; turn left on Vermont Avenue NW at Thomas Circle. Turn right on K Street NW; take a left on 17th Street NW and you're now basically in the city center. Distance is about 34 mi and should take 50 to 60 minutes.

By Public Transit: Amtrak and Maryland Rail Commuter Service (MARC) trains run between BWI and Washington, D.C.'s Union Station from around 6 AM to 10 PM.

> **TIP**
>
> If you plan to take a cab to or from the airport, note that a $1.50 airport surcharge is added to the total at all airports. A $1 surcharge is added to the total for travel during the peak periods of 7 to 9:30 AM and 4 to 6:30 PM. And be aware that unscrupulous cabbies prey on out-of-towners. If the fare seems astronomical, get the driver's name and cab number and threaten to call the D.C. Taxicab Commission.)

The cost of the 30-minute ride is $17 to $41 on Amtrak and $7 on MARC, which runs only on weekdays. A free shuttle bus transports passengers between airline terminals and the train station (which is in a distant parking lot).

Washington Metropolitan Area Transit Authority (WMATA) operates express bus service (Bus B30) between BWI and the Greenbelt Metro station. Buses run between 6 AM and 10 PM. The fare is $3.10.

By Shuttle: SuperShuttle, a fleet of bright blue vans, will take you to any hotel or residence in the city. The length of the ride varies, depending on traffic and the number of stops. The ride from BWI, which takes approximately 60 minutes, averages $35.

By Taxi: The fare from BWI is about $60 to $70.

Contacts Amtrak (☎800/872-7245 ⊕www.amtrak.com). **Maryland Rail Commuter Service** (☎410/539-5000, 410/539-3497 TTY, 866/743-3682

⊕www.mtamaryland.com). **Su-perShuttle** (☎800/258-3826 or 202/296-6662 ⊕www.supershuttle. com). **Washington Metropolitan Area Transit Authority** (☎202/637-7000, 202/638-3780 TTY ⊕www. wmata.com).

GROUND TRANSPORTATION: DULLES

By Car: From Dulles Airport, exit onto Dulles Airport Access Road and follow this for 14 mi; merge onto VA-267 East. Merge onto I-66 East; follow this for approximately 6 mi and exit to the left on E Street Expressway. Take the ramp to E Street NW. Total distance from the airport to downtown is about 27 mi and should take about 45 minutes.

By Public Transit: Washington Flyer links Dulles International Airport and the West Falls Church Metro station. The 20-minute ride is $9 one-way and $16 round-trip for adults, free for children under six. Buses run every half hour from 5:45 AM to 10:15 PM. All coaches are accessible to those in wheelchairs. Fares may be paid with cash or credit card at the ticket counter near Door 4 at the Arrivals/Baggage Claim Level. Board the bus just outside the door.

The Washington Metropolitan Area Transit Authority (WMATA) operates express bus service between Dulles and several stops in downtown D.C., including the L'Enfant Plaza Metro station. Bus 5A, which costs $3.10, runs every hour between 5:30 AM and 11:30 PM. Make sure to have

the exact fare, as drivers cannot make change.

By Shuttle: SuperShuttle, a fleet of bright blue vans, will take you to any hotel or residence in the city. The length of the ride varies, depending on traffic and the number of stops. The roughly 45-minute ride from Dulles runs $32.

By Taxi: The fare from Dulles is about $50 to $60.

Contacts SuperShuttle (☎800/258-3826 or 202/296-6662 ⊕www.supershuttle.com). **Washington Flyer** (☎888/927-4359 ⊕www. washfly.com). **Washington Metropolitan Area Transit Authority** (☎202/637-7000, 202/638-3780 TTY ⊕www.wmata.com).

FLIGHTS

Reagan Washington National (DCA) is served by Air Canada/Air Canada Jazz, AirTran, Alaska, American/American Eagle, Continental, Delta/ Delta Connection/Delta Shuttle, Frontier, Midwest, Northwest, Spirit, United, and US Airways/US Airways Express/US Airways Shuttle.

Baltimore/Washington International (BWI) is served by Air Canada, Air Greenland, Air Jamaica, Air Tran, America West, American, British, Continental, Delta, Icelandair, Midwest, North American, Northwest, Southwest, United Airlines, and US Airways.

Dulles International (IAD) is served by Aeroflot, Air Canada, Air France, Aer Lingus, AirTran, ANA, American/American Eagle, Austrian Air, British Airways, Continental, Delta/Delta Connection,

Ethiopian, Grupo Taca, Iberia, jet-Blue, KLM, Korean Air, Lufthansa, Northwest, Qatar Airways, Saudi Arabian, South African, Southwest, SAS, Sun Country Airlines, Ted, United/United Express, US Airways/US Airways Express, and Virgin America/Virgin Atlantic.

BY BUS

ARRIVING & DEPARTING

Washington's Greyhound bus terminal, a major one for the company, is approximately four blocks north of Union Station. Taxis are always waiting at the terminal, so it's easy to get to other parts of the city. You can purchase your ticket by phone, on the Internet, or at the station before you board the bus. Greyhound accepts cash and all major credit cards. Services at the station are limited, so stock up on snacks and reading material at Union Station ahead of time.

Affectionately known as the Chinatown Express, several bus lines run between Chinatown in New York City and Chinatown in Washington, D.C. The most reliable is called Today's Bus. The buses are clean, the service is satisfactory, and the price—$20 one-way and $35 round-trip—can't be beat.

Information **Greyhound** (✉1005 1st St. NE ☎800/231–2222 for fares and schedules, 202/289–5160 for D.C. terminal ⊕www.greyhound. com). **Today's Bus** (✉610 I St. NW ☎202/408–8200 ⊕www.todaysbus. com).

BY TRAIN

More than 80 trains a day arrive at Washington, D.C.'s Union Station. Amtrak's regular service runs from D.C. to New York in 3¼ to 3¾ hours and from D.C. to Boston in 7¾ to 8 hours. Acela, Amtrak's high-speed service, travels from D.C. to New York in 2¾ to 3 hours and from D.C. to Boston in 6½ hours.

Two commuter lines—Maryland Rail Commuter Service (MARC) and Virginia Railway Express (VRE)—run to the nearby suburbs. They're cheaper than Amtrak, but they don't run on weekends.

Amtrak tickets and reservations are available at Amtrak stations, by telephone, through travel agents, or online. Amtrak schedule and fare information can be found at Union Station as well as online.

Amtrak has both reserved and unreserved trains available. If you plan to travel during peak times, such as a Friday night or near a holiday, you'll need to get a reservation and a ticket in advance. Some trains at nonpeak times are unreserved, with seats assigned on a first-come, first-served basis.

Information **Amtrak** (☎800/ 872–7245 ⊕www.amtrak.com). **Maryland Rail Commuter Service** ([MARC] ☎800/325–7245 ⊕www. mtamaryland.com). **Union Station** (✉50 Massachusetts Ave. NE ☎202/371–9441 ⊕www.union stationdc.com). **Virginia Railway Express** ([VRE] ☎703/684–1001 ⊕www.vre.org).

▌ GETTING AROUND D.C.

Most of the sightseeing neighborhoods (the Mall, Capitol Hill, Downtown, Dupont Circle) are near Metro rail stations, but a few (Georgetown, Adams-Morgan) are more easily reached by the red, white, and blue buses operated by the Washington Metropolitan Area Transit Authority. The No. 42 bus travels from the Dupont Circle Metro stop to and through Adams-Morgan. Georgetown is a hike from the closest Metro rail station, but you can take a Georgetown Metro Connection shuttle to any Metrobus stop from the Foggy Bottom or Dupont Circle Metro stations in D.C. or the Rosslyn Metro station in Virginia. The D.C. Circulator is another option for getting to Georgetown.

Complete bus and Metro maps for the metropolitan D.C. area, which note museums, monuments, theaters, and parks, can be picked up free of charge at the Metro Center sales office.

Fares & Transfers: All regular buses within the District are $1.35; express buses, which make fewer stops, are $3.10. For every adult ticket purchased, two children under the age of four travel free. Children five and older pay the regular fare.

Free bus-to-bus transfers, good for three hours, are available from the driver when you board. To transfer Metro-to-bus, take a pass from the rail-to-bus-transfer machine in the Metro station after you go through the turnstile and before you board your train. When you board the bus, you'll pay a transfer charge (45¢ on regular metrobus routes and $2.20 on express routes). There are no bus-to-Metro transfers.

Payment & Passes: Buses require exact change in bills, coins, or both. You can eliminate the exact-change hassle by purchasing bus fare in advance at the Metro Center sales office, open weekdays from 7:30 AM to 6:30 PM. You can purchase seven-day bus passes for $11. For some bus routes you can get the SmarTrip card, a plastic card that holds any fare amount. The cost of each ride is deducted as you board the bus. You can also order Metrobus passes online with a credit card. There's no charge for shipping and handling, and passes are mailed within two days of your order via first class mail.

D.C. Circulator: The D.C. Circulator has three routes and charges $1. The Circulator, a joint project of the WMATA and the District of Columbia government, is designed to serve only the core of the city and its major attractions.

The Convention Center–Southwest Waterfront Route cuts a path from north to south, running from the D.C. Convention Center at 6th and Massachusetts Avenue NW, to the Southwest Waterfront, at 6th Street and Maine Avenue. The Georgetown–Union Station route goes east to west, journeying from Union Station to Georgetown (intersection of M Street and Wisconsin Avenue NW). Both of these routes are operated daily from 7 AM to 9 PM.

The third loop, operating on weekends only from 10 AM to 6 PM, is the Smithsonian–National Gallery Loop. It circles the National Mall.

Passengers can pay cash when boarding (exact change only) or use Metro Farecards, SmarTrip cards, all-day passes, and Metro bus transfers. Tickets also may be purchased at fare meters or multispace parking meters on the sidewalk near Circulator stops. Machines accept change or credit cards and make change. You only have to wait about 5 to 10 minutes at any of the stops for the next bus.

Information **D.C. Circulator** (☎202/962–1423 ⊕www.dccir culator.com). **Metro Center sales office** (✉12th and F Sts. NW ☎No phone). **Washington Metropolitan Area Transit Authority** (☎202/637–7000, 202/638–3780 TTY ⊕www.wmata.com).

▌ BY CAR

A car is often a drawback in Washington, D.C. Traffic is horrendous, especially at rush hour, and driving is often confusing, with many lanes and some entire streets changing direction suddenly during rush hour. Even longtime residents carry maps in their cars to help navigate confusing traffic circles and randomly arranged one-way streets. Most traffic lights stand at the side of intersections (instead of hanging suspended over them), and the streets are dot-ted with giant potholes. The city's most popular sights are within a short walk of a Metro station anyway, so it's best to leave your car at the hotel. Touring by car is a good idea only for visiting sights in Maryland or Virginia.

Zipcar has been around for a few years now and seems to be growing in popularity. You can rent a car for a couple of hours or a couple of days. Gas, insurance, parking, and satellite radio are included. It's not cheap; $9 an hour or $65 a day, plus a $25 application fee and $50 annual fee, but it may be worth it for the hassle-free convenience. Once you sign up either online or over the phone, a wireless signal is sent to the car, which is parked nearby. When you get to your car, you get in and go, but keep in mind, you're responsible for your own safety seats. You then simply return the car to the same location.

Information **zipcar** (☎866/494–7227 ⊕www.zipcar. com).

GASOLINE
Gas tends to be slightly higher in the District than it is in Maryland or Virginia. As a rule, gas stations are hard to find in the District, especially around Pennsylvania Avenue and the National Mall. Your best bets are a BP station at the corner of 18th and S streets NW, the Mobil station at the corner of 15th and U streets NW, the Exxon station at 2150 M Street NW, and the Mobil station at the corner of 22nd and P streets NW.

LAY OF THE LAND

Interstate 95 skirts D.C. as part of the Beltway, the six- to eight-lane highway that encircles the city. The eastern half of the Beltway is labeled both I–95 and I–495; the western half is just I–495. If you're coming from the south, take I–95 to I–395 and cross the 14th Street Bridge to 14th Street in the District. From the north, stay on I–95 South. Take the exit to Washington, which will place you onto the Baltimore–Washington (B-W) Parkway heading south. The B-W Parkway will turn into New York Avenue, taking you into downtown Washington, D.C.

Interstate 66 approaches the city from the southwest. You can get downtown by taking I–66 across the Theodore Roosevelt Bridge to Constitution Avenue.

Interstate 270 approaches Washington, D.C., from the northwest before hitting I–495. To reach downtown, take I–495 East to Connecticut Avenue South, toward Chevy Chase.

PARKING

Parking in Washington, D.C., is an adventure; the police are quick to tow away or immobilize with a boot any vehicle parked illegally. If you find you've been towed from a city street, call ☎202/727–5000 or log on to ⊕www.dmv.washingtondc.gov. Be sure you know the license plate number, make, model, and color of the car before you call.

Most of the outlying suburban Metro stations have parking lots, although these fill quickly with city-bound commuters. If you plan to park in one of these lots, arrive early.

Private parking lots downtown often charge around $5 an hour and $25 a day. There's free, three-hour parking around the Mall on Jefferson and Madison drives, although these spots are almost always filled. There is no parking near the Lincoln or Roosevelt memorials. The closest free parking is in three lots in East Potomac Park, south of the 14th Street Bridge.

ROADSIDE EMERGENCIES

Dial 911 to report accidents on the road and to reach police, the highway patrol, or the fire department. For police non-emergencies, dial 311.

Emergency Services U.S. Park Police (☎202/619–7300).

RULES OF THE ROAD

In D.C. you may turn right at a red light after stopping if there's no oncoming traffic. When in doubt, wait for the green. Be alert for one-way streets, "no left turn" intersections, and blocks closed to car traffic. The use of handheld mobile phones while operating a vehicle is illegal in Washington, D.C. Drivers can also be cited for "failure to pay full time and attention while operating a motor vehicle."

Radar detectors are illegal in Washington, D.C., and Virginia.

During rush hour (6 to 9 AM and 4 to 7 PM), HOV (high-occupancy vehicle) lanes on I–395 and I–95 are reserved for cars with three or more people. All the lanes of I–66 inside the Beltway are reserved for cars carrying two or more during rush hour, as are some of the lanes on the Dulles Toll Road and on I–270.

In Washington, D.C., Maryland, and Virginia, laws regarding child safety seats are basically the same. Children seven and under (eight and under in Maryland) need to be in appropriate child restraint seats. For children aged four to seven that usually means a booster seat. The law still applies in taxis. Most car rental companies rent child safety seats.

BY METRO

The Metro, which opened in 1976, is one of the country's cleanest, most efficient, and safest subway systems. For train-loving tots, riding the Metro can be as thrilling as exploring D.C. It begins operation at 5 AM on weekdays and 7 AM on weekends. The Metro closes on weekdays at midnight and weekends at 3 AM. Don't get to the station at the last minute, as trains from the ends of the lines depart before the official closing time. During the weekday peak periods (5 to 9:30 AM and 3 to 7 PM), trains come along every three to six minutes. At other times and on weekends and holidays, trains run about every 12 to 15 minutes.

The Metro's base fare is $1.65; the actual price you pay depends on the time of day and the distance traveled, which means you might end up paying $4.50 if you're traveling to a distant station at rush hour. Up to two children under age five ride free when accompanied by a paying passenger.

Buy your ticket at the Farecard machines; they accept coins and crisp $1, $5, $10, or $20 bills. If the machine spits your bill back out at you, try folding and unfolding it lengthwise before asking someone for help. Some newer machines will also accept credit cards. You can buy one-day passes for $7.80 and seven-day passes for $39. Locals use the SmarTrip card, a plastic card that can hold any fare amount and can be used throughout the Metro, bus, and parking system. The cost of each ride is deducted as you enter the subway. Buy passes or SmarTrip cards at the Metro Center sales office or online.

Insert your Farecard into the turnstile to enter the platform. Make sure you hang on to the card—you need it to exit at your destination.

Eating, drinking, smoking, and littering in stations and on the trains are strictly prohibited.

When you leave the train, make sure shoelaces are tied and scarves are tucked in before you ride the escalators, some of which are more than 200 feet long. If your child is afraid of heights or you have a little one in a stroller, take the elevators. All the stations have them, though about a third of them are across the street from Metro entrances.

Metro Information **Washington Metropolitan Area Transit Authority** ([WMATA] ✉12th and F Sts. NW, sales center ☎202/637–7000, 202/638–3780 TTY, 202/962–1195 lost and found ⊕www.wmata.com).

▌ BY TAXI

You can hail a taxi on the street just about anywhere in the city, and they tend to congregate around major hotels. If you find yourself on a quiet street in a residential area, either walk to a busier street or phone for a taxi. Although it depends on your location and the time of day, a taxi ought to arrive in 10 to 15 minutes. There are a number of different cab companies in the city, and as a result, D.C. cabs do not have a uniform appearance (unlike New York's yellow cabs, for example). And you may find yourself in a taxi that's older and a bit run down.

Most District cab drivers are independent operators and may ignore a potential passenger. Cabbies are also known for refusing to pick up passengers after learning of their destination, and the D.C. government rarely enforces the taxi laws that require drivers who are free to either pick up passengers or display an off-duty sign. If after several minutes you haven't been able to get a cab, your best bet is to find the nearest Metro station and take the subway or walk to a nearby hotel and get a cab there.

After 70 years of a zone system, taxis in the District are now on time and distance meters. The base rate for the first 1/6-mile is $3. Each additional 1/6-mile and each minute stopped or traveling at less than 10 mph. is 25¢. The first bag is free, after that there is a charge of 50¢ per bag. There is a $2 surcharge for radio dispatch and $1 surcharge for high fuel prices.

During D.C.-declared snow emergencies, there is an additional 25% surcharge. The maximum fare for trips starting and ending in the District is $18.90 plus applicable surcharges.

Maryland and Virginia taxis also have meters. These taxis can take you into or out of D.C., but are not allowed to take you between points in D.C.

Taxi Companies **Diamond** (☎202/387–6200). **Mayflower** (☎202/783–1111). **Yellow** (☎202/544–1212).

ESSENTIALS

▋ BABYSITTING

Most larger hotels and those with concierges can arrange babysitting services with one of Washington's licensed services, or you can call one of the services listed below. Rates are usually per hour with a four-hour minimum, and you may need to pay the sitter's transportation costs. Fees start at $15 an hour. Additional children may cost more. Most agencies are happy to provide references; some sitters will even take kids sightseeing. You may also arrange for a sitter to stay the night. Agencies can usually arrange for last-minute child care, but advance notice is recommended.

Contacts **WeeSit** (☎703/764–1542 ⊕www.weesit.net). **White House Nannies** (☎301/652–9026 or 800/266-9026 ⊕www.white housenannies.com).

▋ DAY TOURS & GUIDES

We recommend any of the tours offered by the Smithsonian Associates Program, A Tour de Force, and Anecdotal History Tours of D.C. For price and convenience, you can't beat the Old Town Trolley Tours or Tourmobile buses, which take you to all the major historical and cultural landmarks in the city. What's great about those tours is that you can get on and off as you please and stay as long as you like at any spot; you can re-board for free all day long.

From April through October, Washington Walks has two-hour guided tours that are interesting and, at $10 per person, affordable. From February to November, join a free tour of the monuments and memorials with DC by Foot. If it's too hot to walk, hop on board Capitol River Cruises for a look at the city from the water.

For families we recommend the bike or Segway tours, the D.C. Duck tour (younger kids will get a kick out of the quackers that are given to all riders), a mule-drawn barge ride on the C&O Canal, a Bureau of Engraving and Printing tour, and any of Natalie Zanin's historic strolls, especially the Ghost Story Tour of Washington. Traveling on your own? Check out the six-hour D.C. Party Shuttle Tour.

BICYCLE TOURS

Bike the Sites Tours has knowledgeable guides leading daily excursions past dozens of Washington, D.C., landmarks. All tours start at the Old Post Office Pavilion. Bicycles, helmets, snacks, and water bottles are included in the rates, which start at $40 and $30 for kids 12 and under. The Adventure Cycling Association, a national organization promoting bicycle travel, recommends tours around the region.

Contacts **Adventure Cycling Association** (☎800/755–2453 ⊕www.adventurecycling.org). **Bike the Sites Tours** (☎202/842–2453 ⊕www.bikethesites.com).

BOAT TOURS

During one-hour rides on mule-drawn barges on the C&O Canal, costumed guides and volunteers explain the waterway's history. The barge rides, which cost $7 and are run by the National Park Service, depart from its visitor center Wednesday through Sunday from April through November.

Capitol River Cruises offers 45-minute sightseeing tours aboard the *Nightingale* and *Nightingale II*, Great Lakes boats from the 1950s. Beverages and light snacks are available. Hourly cruises depart from Washington Harbor noon to 9 PM April to October. Prices are $12 for adults and $6 for children 3 to 12.

Several swanky cruises depart from the waterfront in Southwest D.C. The sleek *Spirit of Washington* offers lunch and dinner cruises that range from $32 to $105. Sightseeing tours to Mount Vernon on the *Spirit of Mount Vernon* cost $42.95, which includes the cruise and Mount Vernon entrance fee. As of this writing, Spirit Cruises also plans to offer cruises from the new National Harbor on the banks of the Potomac River in Maryland. Located just minutes from D.C., National Harbor is scheduled to open in stages with a hotel and convention center, shops, restaurants, and condominiums.

Departing from Alexandria, the glass-enclosed *Dandy* and *Nina's Dandy* cruise up the Potomac year-round to Georgetown, taking you past many of D.C.'s monuments. Lunch cruises board weekdays starting at 11 AM. Depending on the day, dinner cruises board at 5:45 or 6:30 PM. Prices are $43 to $51 for lunch and $83 to $92 for dinner. The *Dandy* and *Nina's Dandy* also offer special holiday cruises.

From April through October, D.C. Ducks offers 90-minute tours in funky converted World War II amphibious vehicles. After an hour-long road tour of landlocked sights, the tour moves to the water, where for 30 minutes you get a boat's-eye view of the city. During the rides, 'wise-quacking" captains entertain with anecdotes and historical trivia. Tours depart from Union Station and cost $28.80 for adults and $14.40 for children ages 4 to 12; seating is on a first-come, first-served basis.

Contacts **C&O Canal Barges** (⊠Canal Visitor Center, 1057 Thomas Jefferson St. NW, Georgetown ☎202/653–5190 ⊕www.nps.gov/choh). **Capitol River Cruises** (⊠31st and K Sts. NW, Georgetown ☎301/460–7447 or 800/405–5511 ⊕www.capitolrivercruises.com). **Dandy Cruises** (⊠Prince St. between Duke and King Sts., Alexandria, VA ☎703/683–6076 ⊕www.dandydinnerboat.com). **DC Ducks** (⊠50 Massachusetts Ave. NE, Union Station ☎202/832–9800 ⊕www.dcducks.com). *Odyssey III* (⊠600 Water St. SW, D.C. Waterfront ☎202/488–6010 or 800/946–7245 ⊕www.odysseycruises.com). *Spirit of Washington* (⊠Pier 4, 6th and Water Sts. SW, D.C. Waterfront ☎202/554–8013 or 866/211–3811 ⊕www.spiritcruises.com).

BUS TOURS

All About Town has half-day, all-day, two-day, and twilight bus tours to get acquainted with the city. Tours leave from various downtown locations. An all-day tour costs $44 to $56, half-day and twilight tours cost $32.

Capital Entertainment Services offers guided half-day "Monument and Memorial," and "African American Heritage" bus tours priced at $25 for adults and $15 for children ages 5 to 11. One popular tour is "Duke Ellington's Neighborhood Tour," which includes stops at his childhood neighborhood, the African American Civil War Memorial, and the National Museum of American History.

D.C. Party Shuttle Tours offers a daily six-hour "D.C. It All" tour, where you hop on and off with the guide at 12 locations. The cost is $60 for adults and $55 for children under 12. Their three-hour "D.C. The Lights" nightlife tour costs $35 per person.

Gray Line's four-hour tour of Capitol Hill, Embassy Row, and Arlington National Cemetery leaves Union Station at 8 AM (late June–late October) and 2 PM (year-round) and costs $38; tours of Mount Vernon and Old Town Alexandria depart at 8 AM (year-round) and 2 PM (late June–late October) and cost $40. An all-day trip combining both tours leaves at 8 AM (year-round) and costs $60. There's also a two-and-a-half hour tour on Saturday mornings presented in conjunction with the International Spy Museum that showcases more than 25 sites used by infamous spies. Included in the cost of $79 per person is same-day admission to the Museum.

Gross National Product's Scandal Tours, led by members of the GNP comedy troupe, last 1½ hours and cover scandals from George Washington to George Bush. The tours, held on Saturdays at 1 PM, cost $30 per person; reservations are required.

On Location Tours has a three-hour tour that visits more than 30 locations used in the filming of movies and TV shows, including *No Way Out, The Exorcist, Wedding Crashers, All the President's Men, West Wing,* and *24,* among others. Tours run Friday through Sunday beginning at 2 PM and cost $32 per person.

Contacts All About Town (☎301/856–5556 ⊕www.allabout own.com). **Capital Entertainment Services** (✉3629 18th St. NE, Washington, D.C. ☎202/636–9203 ⊕www.washington-dc-tours.com). **Gray Line** (☎301/386–8300 or 800/862–1400 ⊕www.graylinedc. com). **Gross National Product** (☎202/783–7212 ⊕www.gn-pcomedy.com). **On Location Tours** (☎212/209–3370 ⊕www.screen tours.com). **Washington D.C. Party Shuttle** (☎202/756–1983 ⊕www. washingtondcpartyshuttle.com).

GOVERNMENT BUILDING TOURS

Special tours of government buildings with heavy security, including the White House and the Capitol, can be arranged through your representative or senator's office. Limited numbers of these so-called VIP tickets are available, so plan up to six months in advance of your trip. Governmental buildings close to visitors when the Department of Homeland Security issues a high alert, so call ahead.

You can also see the famous domed building with the United States Capitol Guide Service, which leads free tours Monday through Saturday from 9 AM to 4:30 PM. Tickets are distributed on a first-come, first-served basis from the Capitol Guide Service kiosk along the curving sidewalk southwest of the Capitol, near the intersection of First St. SW and Independence Avenue, beginning at 9 AM.

The Bureau of Engraving and Printing has fascinating tours that begin every 15 minutes from 9 to 10:45 and 12:30–2 on weekdays (as well as 2 to 3:45 and 5 to 7 in summer). The free tours are popular with families. During the peak season from March through August, tickets are given out on a first-come, first-served basis at the ticket booth on Raoul Wallenberg Place (formerly 15th Street). The booth opens at 8 AM and closes as soon as all tickets have been handed out; lines form early and tickets go quickly, usually by 9 AM. From September through February, tickets are not required; you line up at the Visitor's Entrance on 14th Street.

Contacts **Bureau of Engraving and Printing** (✉14th and C Sts. SW ☎202/874–2330 or 866/874–2330 ⊕www.moneyfactory.com/locations). **United States Capitol Guide Service** (☎202/225-6827 ⊕www.aoc. gov/cc/visit/index.cfm).

ORIENTATION TOURS

Old Town Trolley Tours, orange-and-green motorized trolleys, take in the main downtown sights and also head into Georgetown and the upper Northwest in a speedy two hours if you ride straight through. However, you can hop on and off as many times as you like, taking your time at the stops you choose. Tickets are $32 ($28.80 on the Web site) for adults. Tourmobile buses, authorized by the National Park Service, operate in a similar fashion, making 25 stops at historical sites between the Capitol and Arlington National Cemetery. Tickets, available at kiosks at Arlington National Cemetery, Union Station, and the Washington Monument, are $25 for adults. Tourmobile also offers three seasonal tours including a "Twilight City Tour," "Mt. Vernon Tour," and "Frederick Douglass Tour."

Contacts **Old Town Trolley Tours** (☎202/832–9800 ⊕www. historictours.com). **Tourmobile** (☎202/554–5100 or 888/868–7707 ⊕www.tourmobile.com).

PRIVATE GUIDES

In business since 1964, the Guide Service of Washington puts together half-day and full-day tours of D.C. sights, including those off the beaten path. A Tour de Force has limo tours of historic homes, diplomatic buildings, and "the best little museums in Washington." Tours are led by Jeanne Fogle, a local historian. Nationally known photographer Sonny Odom offers custom tours for shutterbugs at $50/hour, with a four-hour minimum.

Contacts **Guide Service of Washington** (✉734 15th St. NW, Suite 701, Washington, DC ☎202/628–2842 ⊕www.dctourguides.com). **Sonny Odom** (✉2420F S. Walter Reed Dr., Arlington, VA ☎703/379–1633 ⊕www.sonnyodom.com). **A Tour de Force** (✉Box 2782, Washington, DC 20013 ☎703/525–2948 ⊕www.atourdeforce.com).

SEGWAY & SCOOTER TOURS

Rest your feet and glide by the monuments, museums, and major attractions aboard a Segway. Guided tours usually last from two to four hours. D.C. city ordinance requires that riders be at least 16 years old; some tour companies have weight restrictions and only offer tours from April through November. Tours cost around $65 to $70 per person and are limited to 6 to 10 people.

City Scooter Tours offers three-hour tours on mobility scooters on Wednesday afternoons and Sunday mornings from early spring through early fall. Guides take riders along the National Mall and Tidal Basin and share historical facts and fascinating stories about the nation's capitol. The cost is $75 per person and includes an electronic headset.

Contacts **Capital Segway** (☎202/682–1980 ⊕www.capitalsegway.com). **City Segway Tours** (☎877/734–8687 ⊕www.citysegwaytours.com). **City Scooter Tours** (☎888/441–7575 ⊕www.cityscootertours.com). **Segs in the**

City (☎800/734–7393 ⊕www.segsinthecity.net).

WALKING TOURS

Guided walks around Washington, D.C., and nearby communities are routinely offered by the Smithsonian Associates Program; advance tickets are required. For a free walking tour of D.C.'s monuments and memorials, try DC by Foot. Tour D.C. specializes in walking tours of Georgetown and Dupont Circle, covering topics such as the Civil War, the Underground Railroad, and Kennedy's Georgetown. Anecdotal History Tours leads tours in Georgetown, Adams-Morgan, and Capitol Hill, as well as tours of the theater where Lincoln was shot and the homes of former presidents.

DC by Foot offers free tours (the guides work for tips, which makes them lively and entertaining) to the major memorials and monuments. Tours are at 2 and 6 every day, February 15 through November 15, rain or shine. Look out for the guides in blue T-shirts and orange caps at the start of the tour on the north corner of 15th Street and Constitution Ave, NW; the tours end at the Lincoln Memorial.

Washington Walks has a wide range of tours, including "I've Got a Secret," featuring Washington, D.C., lore; "Moveable Feast: A Taste of D.C.," a walking snack-a-thon through downtown; "Goodnight Mr. Lincoln," a kid's-eye view of Abraham Lincoln for children ages 4 to 9; "In Fala's Footsteps," the life of Franklin Roosevelt from the perspective of his dog Fala; and "Before Harlem There Was U St.," a walk along Washington's "Black Broadway." Each tour costs $10 per person.

The nonprofit group Cultural Tourism DC leads guided walking tours that cover the history and architecture of neighborhoods from the southwest waterfront to points much farther north. Or, if you'd prefer to explore neighborhoods on your own, their Web site features seven self-guided walking tours, all of which are highlighted with historic markers. You also can check out other cultural events, many free, happening around the city on the Cultural Tourism DC Web site. Spies of Washington Walking Tour, led by a retired Air Force officer and former president of the National Military Intelligence Association, visits sites in Washington associated with espionage over the past 200 years. The approximately two-hour tours cost $12 per person.

Step back in time on one of Natalie Zanin's interactive theatrical tours to learn about Washington, D.C. during the Civil War, World War II, or the 1960s. Or you can sign up for a Ghost Story Tour, on which Zanin dresses as Dolly Madison's ghost and shares stories of hauntings around the city, including Lafayette Square Park, where Edgar Allan Poe's spirit is said to wander. Tours cost $10 for adults and $5 for children.

Contacts **Anecdotal History Tours** (☎301/294–9514 ⊕www. dcsightseeing.com). **Cultural Tourism DC** (☎202/661–7581 ⊕www. culturaltourismdc.org). **DC by Foot** (☎571/431–7543 ⊕www. dcbyfoot.com). **HistoricStrolls** (☎301/588–9255 ⊕www.historic strolls.com). **Smithsonian Associates Program** (☎202/357–3030 ⊕www.smithsonianassociates.org). **Spies of Washington Walking Tours** (☎703/569–1875 ⊕www. spiesofwashingtontour.com). **Tour D.C.** (☎301/588–8999 ⊕www. tourdc.com). **Washington Walks** (☎202/484–1865 ⊕www.washing tonwalks.com).

▌ GUIDED TOURS

Children's Concierge arranges specialized, unique itineraries for families that incorporate the interests of each family member. Activities can include scavenger hunts, personal backpacks for each child, and private guides. Collette Vacations, in partnership with Smithsonian Journeys Travel Adventures, has a five-day "Spirit of Washington, D.C." tour that includes guided tours of the Freer Gallery, National Gallery of Art, and National Museum of the American Indian led by Smithsonian historians; a tour of the Library of Congress; and a narrated coach tour of the city's monuments and memorials including a visit to Arlington National Cemetery. Children need to be at least five years old. Globus has two itineraries that include two nights in D.C.: "America's Historic East," an eight-day tour of Washington, D.C., and Philadelphia; and "Eastern U.S. and Canada Discovery." Both trips include a half-day guided city tour and free time, followed by an illumination tour of the monuments. For

Globus, children must be at least eight years old. Mayflower Tours offers a seven-day "Washington, D.C., and Williamsburg" tour that includes four nights in D.C. with visits to the U.S. Capitol, Library of Congress, Arlington Cemetery, and monuments, as well as stops at Mount Vernon and Jamestown. For Mayflower, children should be at least six years old. Tauck Travel also has a "Williamsburg and Washington, D.C." itinerary, which includes two nights in D.C. WorldStrides, which specializes in educational student travel, has 10 "Discover D.C." programs that are designed to enrich the study of U.S. history and government.

Recommended Companies **Children's Concierge** (☎877/888–5462 ⊕ www.childrensconcierge.com). **Collette Vacations** (☎800/340–5158 ⊕ www.collettevacations.com). **Globus** (☎866/755–8581 ⊕ www.globusjourneys.com). **Mayflower Tours** (☎800/323–7604 ⊕ www.mayflowertours.com). **Tauck** (☎800/788–7885 ⊕ www.tauck.com). **WorldStrides** (☎800/468–5899 ⊕ www.worldstrides.com).

SPECIAL-INTEREST TOURS

Elderhostel offers several guided tours for older adults that provide fascinating in-depth looks into the history and beauty of D.C. The nonprofit educational travel organization has been leading all-inclusive learning adventures around the world for more than 20 years. In addition to the programs listed here, Elderhostel also has several other world studies and history programs in D.C. All Elderhostel programs include accommodations, meals, and in-town transportation. Presented in conjunction with the Close Up Foundation, the nation's largest nonprofit citizenship education organization, "Monumental D.C." is a four-night program that includes seminars on many of the figures memorialized on and near the National Mall. Prices start at $973 per person.

"Washington, D.C., A Capital Intergenerational Adventure" is designed for grandparents and their grandchildren ages 11 to 14. The five-night trip starts at $1,133 per person. Highlights include workshops and activities at Mount Vernon, the International Spy Museum, and several Smithsonian museums; as well as a tour of the broadcast studio and control room of "Close-up on C-Span." You'll even have an opportunity to be a part of the audience.

"Discover Washington, D.C.: Our Nation's Capital" enables participants to learn more about our nation's cultural and political foundations through presentations at memorials and museums, visits to historical neighborhoods, meetings and seminars with Washington policy makers, and an evening at the theater. This five-night program starts at $1,073 per person.

Contacts **Elderhostel** (☎800/454–5768 ⊕ www.elderhostel.org).

❚ HOURS OF OPERATION

If you're getting around on the Metro, remember that from Sunday through Thursday the Metro closes at midnight, and on Friday and Saturday nights it stops running at 3 AM. Give yourself enough time to get to the station, because at many stations the last trains leave earlier than the closing times. If it's a holiday, be sure to check the schedule before you leave the station, as trains may be running on a different timetable.

Stores are generally open Monday to Saturday from 10 to 6. Those near Metro stops or along busy streets stay open until 8 or 9. Most open on Sunday sometime between 10 and noon and close at 5 or 6. Museums are usually open daily from 10 to 5:30; some have later hours on Thursday. Many private museums are closed Monday or Tuesday, and some museums in government buildings are closed weekends. The Smithsonian often sets extended spring and summer hours for some of its museums.

ITEM	AVERAGE COST
Cup of Coffee	$1 at a diner, $4 at an upscale café
Glass of Wine	$7–$10 and up
Pint of Beer	$5–$7
Sandwich	$5–$7
One-Mile Taxi Ride in Capital City	$5–$10
Museum Admission	Usually free

MONEY

Washington is an expensive city, comparable to New York. On the other hand, many attractions, including most of the museums, are free.

Prices throughout this guide are given for adults; where available children's prices are listed separately.

PACKING

GEAR

Walk along the National Mall or in Downtown and you can encounter people wearing everything from three-piece suits to shorts and T-shirts. Business attire in D.C. tends to be fairly conservative; it's around the campuses of Georgetown and American University where you can find more eclectic dressing. But D.C. is also understood to be a major year-round tourism destination, so the key is to dress comfortably and for the weather.

In fall, temperatures hover around the 50s and 60s, but it can get cooler, so pants, long-sleeve shirts, and a coat are appropriate. Winter is relatively mild in the D.C. area, with temperatures ranging from the 20s at night to the 40s and 50s and lately even the 60s during the day. There are usually one or two major snowstorms and an occasional ice storm. Pack clothes that can be layered, and bring a warm coat.

D.C. in spring is gorgeous, with lots of sun, an occasional rainstorm, and temperatures ranging from the 40s to 60s. Pack light sweaters, pants, and a lightweight coat. Summer is muggy and hot, with temperatures in the 80s and 90s and high humidity. Sunscreen is a must. Expect an evening thundershower or two. Plan on wearing cool, breathable fabrics like cotton, and bring a sweater for overly air-conditioned buildings.

Most important, D.C. is a walking town. Distances, especially on the Mall, are long. Whatever the reason for your visit, wear comfortable shoes.

STROLLERS

If you want to leave the stroller at home you can rent strollers ($15 day for fold-up umbrella style, $25 for joggers) through Bike and Roll.

Contact Bike and Roll (⌂1100 Pennsylvania Ave., NW ☎202/842–2453 ⊕www.bikethesites.com.).

▋ REST ROOMS

Rest rooms are found in all the city's museums and galleries. Most are accessible to people in wheelchairs, and many are equipped with changing tables for babies. Locating a rest room is often difficult when you're strolling along the Mall. There are facilities at the Washington Monument, the Lincoln Memorial, the Jefferson Memorial, and Constitution Gardens, near the Vietnam Veterans Memorial, but these are not always as clean as they should be. A better option is to step inside one of the museums along the Mall.

Rest rooms are available in restaurants, hotels, and department stores. Unlike in many other cities, these businesses are usually happy to help out those in need. There's one state-of-the-art public rest room in the Huntington Station on the Metro. All other stations have rest rooms available in

cases of emergency. You should ask one of the uniformed attendants in the kiosks.

Find a Loo The Bathroom Diaries (⊕www.thebathroomdiaries.com) is flush with unsanitized info on rest rooms the world over—each one located, reviewed, and rated.

▋ SAFETY

Washington, D.C., is a fairly safe city, but as with any major metropolitan area it's best to be alert and aware. Be aware of your surroundings before you use an ATM, especially one that is outdoors. Move on to a different machine if you notice people loitering nearby. Pickpocketing and other petty crimes are rare in D.C., but they do occur, especially in markets and other crowded areas. Keep an eye on purses and backpacks.

Panhandlers can be aggressive, and may respond with verbal insults, but otherwise are usually harmless. If someone threatens you with violence, it's best to hand over your money and seek help from police later.

The Metro is quite safe, with few incidents reported each year. Buses are also safe, but be aware that a few petty crimes have occurred at bus stops. Stick to those along busy streets.

The only scam you'll encounter in D.C. is an elaborate story from a panhandler. To evoke sympathy, a well-dressed panhandler may pretend to have lost his wallet and need money to get home, or a woman may say she needs cab fare to take a sick child to the hospital. A simple "I'm sorry" is usually enough to send them on their way.

■TIP→**Distribute your cash, credit cards, IDs, and other valuables between a deep front pocket, an inside jacket or vest pocket, and a hidden money pouch. Don't reach for the money pouch once you're in public.**

▌ TAXES

Washington has the region's highest hotel tax, a whopping 14.5%. Maryland and Virginia have no state hotel tax but charge sales tax. Individual counties add their own hotel taxes, which range from 5% to 10%.

Sales tax is 5.75% in D.C., 6% in Maryland, and 4% plus local sales tax in Virginia.

▌ TIPPING

TIPPING GUIDES FOR WASHINGTON D.C.

Bartender	$1 to $5 per round of drinks, depending on the number of drinks
Bellhop	$1 to $5 per bag, depending on the level of the hotel
Hotel Concierge	$5 or more, depending on the service
Hotel Doorman	$1–$5 for help with bags or hailing a cab
Hotel Maid	$2–$5 a day (either daily or at the end of your stay, in cash)

TIPPING GUIDES FOR WASHINGTON D.C.

Hotel Room-Service Waiter	$1 to $2 per delivery, even if a service charge has been added
Porter at Airport or Train Station	$1 per bag
Skycap at Airport	$1 to $3 per bag checked
Taxi Driver	15%, but round up the fare to the next dollar amount
Tour Guide	10% of the cost of the tour
Valet Parking Attendant	$2–$5, each time your car is brought to you
Waiter	5%–20%, with 20% being the norm at high-end restaurants; nothing additional if a service charge is added to the bill
Spa Personnel	15%–20% of the cost of your service
Rest-Room Attendants	$1 or small change
Coat Check	If there is a fee, then nothing

▌ VISITOR INFORMATION

You can gather information about the city before your trip and stop in at the D.C. Visitor Information Center when you arrive. The center is located in the Ronald Reagan Building and International Trade Center, two blocks from the National Mall and one block from the White House Visitor Center. Because it's a government office building, you can enter only after flashing your ID and passing through a metal detector. While there you can pick up maps, guides and brochures; watch a brief film highlighting the city's must-see sights; and speak with staff members. There are also interactive touch-screen kiosks with maps and other information on D.C.

The Washington, D.C., Convention and Tourism Corporation's free 104-page publication, *The Official Visitors' Guide,* is full of sightseeing tips, maps, and contacts. You can order a copy online or by phone, or pick one up in their office.

The most popular sights in D.C. are run by the National Park Service (NPS) or the Smithsonian, both of which have recorded information about locations and hours of operation.

Events & Attractions **National Park Service** (☎202/619-7275 "Dial-a-Park" ⊕www.nps.gov). **Smithsonian** (☎202/633-1000, 202/633-5285 TTY ⊕www.si.edu). **White House Visitor Center** (☎202/208-1631 ⊕www.nps.gov/whho).

Information Center **D.C. Visitor Information Center** (✉1300 Pennsylvania Ave. NW, Washington, DC ☎866/324-7386, 202/289-8317 ⊕www.dcchamber.org).

State Information **State of Maryland** (☎866/639-3526 ⊕www.mdisfun.org). **Virginia Tourism Corporation** (☎804/786-2051 or 800/847-4882 ⊕www.virginia.org).

Tourist Information **Washington, DC Convention and Visitors Association** (✉901 7th St., NW, 4th floor, Washington, DC ☎202/789-7000 or 800/422-8644 ⊕www.washington.org).

▌ WEB SITES

ONLINE TRAVEL TOOLS

ALL ABOUT WASHINGTON, D.C.

Cultural Tourism D.C. (⊕*www.culturaltourismdc.org*) is a nonproft coalition whose mission is to highlight the city's arts and heritage. Their Web site is loaded with great information about sights, special events, and self-guided walking tours.

Billing itself as D.C.'s online community for the Web, **dcregistry.com** (⊕*www.dcregistry.com*) lists more than 4,000 home pages with everything from arts and entertainment to real estate.

Destination DC (⊕*www.washington.org*) gives up-to-date information on special events, grand openings, and hotel packages.

The **Smithsonian Web site** (⊕*www.si.edu*) is a good place to start planning a trip to the Mall and its museums. You can check out the exhibitions and events that will be held during your visit.

Kids & Families **washingtonfamily.com** (⊕www.washingtonfamily.com) features a "Best for Families" as voted on by area families. Families may also want to check out the calendar of events at **washingtonparent.com** (⊕www.washingtonparent.com) and **washingtondckids.com** (⊕www.washingtondckids.com) for kid-friendly activities and events.

INDEX

NOTES

NOTES

ABOUT OUR WRITER

A fourth-generation Washingtonian, freelance writer Kathryn McKay scours the Washington area with her own children plus nieces and nephews looking for the best places to play, eat, and sleep in Washington, D.C. Her current "research assistants" range in age from 6 to 17. Kathryn has written for Fodor's since 1997. She has also written about the Mid-Atlantic region for many local publications, including *Bethesda* magazine, *Northern Virginia* magazine, the *Washington Post* and the *Washington Times*.